Modern Web Development with Angular

Build Cutting-Edge, Scalable Web Apps from Scratch with Angular, TypeScript, and Reactive Programming

Duncan Faulkner

Pierre Bouillon

www.orangeava.com

First Published: November 2024

Published By: Orange Education Pvt Ltd, AVA®

Address: 9, Daryaganj, Delhi, 110002, India

275 New North Road Islington Suite 1314 London,

N1 7AA, United Kingdom

ISBN (PBK): 978-81-96815-09-7

ISBN (E-BOOK): 978-81-96815-07-3

Scan the QR code to explore our entire catalogue

www.orangeava.com

Dedicated To

To my beautiful wife, Tracey, and my three amazing boys, Tyler, Callum, and Daniel. Your support and encouragement mean everything to me.

To my late grandfather, who gave me my first computer (a ZX81) and got me interested in computing.

-- Duncan Faulkner

To my family and my wife, Johanna, whose unwavering support and patience made this book possible. To my former colleagues, whose insightful suggestions and relevant insights shared over cups of coffee were invaluable. And to my uncle, whose passion for computers sparked my own.

-- Pierre Bouillon

Forewords

Alain Chautard

Google Developer Expert in Angular and Microsoft MVP

Web applications have become increasingly prevalent in modern development, and for a couple of years, front-end and full-stack developers have been among the roles with the most open positions.

Nowadays, it is rare to find any developer who does not know, at least, the names of the most commonly used web technologies, and learning these technologies is a valuable skill for staying up-to-date in the current tech landscape.

Among these technologies, Angular has helped engineers develop web applications since 2011, first as a pure JavaScript framework and later revamped as a TypeScript-based framework since Angular 2.0.

As a teacher and mentor, I can say that Angular is the de facto choice for enterprise applications. The framework is opinionated, strongly typed, and enjoys incredible support from Google and the community, making it a safe choice for large-scale web applications. I have seen dozens of teams succeed with Angular, despite being new to web development and more back-end oriented.

Angular continues to improve with new features and refinements, ensuring the framework is ready for the years ahead by focusing on performance, developer experience, simplified learning, and migration paths.

As the Angular team puts it, their goal is to make Angular an excellent choice today, one that will remain so ten years from now. You have chosen to read this book, and I am confident that it will prove to be a good decision.

Lars Gyrup Brink Nielsen

Angular Hero of Education and Co-founder of 'This is Angular'

Duncan Faulkner and Pierre Bouillon are active contributors to the Angular community and ecosystem, and you can meet them at events such as the 'Angular Community Meetup' and 'This is Angular' community. This book serves as their comprehensive and a step-by-step guide to all foundational aspects of Angular application development.

Whether you are new to software development or looking to learn another web application framework, special care has been taken to guide you from the very beginning. This includes learning TypeScript, setting up Node.js and the Angular CLI, as well as generating and running your first Angular applications.

Classic Angular concepts such as components, directives, pipes, and services are covered, including both standalone and Angular module-based versions. You will learn about both RxJS and Angular Signals for reactive state management, as well as essential component communication and data flow patterns.

Angular is a fully-featured framework and includes the powerful Angular Forms package. In this book, you will learn about both template-driven and reactive Angular forms, as well as form validation and submission.

Any non-trivial web application needs routing to orchestrate component activation based on the URL and user interactions. Vital parts of Angular's robust Router package are covered, including lazy-loaded routes, nested routes, and route parameters.

To complete your Angular skill tree and prepare you for contributing to production-ready Angular projects, Duncan and Pierre will guide you through Angular component testing, which are unit tests using Karma or Jest with Angular's TestBed API.

Brecht Billiet

Software Architect/Founder

Duncan is an experienced architect with a remarkable ability to translate complex ideas into clear, easy-to-understand language. His talent for breaking down complex concepts makes this book an invaluable resource for anyone looking to dive into Angular, even if they have no prior knowledge of the framework.

If you are starting from scratch and want a straightforward, practical book, this is your go-to resource. It's packed with useful tips on how to set up everything properly and covers all the essential aspects of Angular, which will help you tackle real-world projects.

Whether you are a complete beginner or someone looking to sharpen your skills, this book will help you become proficient in Angular in record time. Duncan has done an exceptional job of making an intimidating framework accessible. I have no doubt you will find this book both educational and enjoyable.

About the Authors

Duncan has been a software developer for over twenty years and has developed applications across various industries, from Hedge Fund and Investment Management to Satellite Communication Management. He was introduced to AngularJS by a colleague around version 1.3 and shifted from full-stack developer to front-end development using Angular. Duncan was an early adopter of Angular (formerly, Angular 2) and has spent more than eight years learning Angular. He has authored several short books and numerous articles on Angular and Angular Material (called *Shooks*).

Pierre has been working with Angular as a Full Stack Software Engineer for six years in various domains. Since then, he has written several articles on the framework and been involved in open-source projects and communities.

About the Technical Reviewers

Deeksha Kusuma "Code Wrangler" is a software engineer with over 14 years of experience, specializing in Angular, TypeScript, Node, .NET, and Microservices to build scalable enterprise solutions. With her background in tackling complex code challenges and her deep familiarity with diverse APIs, Deeksha has honed an exceptional skill for identifying edge cases. Her commitment to clean, maintainable codes is unwavering, and she reviews technical content with the same passion she has for debugging.

Beyond her professional expertise, Deeksha often helps her non-technical friends understand topics such as cloud technology. She ensures each book meets high standards of excellence and surpasses expectations. Her expertise and passion lie in software development and leading teams.

Siddhartha Shrivastava has over 9 years of experience in the IT industry, specializing in Software Development and the SDLC process. He has extensive expertise in developing web applications using technologies such as JavaScript, jQuery, Angular 8, React, Next.js, SASS, MVC, web services, and API integration.

Siddhartha is proficient in CI/CD tools such as Jenkins and uDeploy, with significant experience in front-end technologies and API integration. He has also worked with tools such as Jupyter, PyCharm, Visual Studio Code, Eclipse, and Sublime.

Acknowledgements

My heartfelt thanks to those whose support and guidance shaped this book. Their insightful feedback enriched its content.

Lars Gyrup Brink Nielsen: Thank you for helping me get started and for the early technical reviews and feedback. I also appreciate for introducing me to Pierre Bouillon.

Pierre Bouillon: Your support and encouragement have been invaluable in inspiring this book. It took longer than expected, but without your help, I might still be on Chapter 2.

Priyanka Arora and Sonali Biswas: Thank you for your support and perseverance in keeping me focused. It's been a pleasure working with you both, and I hope we collaborate again soon.

I would also like to thank the following people for their forewords:

- **Brecht Billiet** of Simplified Courses
- Lars Gyrup Brink Nielsen
- Alain Chautard of Angular Training

I would like to express my gratitude to the technical reviewers Deeksha Kusuma and Siddharth Shrivastava for their invaluable feedback in shaping this book.

-- Duncan Faulkner

A special thanks to Lars Gyrup Brink Nielsen for introducing me to the opportunity to contribute to my first book.

Thank you, Duncan Faulkner, for your experience, kindness, and advice that helped me start this book. Your support made it possible, one page at a time.

My heartfelt thanks to all the reviewers, whether technical or not, who contributed to making this book the highest quality it can be for the readers.

Thank you, Priyanka Arora and Sonali Biswas, for your relentless professionalism and support. Completing this book took immense effort, and it wouldn't have been possible without you. I hope that this book is the first of many, and I look forward to working with you in the future.

-- Pierre Bouillon

Preface

The vision of the book is to make sure everyone, with or without basic knowledge of Angular, can understand and gain expertise in web application development using Angular. After going through all the chapters in this book, readers will be able to quickly and confidently create a live web application using Angular within a few hours. This book uses simple language to make sure that everyone who reads this book can understand each concept without any complexity.

Chapter 1. Setting Up Angular: In this chapter, we will show how to get started with Angular by setting up our environment, from getting Node and Angular installed to creating a test application.

Chapter 2. Angular Application: In this chapter, we will cover workspaces and singular applications. The chapter explores both NgModules and Standalone applications, creates a new application, and introduces routing. We will finish this chapter with lazy loading.

Chapter 3. Introduction to TypeScript: In this chapter, we will introduce TypeScript, which Angular uses for its code files. The chapter covers what TypeScript is, how it differs from JavaScript, and explores data types and accessors.

Chapter 4. Components, Directives, Pipes, and Services: In this chapter, we will cover various types of components we can create to build our applications. The chapter covers components, directives, pipes, and services, explaining when and how to use them.

Chapter 5. Getting Started with Reactivity: In this chapter, we will learn about reactive programming, RxJS, and the newly introduced signals.

Chapter 6. Component Communication and Data Flow: In this chapter, we will learn about smart components, presentational components, and some advanced communication strategies. We will dive into passing data between components, for example, when using @input and @output decorators, as well as one-way and two-way data binding.

Chapter 7. Reactive and Template-Driven Forms: In this chapter, we will learn about Angular's two types of forms: template-driven (mostly done in HTML) and reactive forms (mostly done in the code-behind file).

Chapter 8. Form Validation: In this chapter, we will learn about validation and how to apply it to our components/forms. This allows us to test and inform users that their entered data meets certain rules and validation, preventing the entry of (potentially) invalid data that could affect our API or database.

Chapter 9. Routing: In this chapter, we will learn about Angular Routing. We will cover creating and consuming routes, controlling navigation, and configuring our routes for lazy loading. We will also learn how to create child routes and pass parameters to our routes.

Chapter 10. Unit Testing: In this chapter, we will focus on unit testing and the importance of having unit tests in our application. We will begin with using Karma (the default test runner with Angular) and then set up and configure our Angular applications to use Jest as an alternative, as Karma is now deprecated.

Get a Free eBook

We hope you are enjoying your recently purchased book! Your feedback is incredibly valuable to us, and to all other readers looking for great books.

If you found this book helpful or enjoyable, we would truly appreciate it, if you could take a moment to leave a short review with a 5 star rating on Amazon. It helps us grow, and lets other readers discover our books.

As a thank you, we would love to send you a free digital copy of this book, and a **30%** discount code on your next cart value on our official websites:

www.orangeava.com

www.orangeava.in (For Indian Subcontinent)

☑ **Here's how:**

Leave a review for the book on Amazon.

Take a screenshot of your review, and send an email to **info@orangeava.com** (it can be just the confirmation screen).

Once, we receive your screenshot, we will send you the digital file, within 24 hours.

Thank you so much for your support – it means a lot to us!

Downloading the code bundles and colored images

Please follow the links or scan the QR codes to download the ***Code Bundles and Images*** of the book:

https://github.com/ava-orange-education/Modern-Web-Development-with-Angular

The code bundles and images of the book are also hosted on ***https://rebrand.ly/ik4sgj3***

In case there's an update to the code, it will be updated on the existing GitHub repository.

Errata

We take immense pride in our work at **Orange Education Pvt Ltd,** and follow best practices to ensure the accuracy of our content to provide an indulging reading experience to our subscribers. Our readers are our mirrors, and we use their inputs to reflect and improve upon human errors, if any, that may have occurred during the publishing processes involved. To let us maintain the quality and help us reach out to any readers who might be having difficulties due to any unforeseen errors, please write to us at :

errata@orangeava.com

Your support, suggestions, and feedback are highly appreciated.

DID YOU KNOW

Did you know that Orange Education Pvt Ltd offers eBook versions of every book published, with PDF and ePub files available? You can upgrade to the eBook version at **www.orangeava.com** and as a print book customer, you are entitled to a discount on the eBook copy. Get in touch with us at: **info@orangeava.com** for more details.

At **www.orangeava.com**, you can also read a collection of free technical articles, sign up for a range of free newsletters, and receive exclusive discounts and offers on AVA® Books and eBooks.

PIRACY

If you come across any illegal copies of our works in any form on the internet, we would be grateful if you would provide us with the location address or website name. Please contact us at **info@orangeava.com** with a link to the material.

ARE YOU INTERESTED IN AUTHORING WITH US?

If there is a topic that you have expertise in, and you are interested in either writing or contributing to a book, please write to us at **business@orangeava.com**. We are on a journey to help developers and tech professionals to gain insights on the present technological advancements and innovations happening across the globe and build a community that believes Knowledge is best acquired by sharing and learning with others. Please reach out to us to learn what our audience demands and how you can be part of this educational reform. We also welcome ideas from tech experts and help them build learning and development content for their domains.

REVIEWS

Please leave a review. Once you have read and used this book, why not leave a review on the site that you purchased it from? Potential readers can then see and use your unbiased opinion to make purchase decisions. We at Orange Education would love to know what you think about our products, and our authors can learn from your feedback. Thank you!

For more information about Orange Education, please visit **www.orangeava.com**.

Table of Contents

Introduction

Web applications have become more prevalent in modern development, and both front-end and full-stack developers have been among the roles with the most open positions for a couple of years.

Nowadays, you will hardly find any developer that does not know at least the names of the most used web technologies and it is a valuable skill to learn to stay up-to-date in the current tech landscape.

Amongst those technologies, Angular has helped engineers develop powerful web applications since the end of 2016, cumulating more than 3 million downloads per week at the time of writing. While it already has some incredible features such as a powerful dependency injection system, an opinionated separation of concerns, and more, lately, this number kept on increasing with new features and improvements making Angular ready for the years to come by focusing on performances, standard adoptions, developer experience and enhanced learning paths.

Today, Angular is definitely a strong choice to consider when developing a new project, or as another tool to have on your belt, and, in my biased opinion, this book is a great starting point, and we hope you will enjoy reading it as much as we enjoyed writing it.

Audience

This book is aimed at developers interested in learning how to develop web applications, whether you are beginning in web development, wanting to transition to a new technology or simply seeking to learn or deepen your knowledge in Angular.

Prior experience with another framework or library is not required, but some knowledge of JavaScript, TypeScript, and/or HTML would be beneficial.

What is Angular?

Before diving into the actual code and the technical details, let's first explore what Angular is.

A Bit of History

In 2010, in the early days of JavaScript frameworks, Miško Hevery developed a strongly opinionated tool to write web applications which was named AngularJS.

This framework focused on using a declarative approach to build web interfaces and enhanced HTML using a special syntax to enhance its behavior. It aimed to enforce a specific way of developing web applications to ease their creation and testing while pushing towards a specific technology stack.

As groundbreaking as it was, soon other competing technologies emerged, simpler and more efficient such as React, later VueJS, and so on.

As a result, AngularJS was discontinued, and Google released Angular at the end of 2016. Even though the name is almost the same, the two frameworks are vastly different and Angular is not just a more recent version of AngularJS. In fact, companies using AngularJS had no choice but to rewrite their whole code for Angular if they wanted to get the latest updates and features. It resulted in a huge impact on the framework's popularity, and a lot of projects migrated to React or other alternatives.

Since 2016, however, Angular has had a stable and steady release cycle of a new major version every six months, with a detailed update guide, automatic code migrations, and, most importantly, enforces that every update is backward compatible. This means that a project written in Angular 14 won't need any rewrite if migrated to Angular 18.

Angular Nowadays

Still suffering from the confusion with AngularJS, Angular has come a long way since its early days and has been experiencing what is commonly called "*Angular Renaissance*" since its v14 with the team focusing on backward compatible and innovative features. This *renaissance* led to a regain in popularity and a bump in the available job offers, mostly in North America, Europe, and India, and the birth of new technologies and initiatives such as AnalogJS, a meta-framework for Angular, more or less like Next for React.

Lately, pieces of Angular code have been incorporated into YouTube, and the implementation of Signals, which is a primitive that is considered to be integrated into JavaScript natively, has been selected by the TC39, the expert group that decides the future of JavaScript.

More than ever, the Angular core development team has been working on improving performances and enhancing the developer experience and the learning path. They reworked their documentation from the ground up (which I highly encourage you to browse at https://angular.dev), revamped the framework's tutorial, created a Discord community, and showcased their work on YouTube through live coding sessions and presentations.

Any major change is now going through an RFC (Request For Comment) on GitHub in which it is debated with the community and released in developer preview for a couple of versions to get as much feedback as possible before making any actual change to the framework, which is made with an upgrade plan and automatic tools.

While still preparing for the future and improving the framework, they can already count on the most known and interesting feature Angular has, namely its dependency injection system that is very efficient, and allows for an organized and flexible way of creating your web applications; but also its CLI (Command Line Interface) that acts as a partner when coding by running migrations for you or scaffolding and organizing most of the code as you will soon see in the next chapters.

Angular in the JavaScript Landscape

With all those years of existence, Angular is one of the oldest JavaScript frameworks and countless websites of any size were built with it. To name a few there are:

- KLM (Dutch airline) main website (https://www.klm.nl/en)
- Google Gemini (https://gemini.google.com/)
- Activizion Blizzar's Battle.net e-shop (https://us.shop.battle.net/en-us)
- More than "4500 *Angular applications*" in Google's private monorepo according to Minko Gechev, DevRel lead at Google

Those are only some of the most known ones, but applications spread from internal business applications, e-commerce websites, landing pages, and more.

Thanks to the duration of its existence and Google backing it up, the framework still evolves and attracts new developers, staying relevant and competing against old frameworks (React, Vue) but also among newer ones (Svelte, Lit, and more).

From a company's point of view, Angular is definitely a safer choice for several reasons. Its release cycle is carefully scheduled and communicated upfront with new features coming every 6 months and provided as functionalities you can opt-in if you want to, or simply ignore without being left behind. Angular also packs a powerful CLI that standardizes the development process. It also comes with a lot of the functionalities you can expect from a web framework out of the box: a router, an HTTP client, and so on. Thanks to that, the number of dependencies and third-party tools is greatly reduced which dramatically simplifies maintenance and allows for a reasonable level of confidence in the tools your project is using since most of them are used and battle tested in Google immense Monorepo before being even available to the public.

What's in This Book?

At the end of this book, you will be able to navigate the codebase of existing Angular projects and build your own web applications.

Each chapter is designed as a building block on top of the previous one and features an exercise at the end, when applicable. While optional, we strongly encourage you to complete these exercises to gradually apply the concepts as we cover them. Some chapters might feature a lot of information and new concepts; take the time to read them more than once if needed, and don't hesitate to go through again if something is unclear.

The learning path will be the following:

- **Setting up Angular:** We will cover the technical installation of the framework and set up your development environment;
- **Creating our First Application:** This will be our starting point to explore how an Angular application is structured.
- **Introduction to TypeScript:** The language that Angular is using and that you will need to manipulate;
- **Components, Directives, Pipes, and Services:** We will unravel the main building blocks of any Angular application;
- **Getting Started with Reactivity:** We will explore the concept of reactivity, which, while not inherent to web development, can help you write efficient and maintainable code;
- **Component Communication and Data Flow:** We will cover how to orchestrate your building blocks in a cohesive structure;
- **Reactive and Template-Driven Forms:** This chapter will discuss various ways of creating forms to retrieve user input, which is at the core of any web application;
- **Form Validation:** We will learn how to sanitize inputs and provide a good user experience while the user provides input;
- **Routing:** We will explore how to create a multi-page web application and strategies to secure them and improve performance;
- **Unit Testing:** We will see how to test our code to ensure that our code behaves as expected and prevent unexpected bugs and regressions.

With that covered, this ends the introduction of this book. and we can start diving right in!

Chapter 1
Setting up Angular

Introduction

This chapter is all about getting our development environment up and running to enable us to develop Angular applications. We'll set up and install a few packages and go through the installation process using Linux and will cover where it differs on Windows.

We'll look at the various Integrated Development Environments (IDEs) that allow us to write code, but also provide code checking in the form of errors, intellisense that provides us with additional information on what the properties, methods and data types do and how we can use them.

Structure

In this chapter, we will cover the following topics:

- Setting up Node Version Manager (NVM): Install multiple versions of Node
- Setting up Volta – an alternative to NVM: Install and pin versions of Node
- Setting up Git: Git is a distributed version control system (VCS)
- Setting up Angular: Install the framework so we can develop Angular applications
- Setting up our Integrated Development Environment (IDE): This will allow us to write code and provide us with IntelliSense, color-coded text to make our code easier to distinguish between keywords, variables, and data types.

Setting up Node

Angular is a JavaScript framework that requires Node to enable the framework to run in our development environment.

There are four distinct Node packages available:

- **Pending version** is the next version, still very much under development and unstable.

- **Current version** is usually the bleeding edge version and is the most up-to-date, but it takes time for that version to be supported by other vendors including Angular.
- **Long-Term Supported (LTS)** is usually a version behind the current version but is more stable and more widely supported by other vendors.
- **Maintenance version** is for the two versions prior to the LTS version that is out of long-term support but is likely to still be in production applications, these would only receive security and bug fixes that are deemed to be critical.

Note: *Node's versioning is structured so that even-numbered versions are released in April and odd-numbered versions in October. The October release pushes the even-numbered release into Long Term Support, with twelve months of active support, and after the twelve months, it moves into maintenance support for eighteen months.*

There are a couple of options to install Node on our computers, we could download and install it, which will work fine. The main downside to this comes when we need to upgrade (or downgrade to an earlier version) this means we must uninstall it and then install the next (or previous) version, this can be time-consuming and not particularly helpful if we need to switch between the versions regularly.

For that reason, we use a Node Version Manager (NVM), which gets installed before we install Node. This package will let us install multiple versions of Node and gives us the ability to switch between versions with a couple of simple commands.

Note: *We'll go through each setup, on each of the main Operating Systems (OS) starting with Linux and Windows. You can skip this section if you have a Node or Node Version Manager installed on your OS. If using a Mac, please follow the instructions for Linux as these are similar.*

Linux/Mac OS

We'll use the terminal to install all the packages in this section and we'll use **`Curl`** to install NVM. Depending on what's installed on your computer, you may already have **`Curl`** installed, if you do have it installed then you can skip this part of the process.

Tip: **`Curl`** *is a way to transfer data from a server to your local computer.*

To check if it's installed from the terminal window, type:

```
curl --version
```

If it returns a version number then you know it's installed (currently, the latest version on Ubuntu is 7.81).

If not, start by updating your system, open a new terminal and type:

```
sudo apt update
```

Enter your password and wait for it to complete, then type:

```
sudo apt upgrade
```

Once complete, type:

```
sudo apt install curl
```

Note: *Since we're using the* **sudo** *command, we will need to enter the user's password.*

Once installed, we can check the version again, but also to test that curl is working, we can download an example page, on the terminal type:

```
curl example.com
```

We should see a copy of the website's page in HTML format.

```
<!doctype html>
<html>
<head>
    <title>Example Domain</title>

    <meta charset="utf-8" />
    <meta http-equiv="Content-type" content="text/html;
    charset=utf-8" />
    <meta name="viewport" content="width=device-width,
    initial-scale=1" />
    <style type="text/css">
       // styling removed for brevity
    </style>
</head>
<body>
<div>
    <h1>Example Domain</h1>
       <p>This domain is for use in illustrative examples in
       documents. You may use this domain in literature without
       prior coordination or asking for permission.</p>
<p><a href="https://www.iana.org/domains/example">More
information...</a></p>
</div>
</body>
</html>
```

Note: *This won't download any files; it will just display an HTML page in the terminal window.*

Node Version Manager

With **Curl** installed, we can now install Node Version Manager (NVM). Back in the terminal window, type the following:

```
curl -o- https://raw.githubusercontent.com/nvm-sh/nvm/v0.39.3/
install.sh | bash
```

Note: *Ensure that you are using the latest version and update the version number (v0.39.3) in the preceding link before running it.*

NVM has now been cloned into the **~/.nvm** directory and will update the profile file script, (for example **~/.bashrc**). Once this is complete, either close and reopen the terminal or type:

```
source ~/.bashrc
```

This command will reload your profile. At this point, we should now have a Node Version Manager installed. To test this, type:

```
nvm -v
```

which should return the current version number (at the time of writing this is 0.39.3).

Tip: *Useful Node Version Manager commands:*	
`nvm ls`	Lists all versions of the node locally installed
`nvm ls-remote`	Lists all remote versions (this is a very long list!)
`nvm use (node-version)`	Selects the version of the node to use
`nvm alias default (node-version)`	Sets the default version of Node to use
`nvm install (node-version)`	Installs a specific version of the node
`nvm install --lts`	Installs the latest Long-Term Support version
`nvm -v`	Displays version of NVM

***Table 2.1**: List of regularly used Node Version Manager commands*

With NVM installed, we can now use NVM to install Node, from the terminal type:

```
nvm install 20.13.1
```

This will install the latest (at the time of writing) Long Term Support version and will set this to be the default version. We could have also typed:

```
nvm install -lts
```

It would have installed the same version. Now, if we type:

```
nvm ls
```

We can get a list of installed Node versions.

```
$ nvm ls

        -> v20.13.1

Default->  20.13.1 (-> v20.13.1)
```

We now have one version of Node installed, let's install another version. At the terminal, type:

```
nvm install 22.2.0
```

```
$ nvm install 22.2.0
Downloading and installing node v22.2.0...
Downloading https://nodejs.org/dist/v22.0.0/node-v22.0.0-li-
nux-x64.tar.xz...###100%
Computing checksum with sha256sum
Checksums matched!
Now using node v22.2.0 (npm v10.7.0)
```

This will install the latest, the current version, run this command again to see both versions:

```
nvm ls
$ nvm ls
-> v22.2.0
Default-> 20.13.1 (-> v20.13.1)
```

Notice that we didn't uninstall the previous version of Node.

NVM has now made version **`22.2.0`** the latest but creating a new project will still use the default 20.13.1, to use the latest version (**`22.2.0`** in this case), we need to let NVM know we want to use that version. In the terminal, type:

```
nvm use 22.2.0
```

Now, any new project created with this currently open terminal will now use this version; once this terminal has been closed then NVM returns to the default version.

With NVM and Node installed, in a way that if we need to change our Node version, then this is a simple command to switch to the new version or quickly install another without having to worry that we have broken other applications.

Tip: *If we want to change the default at any time, then we use the alias command, in a terminal type:*

```
nvm alias default <insert version of Node>
```

Windows – 10/11

There isn't an official version of NVM that supports Windows, but there is **`nvm-for-windows`** (this is a similar package to NVM mentioned in the Linux section, but it's not identical). In this section, we'll walk through installing Node Version Manager for Windows and installing Node on Windows.

Note: *Before you start, uninstall any previous versions of the Node and delete the existing Node installation directories before installing the Node Version Manager for Windows.*

Download the installer for Node Version Manager for Windows from the GitHub repository and run the installer using the default settings.

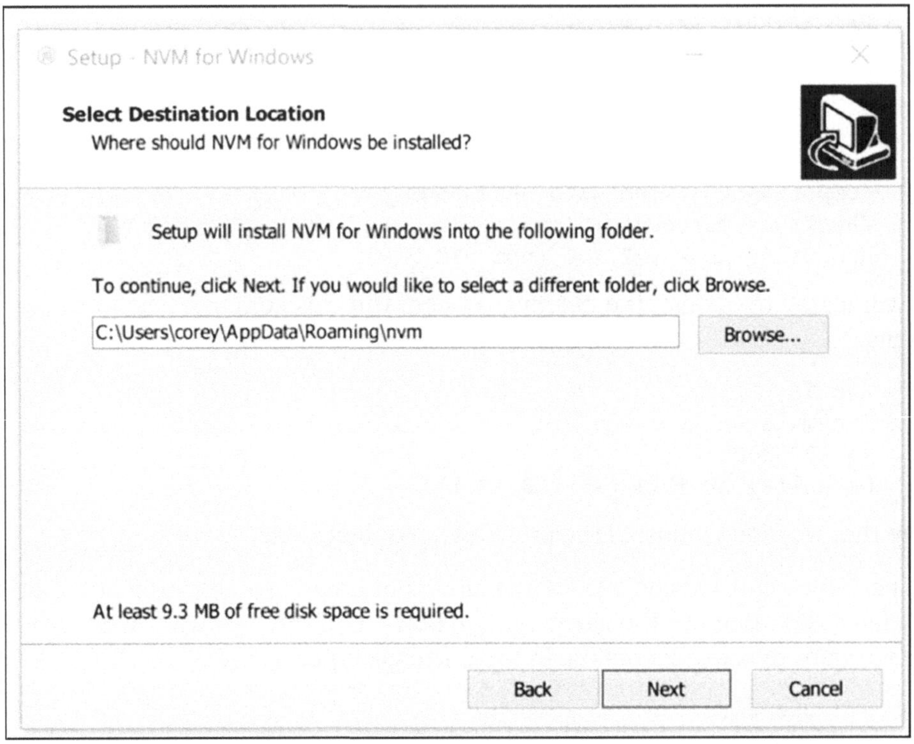

***Figure 1.1**: Installation Wizard for Node Version Manager for Windows*

To ensure that the Node Version Manager for Windows has been installed, open a command line or PowerShell window and type:

```
nvm version
```

This will return the version number which confirms it's now installed and working.

Note: *The Node Version Manager for Windows requires either PowerShell or a Command line with admin privileges.*

Tip: *To open a PowerShell or command line window with Admin privileges, use the search menu to locate PowerShell or command line application and right-click the application and from the context menu, select "`Run as Admin`".*

With the terminal window open let's install Node, type:

```
nvm install 20.13.1
```

This will install Node version 20.13.1, type:

```
nvm list
```

This will list the version of Node installed.

```
C:\nvm list
-> v20.13.1
Default-> 20.13.1 (-> v20.13.1)
```

Running the install command again:

```
nvm install 22.2.0
```

Will now install version 22 of Node, and running,

```
nvm list
```

This will list both versions of Node installed.

```
C:\nvm list
-> v20.13.1
-> v22.2.0
Default-> 20.13.1 (-> v20.13.1)
```

To use a specific version of Node type:

```
nvm use 20.13.1
```

or you can specify, **`latest`**, **`lts`**, or **`newest`** instead of the version number. We are now ready to install Angular and switch between versions of Node with ease.

Note: *One main difference between* NVM *and* Node Version Manager *for* Windows, *every time we install a new version of* Node, *we will need to re-run any globally installed packages, for example, yarn.*

```
nvm use 22.13.1
npm install -g yarn
```

Node Version Manager for Windows – common commands	
`nvm list [available]`	Lists versions installed or available
`nvm use`	Switches the version of Node
`nvm install (version or lts, latest or newest)`	Installs the specified version
`nvm version`	Displays the version number

***Table 2.2**: NVM commands*

Setting up Volta

In recent years, Volta has been gaining traction as an alternative to Node Version Manager for Windows. Volta takes a slightly different approach to managing versions of Node by allowing to pin a version of Node to your application, so you can easily swap between different projects using different versions of Node and it will swap automatically.

Note: *Volta's role is to manage command line tools, such as yarn, npm, or executables that are part of JavaScript packages.*

Download the installer from the Volta website (https://docs.volta.sh/guide/getting-started) and then run the installation. Open the Command line window and type:

```
volta install node@20
```

This will install the latest version of Node 20, to pin a version of Node to your project type:

```
volta pin node@20
```

This will add an entry to the project's `package.json` file, so each time you run the project the version of Node is switched to the pinned version automatically. This becomes more beneficial when there is a team of developers as the project is controlling the version of Node to use; it's a great way to guarantee consistency across teams.

Note: *Angular 18.0.0 officially supports LTS versions of Node, so while setting up* NVM *or Volta please install one of the following versions.*

```
^18.20.2 || ^20.9.0
```

Understanding Version Control

When developing software applications, there are times when we will often need to refer to a previous version of a file (often many files). To enable developers to have the ability to travel back in time, we need to be able to periodically store revisions of our codebase and for that, we need to use a version control system (VCS). The most popular VCS is Git; there are others like Azure DevOps (formerly Team Foundation Services), Subversion and Mercurial, to name a few. There are two types of Version Control Systems, a distributed and a central version control system.

Centralized Version Control

The centralized version control system relies on a central server to host all the repositories where developers commit changes. There are some disadvantages to centralized version control, for example:

- **Single point of failure**: If the server goes down.
- **Corrupt codebase**: Unable to access the code or previous versions.
- **Remote commits**: Can be slow as it needs to go through a network to the central repository.

- **Merging and branching**: Needs to be done in a single check-in.

Distributed Version Control

The distributed version control system does not have a centralized server, removing the main single point of failure. Developers clone the repository locally thus creating multiple copies of the repository and all the version history so if the codebase becomes corrupt, then it can be easily restored using one of the distributed copies. Because developers have a local copy of the repository, commits can also be done offline, merging and branching are faster as there is no communication to a remote server.

Setting up Git

To be able to use Git we first need to install it, head over to https://git-scm.com and download the version for your operating system.

Linux

At the command line type:

```
add-apt-repository ppa:git-core/ppa
apt update
apt install git
```

Depending on your setup you may need to use the **`sudo`** and supply your **`password`**. Once complete, type:

```
git --version
```

It should return the version 2.45.1 (at the time of writing).

Windows

With Windows, we need to download the 64-bit executable. Once downloaded, launch the executable and follow the steps, except all the default settings; once installed, open a command line and check that the version is returned using the same command above.

Setting up Angular

With NVM (or Volta) installed on our computer along with an LTS version of Node, we are now able to install Angular with the Command line interface (CLI). The CLI will help us build our applications, scaffold components, services and directives; while the Angular framework helps us to build our web applications by extending the HMTL syntax.

Linux

With the terminal open, type:

```
npm install -g @angular/cli@latest
```

The '**-g**' flag will install Angular globally on our computer.

Note: *It's possible to shorten the command for installing applications or packages using npm, for example, we can use:*

```
npm i -g @angularcli@latest
```

Instead of

```
npm install -g @angular/cli@latest
```

There are many other commands we can shorten and will point these out as they appear.

Once the installation is complete, we should be able to see the version number by typing:

```
ng version
```

The results should look something like this.

```
Angular CLI: 18.0.0
Node: 20.13.0
Package Manager: NPM 10.5.0
OS: linux x64

Angular: 18.0.0
… animations, common, compiler, compiler-cli, core, forms
… platform-browser, platform-browser-dynamic, platform-server
… router

Package                              Version
----------------------------------------------------------
@angular-devkit/architect            0.180.0
@angular-devkit/build-angular        18.0.0
@angular-devkit/core                 18.0.0
@angular-devkit/schematics           18.0.0
@schematics/angular                  18.0.0
rxjs                                 7.8.1
typescript                           5.4.5
zone.js                              0.14.6
```

Windows

With Node Version Manager for Windows or Volta installed, we can now install Angular; the setup is the same as on Linux. From the command line type:

```
npm install -g @angular/cli@latest
```

The '**-g**' flag will install Angular globally on our computer.

If you prefer to use Powershell scripts, you may need to set the execution policy as the execution of scripts is disabled by default. To set the policy, run the following command from a Powershell window.

```
Set-ExecutionPolicy -Scope CurrentUser -ExecutionPolicy
RemoteSigned
```

Note: *When setting the execution policy it will display a message, please read and understand what the implications are when setting the execution policy.*

Creating our First Angular Application

We now have everything set up with NVM (or Volta), Node and the Angular framework and CLI, we are now ready to create our first Angular application. The Angular CLI is a powerful tool, and it can do many things for us, (we'll discuss it in later chapters), but one of these things it allows us to create is a new project.

Linux/Windows

Open the terminal/command line/Powershell window, navigate to a directory (or create a new directory) and type:

```
ng new <project-name>
```

Replace **`<project-name>`** with a name, for example.

```
ng new myfirstapp
```

Angular will now gather some additional information from us by asking a couple of questions; the first is whether we would like to set up routing. In this example, we'll say No, and we'll discuss what routing is in a later chapter.

```
? Would you like to add Angular routing? (y/N)
```

Tip: *The capital letter in brackets '(y/N)' is the default and pressing the enter key will accept the default.*

Next, Angular will ask us which of the four stylesheet formats we would like to use.

```
? Which stylesheet format would you like to use? (use arrow keys)

> CSS

SCSS [https://sass-lang.com/documentation/syntax#scss]

Sass [https://sass-lang.com/documentation/syntax#the-
indented-syntax]

Less [http://lesscss.org]
```

For this example, we'll select the first one, CSS (we'll discuss the rest in a later chapter), and the CLI will now create our application (this may take a few minutes to complete). To run the application, we have a couple of options, new in Angular 18 we can type:

```
ng dev
```

This will compile an in-memory version of our application and get the application ready to serve, once compiled there will be a link in the terminal to launch the application. Alternatively, there is:

```
ng serve
```

Or finally, we can use the script from the **package.json** file:

```
npm run start
```

Open a new tab and load the application into that browser tab. Congratulations! We've successfully created our first Angular application, and you should see a page that looks like this (see the following image) in your browser.

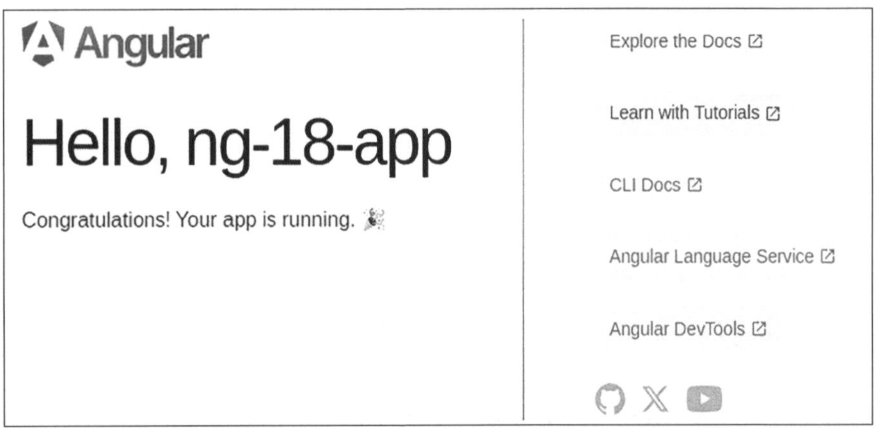

***Figure 1.2**: Page from the first application*

Note: *The creation of a new Angular project is the same across Operating Systems.*

Setting up Integrated Development Environments (IDE)

With our first application successfully created and under our belt, we need a way to edit the files and the best way to do that is through an Integrated Development Environment (IDE). There are plenty of IDEs available, some are paid and some are free.

Here is a list of the most popular ones.

- Visual Studio Code (also known as VS Code) is a free IDE from Microsoft and runs on Linux, Mac and Windows. This editor can support pretty much every programming language using extensions the IDE is also very customizable supporting different themes, colours, and fonts.

- Visual Studio Community Edition, Professional/Enterprise, the community edition is free for non-commercial use with some limited capabilities, the Professional and Enterprise editions are paid usually via an MSDN subscription.
- WebStorm is a low-cost IDE from JetBrains, very extensible, supports a wide range of programming languages and has recently undergone a makeover.
- Stackblitz is a web-based browser IDE; there are free versions and paid subscriptions. This IDE will allow users to create a wide range of applications using a handful of different application types, for example, Angular, JavaScript, Node, NextJS, Vue, React, Nuxt, NestJS, Express, and React-Native for mobile development.
- Notepad/Text/VIM, it is possible to write a website in a text editor, but the main downsides to this are no intellisense, no auto imports of libraries, no colour coding of keywords, and no design time error checking.
- Sublime Text is a paid-for product with different payment structures depending on whether the licence is for personal or commercial use.

Throughout this book, we will be using VS Code, this is a lightweight and extremely customizable IDE, with a considerable collection of third-party extensions for pretty much anything you can think of. If you prefer a different IDE to VS Code, then all the examples in this book will work just as well.

To install VS Code, go to the website for VS Code (https://code.visualstudio.com/) and download the version for your operating system.

Linux

For Linux, there are Debian and Ubuntu packages (.deb and .rpm) but are also available on Snap as well as compressed format (.tar.gz) files or CLI.

Windows

For Windows, there are user installers, system installers, and compressed files (.zip) or CLI.

Mac

For Mac, there are compressed files (.zip) or CLI.

Insiders' version

There are insider versions called VS Code-insiders, these versions are a bit more bleeding edge with nightly builds. The VS Code team works on a four-week cadence cycle, so what's being worked on today will be released the following month.

VS Code

Once installed, we can open VS Code from the operating systems menu or the terminal window. With the terminal window open, navigate to the directory of the application we created above and type:

```
code .
```

Or if you are using the insider's version, type:

```
code-insiders .
```

Note: *There is a space and a full stop after the word **code*** (or **`code-insiders`**).

VS Code should now be open; if you opened VS Code using the command line then our project will be loaded, otherwise, you will need to locate and open the folder in VS Code. One of the first things you will notice with VS Code is the clean user interface. Menu items and panels are all hidden away in a discrete Activity bar - the default would be across the top for the menu items, but as the following image shows these can be placed top, bottom left-hand, or right-hand side of the user interface. It's also possible to hide everything to maximize the screen of real estate.

Activity bar

The activity bar is where most VS Code extensions reside; these are usually extensions that have Graphical User Interface (GUI), extensions, such as Git, File Explorer, Debug and Extensions for example.

Figure 1.3: *Activity bar*

For an easier way to search for VS Code extensions, visit the VS Code Marketplace.

Explorer

The main panel is the Explorer panel, this is a tree view of the working directory, and we can expand items using the chevron '**>**'.

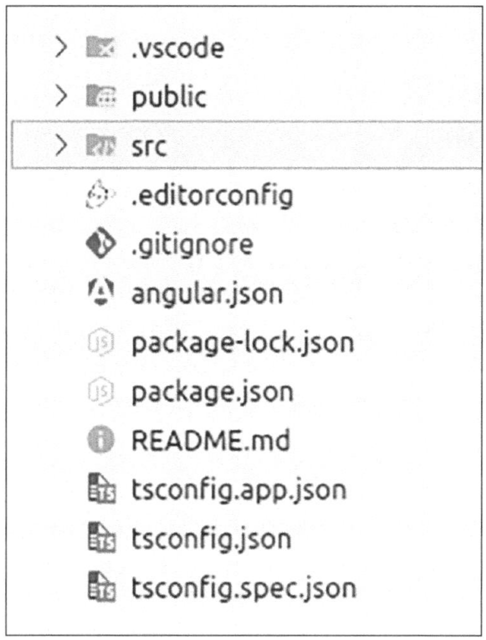

Figure 1.4: *VS Code Explorer*

There are several other panels located at the bottom of the explorer panel:

- **Outline:** This panel shows a tree view of your HTML page.
- **Timeline:** This records when you perform an action, save the page, and commit to source control.
- **NPM Scripts:** This lists all the NPM scripts that are in the projects **`package.json`** file and is a shortcut to running or debugging your applications.

Search

This panel performs two operations, the first is to search, this can be a word, a phrase, keywords basically anything and it can be in any file as well. The second operation is to replace, this will find all occurrences of a word or phrase and replace it, VS Code does display a confirmation dialog box before a replace happens, to make sure you meant to do it. Under the **`Search/Replace`** text input box there are three ellipsis (...) that allow you to specify files to include or exclude, for example, to exclude all spec files enter **`*.spec.ts`**.

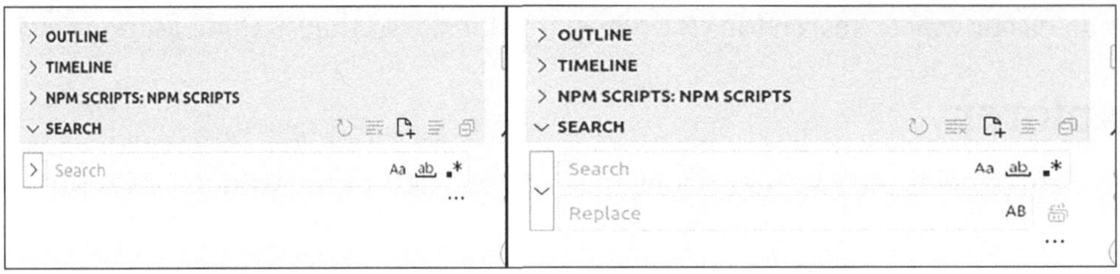

(a) (b)

***Figure 1.5**: (a) Search (b) Search and Replace*

Source Control

This panel performs all the source control functions of which there are quite a few. Earlier, we installed Git, which now connects to source control in VS Code, for us to be able to publish (or push) our commits to a central location, we need to connect to a repository host, like GitHub. We won't cover signing up for a GitHub account as it's outside the scope of this book, but it's quite a straightforward process. At the end of the process, you should be able to create a repository and be able to push a local repo up to it.

Tip: *There are a couple of settings that will make adding project changes a bit easier, and that's to set up the global config. At a terminal type:*

`git config -list`: *this will list your current config settings. The two we are most interested in are the username and email, if these settings aren't present or have no value set, then we can add them.*

These credentials are used when creating a commit, your username, and email address are added to the commit as a reference. To add your username and email to the global config (by setting it globally it will cover all projects), type:

`git config -global user.name "Your Name"`

For example, and for the email:

`git config -global user.email` Your-Name@Your-domain.com.

This will remove the need to enter your username and email address with each commit.

This panel shows the files that have been changed and show up in the changes section, to commit them to our local repository, they first need to be staged, we can then add a commit message and then commit the changes. These have now been committed locally and can be published (or pushed) to our GitHub repository.

Note: *When you create a new repository in GitHub, it will display various options with commands that we need to run on our projects' directory to link up our local repository with the GitHub repository, and follow the commands to set the origin. To check that our local repositories origin is set type:*

```
git remote -v
```

This should return:

```
origin git@github.com:<repository-name> (fetch)
origin git@github.com:<repository-name> (pull)
```

The **`commit`** button changes from commit to publish after a commit has been committed locally.

Note: *Though a commit message is optional, it's considered best practice to write a good commit message.*

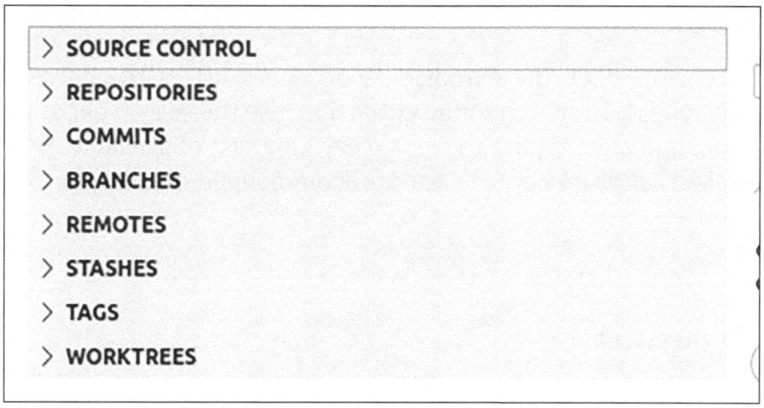

***Figure 1.6**: Source control*

Debug

The Debug panel allows applications to run in debug mode. Debug mode allows us to add breakpoints in our code, so when our application is running, we can stop the application at these breakpoints to inspect the state of our application and check on various conditions or variable values.

The debug process allows us to continue executing the code line by line, or we can choose to fast-forward through our code by stepping over it or by short-circuiting our journey through our code and returning once a function or method has completed, handy if we know that the error occurs after a particular function so we don't need to follow that code, we can just skip through it.

The debug panel also shows our variables as we step through; we can see the stack trace and our breakpoints, we are also able to add a watch, this is where we can create a condition that once met the application will stop at that point.

When we start VS Code in debug mode, VS Code will create an instance of the browser (removing all menus and toolbars), this browser is closed when we stop the debug process.

Figure 1.7: *Debug*

Extensions

To add an extension, click the extension icon and a list of the currently installed extensions will appear. To search for an extension, use the search bar at the top of the extension menu, and start typing to see a (very long) list of available extensions. The currently installed list given here is a list of recommended extensions.

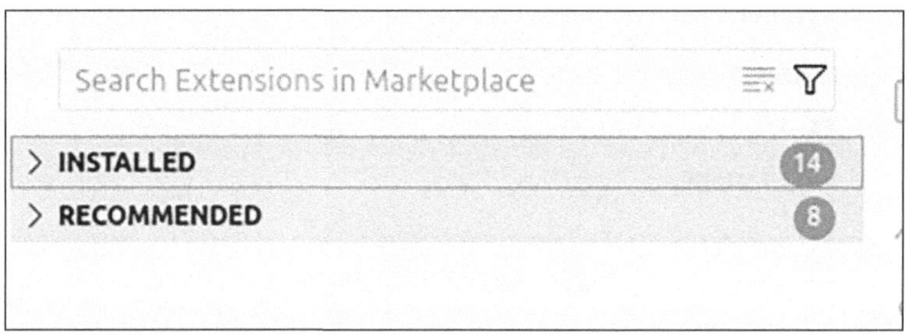

Figure 1.8: *Extensions*

There is a lot more to VS Code, but this should be enough for us to navigate around the application for the moment.

Project Files

Let's go through the files that CLI created for us; we'll cover the **`.vscode`** and **`src`** directories in a bit.

Files	**Application**
`.editorconfig`	This is an extension that's part of VS Code and sets a few editor settings.
`.gitignore`	This is the ignore file for git, when we check files into a repository, files listed in this file are not committed to the repository.
`angular.json`	This is the main file that lays out the project structure and sets configuration values for the development, build, production, and test sections of our project; this will also include libraries.

`package-lock.json`	This file specifies the installed packages, meaning that everyone who installs this application should get the same versions of the packages. It also improves the performance of the installation.
`package.json`	This is the file that stores which files are required for production and which are for development only.
`README.md`	This is a markdown file and explains how to set up the project.
`tsconfig.app.json`	This extends the **`tsconfig.json`** file to application-specific settings.
`tsconfig.json`	This sets several defaults for the application, what version to build the application in, whether to target a different version and some project default settings for Typescript.
`tsconfig.spec.ts`	This extends the **`tsconfig.json`** file to specification-specific settings (used in unit tests).

***Table 2.3**: Default files in Angular application*

The **`.vscode`** directory is where VS Code stores files for workspace settings that override the user settings, this allows consistency across teams. For example, if your team wants to use a particular font, formatting or pretty much any other setting. This file needs to be checked into source control so it can be shared.

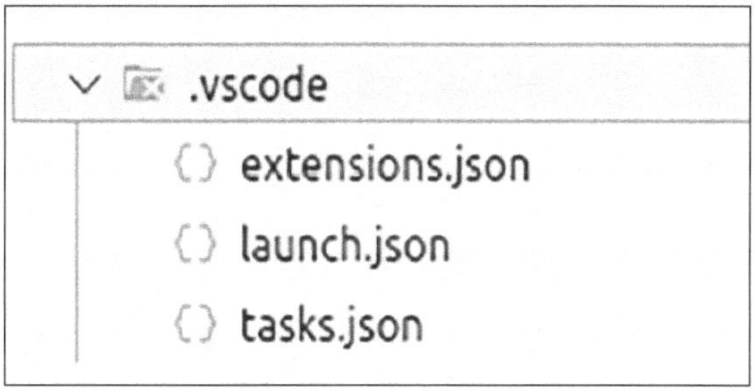

***Figure 1.9**: VS code files*

The **`src`** directory (short for source) is the main directory for our projects. Within this directory, there is another directory called app, which is the root of the application; and within the app directory, the CLI has created a default set of components to get us started.

***Figure 1.10**: Source (SRC) code files*

There are five files within the app directory and these are:

- **`app.component.css`**: This is the Cascading Style Sheet, other variations could be **`.scss`**, .sass, or **`less`**.
- **`app.component.html`**: This is the Hyper Text Markup Language file this is what gets displayed on our web page.
- **`app.component.spec.ts`**: This is the unit test file; we use Jasmine to write unit tests using libraries like Karma or Jest.
- **`app.component.ts`**: This is the Typescript code file; we use this to write logic, set up form controls and initialize our component.
- **`app.module.ts`**: This is a special file that allows us to pull in other files or third-party libraries for use within our component.

The assets directory is where we can add images, fonts, language files, and icons for our applications. The **.gitkeep** file is an empty file and it is there to allow distributed version control systems like Git to include empty directories.

Figure 1.11: *favicon*

Starting in version 18, the favicon is now moved to the **public** folder, the little icon in the browser tab, which can be replaced with any other icon (icon files have the **.ico** extension); it is called favicon.

The **index.html** is the only page in an Angular project. Remember that Angular projects are Single Page Applications (SPA), and this is the single page, this can be confusing to start with as we create lots of other HTML pages, but they are all loaded into this one HTML file.

The **main.ts** file is the bootstrap file and points to the **app.module** file, this in turn loads the **app.component.ts** file.

If we look at the HTML in the **index.html** file, then we'll see the following HTML:

```
<!doctype html>
<html lang="en">
<head>
  <meta charset="utf-8">
  <title>Demo</title>
  <base href="/">
  <meta name="viewport" content="width=device-width, ini-
tial-scale=1">
  <link rel="icon" type="image/x-icon" href="favicon.ico">
</head>
<body>
  <app-root></app-root>
</body>
</html>
```

The important part here is the **<app-root></app-root>**; this element comes from the **app.component.ts** file. This is how the code will look like in that file:

```
import { Component } from '@angular/core';

@Component({
  selector: 'app-root',
```

```
  standalone: true,
  imports:[RouterOutlet],
  templateUrl: './app.component.html',
  styleUrls: ['./app.component.scss']
})
export class AppComponent {
  title = 'Demo';
}
```

Here we can see the selector, '**app-root**', which matches the **<app-root>** element in the index.html.

So, this is how the application starts:

- **index.html** file sets up the HTML document
- Angular, third party libraries and the application
- **main.ts** file application entry point
- **app.component.ts**
- **app.component.html**

The **style.css** file (this could also be **.scss .sass** or **.less**) is the global style sheet for the application.

We now have our computer set up with NVM, Node and the Angular framework; we have also created a sample application to prove that our system works as it should and we are ready to take a deeper dive into Angular.

Making a Change

At this point, we have a working application and an IDE that we can use to view and make changes to our code (keep the application running, as this will demonstrate Angular's Live reloading). Let's make some changes to our application. Delete all the styles and html in the **app.component.html** file and add the following:

```
// in the app.component.html file add:
<div class="wrapper">
    <h1>Our First Application</h1>
    <div class="button-container">
      <button type="button" (click)="start()">Start</button>
      <button type="button" (click)="middle()">Middle</button>
      <button type="button" (click)="end()">End</button>
    </div>
  </div>

// in the app.component.css file add:
.wrapper {
```

```
    display: flex;
    flex-direction: column;
  }

  .button-container {
    display: flex;
    flex-direction: row;
    justify-content: space-around;
  }

  // in the app.component.ts file add:
  export class AppComponent {
    title = 'myfirstapp';

    start(): void {
      this.message('start');
    }
    middle(): void {
      this.message('middle');
    }
    end(): void {
      this.message('end');
    }

    message(name: string): void {
      alert(`myfirstapp ${name}`);
    }
  }
```

Save the files and go back to the browser. The page should have been reloaded (if the application is still running) and should look a little different too. We should just see an h1 header "**`Our first application`**" and three evenly spaced-out buttons with "**`start`**", "**`middle`**", and "**`end`**" as button captions. Clicking any of the buttons creates an alert dialog to be shown with the position of the button.

Ignoring the styling code for the moment, the code should be self-explanatory, but some of the key points are the **`(click)="start()"`**, **`(click)="middle()"`**, and **`(click)="end()"`** are events, when a user clicks one of the buttons, the corresponding event in the **`app.component.ts`** file is called, this in turn, calls the function `message` passing in the name as parameter, the message function calls the alert function of the browser displaying a modal dialog box.

The CSS uses **flexbox**, we set the **`wrapper`** class to **`column,`** the **`button-container`** class to **`row,`** and the buttons with space around each button.

Conclusion

In this chapter, we covered setting up our computer with Node Version Manager (NVM) on Linux and Windows, installed a couple of versions of Node and learnt how to swap between the different versions.

We installed the Angular framework and created a new project. Also, we installed VS Code and walked through some of the key points of the application and finally, we looked at some of the files that the Angular CLI generates when creating a new application for us.

In the next chapter, we are going to learn the new Angular standalone feature and also look at the existing method using NgModules, plus add routing to our application as well.

References

Here is a list of resources that we used in this chapter.

- To download NVM for Linux, go to: https://github.com/nvm-sh/nvm
- To download Node Version Manager for Windows, go to: https://github.com/coreybutler/nvm-windows
- To download Volta, go to: https://volta.sh/
- To download Node, go to: https://nodejs.org
- To find all the available extensions for VS Code, go to: https://marketplace.visualstudio.com/vscode

CHAPTER 2
Angular Application

Introduction

Now that we have everything set up, let's dig a little deeper and create an Angular application with multiple pages (technically, we'll still have only one page). We'll add routing so that we can navigate around the application.

In this chapter, we will create two separate applications; we'll create a workspace where we can have one or more projects that we can easily share code or common components or libraries. Our first application will use the **`NgModules`** and the second will use the new `Standalone` feature that was released in Angular version 15, and makes **`NgModules`** optional, although an application can contain both with some conditions.

When creating a new Angular workspace, we can choose to create either a workspace for one project per repository (multi-repo) or multiple projects per repository (mono-repo). We'll look at both approaches to these project structures, compare them and discuss their pros and cons for each.

When both applications have been created, we'll create a couple of additional components and set up the routing, which gives users the ability to navigate between components. Finally, we will introduce lazy and eager loading of modules and components in both projects.

Structure

In this chapter, we will cover the following topics:

- Creating an Angular Workspace
- Creating Angular Applications
- Using NgModules Feature
- Using the Standalone Feature
- Adding a Couple of New Pages to Our Applications
- Adding Routing to Our Applications and Setting up Navigation
- Discuss Eager Loading

- Discuss Lazy Loading
- Route Ordering
- Redirecting to Another Page

Note: *All commands are the same regardless of which Operating System you are using.*

Creating an Angular Workspace

All new Angular projects start with a workspace. There are two variations on the workspace, you can have one application per workspace or multiple projects per workspace. Which one should you use? If you know your project will be the only project in the workspace, and you're not going to be developing libraries for your project to use, then a multi-repo, otherwise if your application will (or could) contain other projects and shared libraries, then use the mono-repo. To create a new Angular application, we'll use the Angular CLI we installed in the previous chapter. The CLI allows the creation of several different things, for example: projects, components, directives, pipes and services. To create a new project, we'll use the ng command and pass in various parameters and flags to generate a host of different things. Using the CLI to do this will not only save us time by doing it all at once but also ensure that all the required items are created and contain default boilerplate code to get us started.

We will be using the ng command quite a bit throughout this book, and as developers, a good understanding of the ng command will help us in our day-to-day lives. At the command line type:

```
ng --help
```

This will bring up a list of commands, here is a selection of some of the ones that we will be using throughout this book.

Commands		
ng add <collection>	Adds support for external library to your project	None
ng build	Compiles the application or library to the output directory named **dist**	[alias: b]
ng generate	Generates and/or modifies files based on a schematic	[alias: g]
ng lint [project]	Runs linting tools on Angular code in each project	None
ng new [name]	Creates a new Angular workspace	[alias: n]
ng run <target>	Runs an Architect target defined in your project	None
ng serve [project]	Builds and serves your application, with rebuilding on file changes.	[alias: dev, s]

`ng test [project]`	Runs unit tests in a project	[alias: t]
`ng update [packages...]`	Updates the workspace and its dependencies	None
`ng version`	Outputs the Angular CLI version	[alias: v]

***Table 3.1**: Angular CLI commands*

Having one project per workspace is referred to as a multi-repo and can be created using the Angular CLI command:

```
ng new <project-name>
```

If your project has multiple projects and/or libraries, then you need to create a new workspace without an initial application. By doing this, the CLI will create a folder named Projects where we can add multiple projects afterwards. To create a multi-project workspace, referred to as a mono-repo, we use the Angular CLI command:

```
ng new <workspace-name> --no-create-application
```

The main benefit of a multi-project workspace is that we can easily share code and libraries between multiple applications, meaning that we can write code once and use it across multiple applications. Writing small reusable components or libraries means that these small self-contained units of code can be well-tested and become stable and reliable over time, making our applications more robust in production.

In this chapter, we'll create a multi-project workspace. This is recommended for more advanced users, but this option offers greater flexibility and future-proof the project should the scope change in the future:

Open a terminal/command window and navigate to a directory to create our workspace and type:

```
ng new angular-guide --no-create-application
```

The Angular CLI will now create an empty workspace. This workspace will contain the following files and directories:

- **`angular.json`**: This is the project structure file.
- **`package.json`**: List of all dependencies installed (files for development and production).
- **`package-lock.json`**: This is a lock of the **`package.json`** file.
- **`README.md`**: project readme file.
- **`tsconfig.json`**: This is the Typescript configuration file.
- **`node_modules`**: This directory stores all the node module files (though this is hidden by VS Code).
- **`.vscode`**: Folder for VS Code settings, tasks, launch, and extensions.
- **.editorconfig**: VS Code default settings.

With a multi-project Angular workspace complete, we can now add one or more applications. Before we get started, let us focus on the **angular.json** file. If we open this file now, then we'll see it only has the following four lines:

```
{
  "$schema": "./node_modules/@angular/cli/lib/config/schema.json",
  "version": 1,
  "newProjectRoot": "projects",
  "projects": {
  }
}
```

This file is where all the project information is stored. When we create our applications, this file will be updated with the project configuration details so that the Angular framework knows where to find styles, where to output builds to, along with different configurations for development, testing and production. When we've created our first application, we'll return to this file to see what Angular has added.

In this chapter, we'll be creating two projects, one using the **NgModules** and one using the **Standalone** feature. With Angular now defaulting to **Standalone** applications, **NgModules** will be around for many years to come, but you can skip this section if you are only interested in **Standalone** applications.

NgModule

Prior to version 14 of Angular, every application had to use **NgModules**. An **NgModule** pulls together all the imports from Angular modules and third-party libraries, as well as components, directives, pipes, and services we write within our application. Since the release of Angular 17, **Standalone** components are now the default project type, and you must provide a flag now if you want to create an application that uses **NgModules**.

```
ng new angular-guide --no-standalone // or --standalone false
```

Even though **NgModules** are now an optional feature, they will be around for many years to come as there are a lot of applications that still use them and not all applications will be converted to Standalone. While they may not be as relevant these days, some understanding of **NgModules** is still valuable. An **NgModule** is there to register your application imports and to make them available for use in other components. For example, **CommonModule** and **FormsModule** are Angular libraries and have an **NgModule** along with other external libraries such as Angular Material and frameworks like Ionic.

NgModules can be categorized into various types. Every Angular application will have a root **NgModule**, which is usually called **app.module.ts.** Other types can include Routing, Shared, and Core.

We'll create the **NgModule** application shortly, let's look at some code and explain what the **NgModule** is.

```
import { NgModule } from '@angular/core';
import { BrowserModule } from '@angular/platform-browser';
import { AppRoutingModule } from './app-routing.module';
import { AppComponent } from './app.component';

@NgModule({
  declarations: [
    AppComponent
  ],
  imports: [
    BrowserModule,
    AppRoutingModule
  ],
  providers: [],
  bootstrap: [AppComponent]
})
export class AppModule {}
```

At the top of the file, we have a few imports. The first one is for the **NgModule** itself and this comes from **@angular/core**. The **BrowserModule** provides services to run browser applications, the **AppRoutingModule** is for the routing configuration module that sets up the application navigation, and lastly, the **appComponent** is the root component and is bootstrapped from **main.ts**.

Note: **BrowserModule** *should only appear once in an application and only in the root module.*

Next, we have this strange-looking syntax starting with **@NgModule**, this is called a decorator; all components, directives and pipes use this method to provide configuration metadata. In its simplest form, the `decorator` is just a special type of function. Within this special function, we can pass in various items of metadata, for example **declarations**, **imports**, and **providers** each take an array of items. Declarations reference other components, directives, and pipes that are within our application that we have written. Imports reference other modules within our application but also third-party external modules, for example, Angular Material modules. Providers take an array of injectable objects, like services, for example the last part is the Bootstrap section this is the entry for the component to the application and can only appear once in an application.

The **main.ts** file bootstraps the application and is called as the application starts. The **index.html** file is loaded, and this file then hands control over to the Angular framework.

```
import { platformBrowserDynamic } from '@angular/platform-
browser-dynamic';
```

```
import { AppModule } from './app/app.module';

platformBrowserDynamic().bootstrapModule(AppModule)
  .catch(err => console.error(err));
```

NgModule Application

We previously set up our workspace, now we can start adding our applications to the workspace. First, change into the **angular-guide** directory and type:

```
ng generate application ngmodule-app --no-standalone
// or ng g application ngmodule-app --standalone false
```

Now the CLI will prompt us with a couple of questions.

```
Would you like to add Angular Routing? (y/N)
```

We'll be looking at routing in a later chapter, so let's add routing. The next question we're asked is about styling:

```
Which stylesheet format would you like to use?
 CSS
>SCSS [ https://sass-lang.com/documentation/syntax#scss ]
 Sass [ https://sass-lang.com/documentation/syntax#the-
indented-syntax ]
 Less [ http://lesscss.org ]
```

The default is CSS, but for this example, we'll select the SCSS option.

Starting in Angular 18, we get a new question:

```
Do you want to enable Server-Side Rendering (SSR) and Static Site
Generation (SSG/Prerendering)? (y/N)
```

For this option, select **No**.

After a few minutes, the Angular CLI will be completed, and we should be able to serve our application. To test this out, change into the **angular-guide** directory and at the terminal/command window, enter the following command:

```
ng serve
```

Or newly introduced into Angular 18:

```
ng dev
```

The Angular compiler will build the application in memory and once built, either *shift+click* the link in the terminal window or open a new browser tab and enter **localhost:4200**. we should see something like the following screenshot.

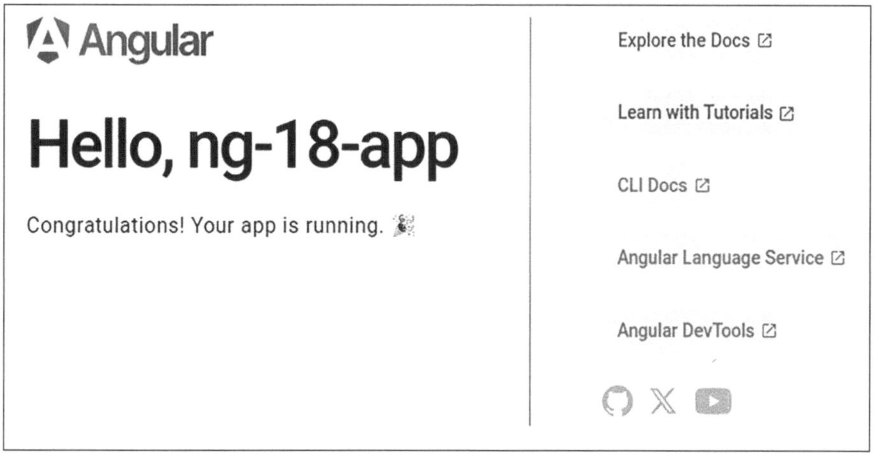

Figure 2.1: *Screenshot of default Angular application*

Now we have created our first project. Let's take another look at the **`angular.json`** file to see what Angular has added. As we can see in the following image quite a bit has been added, let's break each section down to see what Angular has added.

```
{
  "$schema": "./node_modules/@angular/cli/lib/config/schema.json",
  "version": 1,
  "newProjectRoot": "projects",
  "projects": {
    "ngmodule-app": {
      "projectType": "application",
      "schematics": {…
      },
      "root": "projects/ngmodule-app",
      "sourceRoot": "projects/ngmodule-app/src",
      "prefix": "app",
      "architect": {
        "build": {…
        },
        "serve": {…
        },
        "extract-i18n": {…
        },
        "test": {…
        }
      }
    }
  }
}
```

Figure 2.2: *Angular json file*

The first section sets the application name (**ngmodule-app**), the type of project (**application**) and sets the defaults for the schematics, for components we set the style to be SCSS and because this is an **NgModule** application **Standalone** is set to false.

```
{
  "$schema": "./node_modules/@angular/cli/lib
  "version": 1,
  "newProjectRoot": "projects",
  "projects": {
    "ngmodule-app": {
      "projectType": "application",
      "schematics": {
        "@schematics/angular:component": {
          "style": "scss",
          "standalone": false
        },
        "@schematics/angular:directive": {
          "standalone": false
        },
        "@schematics/angular:pipe": {
          "standalone": false
        }
      },
```

Figure 2.3: *Project type*

The next section sets the directories for root and the source code root; the prefix is used when creating components, this appears in the component decorators' selector section (see *Figure* 2.5). If you want to use a different prefix, then change it here without forgetting to update any existing components, or else linting will fail (more on linting will be covered later).

```
"root": "projects/ngmodule-app",
"sourceRoot": "projects/ngmodule-app/src",
"prefix": "app",
```

Figure 2.4: *Root directory and prefix*

```
@Component({
  selector: 'app-root',
  templateUrl: './app.component.html',
  styleUrl: './app.component.scss'
})
```

Figure 2.5: *Selector*

The next section is all about the project build configuration; this is for a common set of options, the type of builder (**`application`**), the output paths, and the location of the **`index.html`**, **`main.ts`** files, along with assets and styles, followed by the configurations for the production budgets, where we can raise a warning or error when these have been exceeded.

```
"architect": {
  "build": {
    "builder": "@angular-devkit/build-angular:application",
    "options": {
      "outputPath": "dist/ngmodule-app",
      "index": "projects/ngmodule-app/src/index.html",
      "browser": "projects/ngmodule-app/src/main.ts",
      "polyfills": [
        "zone.js"
      ],
      "tsConfig": "projects/ngmodule-app/tsconfig.app.json",
      "inlineStyleLanguage": "scss",
      "assets": [
        {
          "glob": "**/*",
          "input": "projects/ngmodule-app/public"
        }
      ],
      "styles": [
        "projects/ngmodule-app/src/styles.scss"
      ],
      "scripts": []
    },
    "configurations": {
      "production": {
        "budgets": [
          {
            "type": "initial",
            "maximumWarning": "500kB",
            "maximumError": "1MB"
          },
          {
            "type": "anyComponentStyle",
            "maximumWarning": "2kB",
            "maximumError": "4kB"
          }
        ],
        "outputHashing": "all"
      },
      "development": {
        "optimization": false,
        "extractLicenses": false,
        "sourceMap": true
      }
    },
    "defaultConfiguration": "production"
  },
```

Figure 2.6: *Architecture*

Next comes the configuration for serving our application in both development and production.

```
"serve": {
  "builder": "@angular-devkit/build-angular:dev-server",
  "configurations": {
    "production": {
      "buildTarget": "ngmodule-app:build:production"
    },
    "development": {
      "buildTarget": "ngmodule-app:build:development"
    }
  },
  "defaultConfiguration": "development"
},
```

Figure 2.7: *Serve configuration*

The last two sections are one for internationalization (i18n) and one for testing.

```
"extract-i18n": {
  "builder": "@angular-devkit/build-angular:extract-i18n"
},
"test": {
  "builder": "@angular-devkit/build-angular:karma",
  "options": {
    "polyfills": [
      "zone.js",
      "zone.js/testing"
    ],
    "tsConfig": "projects/ngmodule-app/tsconfig.spec.json",
    "inlineStyleLanguage": "scss",
    "assets": [
      {
        "glob": "**/*",
        "input": "projects/ngmodule-app/public"
      }
    ],
    "styles": [
      "projects/ngmodule-app/src/styles.scss"
    ],
    "scripts": []
  }
}
```

Figure 2.8: *Testing configuration*

The testing lets Angular know what testing framework we are using (at present Karma is still the default), the **polyfills** for **zone.js**, the location of the **tsconfig** for the spec files and the location of the assets and styles. Any new application or library we add, subsequently will be added to the **angular.json** file.

Tip: *Removing an application or library from an Angular workspace is a manual task; first we can delete the project or library folder and then clean up the* **angular.json** *file by removing the application or library section(s).*

Standalone Application

With the release of Angular 14, the Angular Team released a preview of the Standalone feature which makes **NgModule** optional. This feature was made stable in Angular 15 and has been the default setting for all new Angular projects since Angular 17.

At the terminal/command window, type:

```
ng generate application standalone-app

//or ng g application standalone-app
```

We'll use the same defaults as per the previous example. Once the command completes, the CLI will have generated our second application; if you still have VS Code open from the last section, then you should be able to see both applications in the project directory, if not, navigate into the **standalone-app** directory and open VS Code by entering the following command at the terminal/command window:

```
code . // Or code-insiders .
```

Expanding the projects directory should show the two applications we just created - **ngmodule-app** and **standalone-app**. Let's expand the **standalone-app**, **src** directory, and lastly, the **app** directory.

The **main.ts** in the standalone application has changed and there is no **app.module.ts** file to connect to, instead, we now bootstrap to the **app.component.ts**. The **main.ts** now looks like the following:

```
import { bootstrapApplication } from '@angular/platform-browser';

import { AppComponent } from './app/app.component';


bootstrapApplication(AppComponent).catch((err) => console.
error(err));
```

Open the **app.component.ts** file, and the code should now look like the following:

```
import { CommonModule } from '@angular/common';
import { Component } from '@angular/core';
import { RouterModule } from '@angular/router';
```

```
@Component({
  selector: 'app-root',
  standalone: true,
  imports: [CommonModule, RouterModule],
  templateUrl: './app.component.html',
  styleUrls: ['./app.component.scss'],
})
export class AppComponent {
  title = 'standalone-app';
}
```

Here we can see the CLI has now added the `Standalone` property and set it to **`true`**. To run the Standalone application, we need to pass in the project name (this is only necessary as we now have multiple applications). From the terminal/command window, enter:

```
ng dev --project standalone-app
```

And we should see something like the following figure.

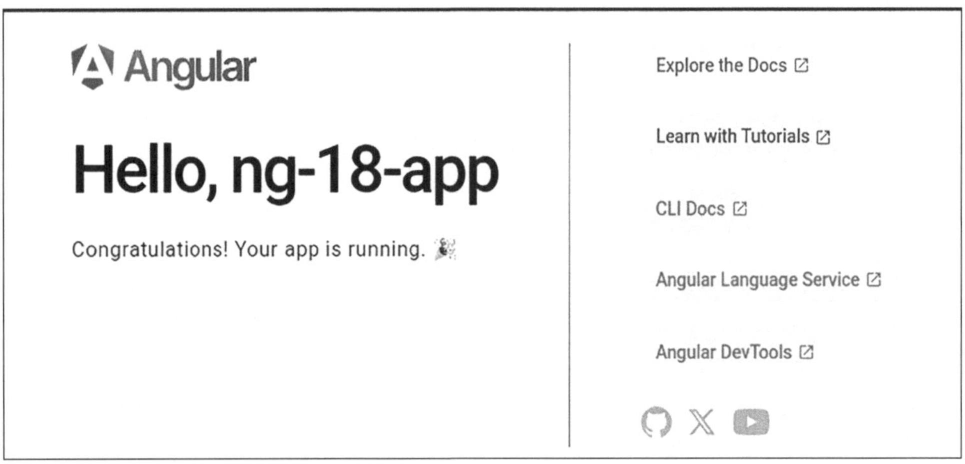

***Figure 2.9**: Screenshot of default Angular application*

Tip: To simplify running the serve command, we can add a script to the **`package.json`** file. Open the **`package.json`** file, find the scripts section (near the top of the file) and within the curly braces, add one entry for the **`ngmodule-app`** and one for the **`standalone-app`**, for example:

```
"scripts":{
       "ng": "ng",
       "start": ...
"std:app": "ng dev --project standalone-app",
"mod:app": "ng dev --project ngmodule-app"
}
```

Then, from the terminal/command line, we can now use:

```
npm run std:app
```

Or

```
npm run mod:app
```

You can use any name for the scripts; it doesn't have to be "**std:app**" or "**mod:app**".

We now have two separate applications that do the same thing but use two different approaches.

Comparing the two applications the most obvious difference we find is that the Standalone application does not have module files and bootstraps straight to the **app.component.ts** instead. The **NgModule** application uses module files and bootstraps to the **app.module.ts** file.

You might be wondering why the Angular team did not add Standalone from the beginning. This was mainly down to the compiler at the time called **ViewEngine** and the way it needed to understand the compilation context. The compilation text refers to how the compiler determines which piece of code can call a particular component. The following code of the **NgModule** shows the compilation context (marked in bold).

```
import { NgModule } from '@angular/core';
import { BrowserModule } from '@angular/platform-browser';
import { AppRoutingModule } from './app-routing.module';

@NgModule({
 declarations: [AppComponent],
  imports: [BrowserModule, AppRoutingModule],
  providers: [],
  bootstrap: [AppComponent]
})
export class AppModule {}
```

With the introduction of Ivy (the replacement compiler for **ViewEngine**), this compilation context can be moved to the components. All we need to do is tell the compiler that the component (directive or pipe) is standalone, by setting this property to true and passing the declarations/imports the application requires. This can also include modules from either within the application or third-party libraries.

Note: *Services don't require the standalone property as they use the* **providedIn** *in the Injectable decorator.*

Benefits of Standalone

The main benefits are as follows:

- Import only what your component needs, reducing file sizes.
- Reduces the learning curve.
- Provides a simplified approach to building applications.

One of the main sticking points with Angular has always been its learning curve. Angular is a large and complex framework with lots of concepts to learn, which can be difficult at the start. Angular is an opinionated framework, which requires developers to work in a certain way and this can be challenging at first.

Even though Standalone components are the default for new projects, **`NgModules`** will be around for quite some time to come, so understanding how Modules work will be beneficial.

Note: *There are currently no plans to remove* **`NgModules`** *from the framework at present. With every new feature introduced into the framework (For example, Standalone) the Angular team ensures that the framework remains backwards compatible.*

Folder Structure

To get a better understanding of how **`NgModules`** work, we need to know why it existed in the first place. We need to have some understanding of how applications are structured. There are several ways we can achieve this, but the more common practice is to structure our directories by feature type:

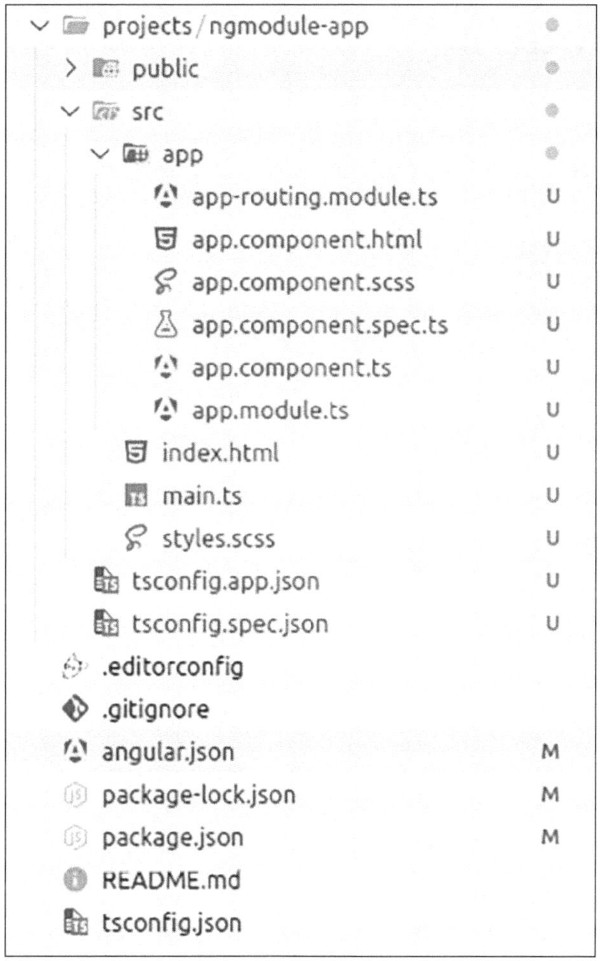

Figure 2.10: *Project layout*

We'll be adding to our example in a moment, here we'll create a dashboard component called a feature, and within this feature, we have our component files (`.ts`, `.html`, `.scss` and `.spec.ts`) and a `dashboard.module.ts`. In this file, we would import only the things that this feature required, and this is what an `NgModule` file is for, keeping the imports, declarations, and providers all in one place.

One of the side effects of this approach is that we can take advantage of lazy loading this feature where it will only be loaded when the user navigates to the dashboard.

The same principle applies to standalone components, the imports, declarations, and providers have just moved to the component level within the decorator.

Even though the Standalone feature removes the need for NgModules, it's still worth learning about NgModules as they will be around for quite some time and there are a lot of legacy applications that will still need new features and maintenance.

Adding Routing

Before we start with the routing, we need to add another component so that we have somewhere to navigate. We'll start with the **ngmodule-app** first and then, repeat this process for the **standalone-app** and compare the differences.

Ngmodule-app

Let's add a new component to our **ngmodule-app**, navigate into the project's directory using the terminal/command line and enter:

```
ng generate component src/app/dashboard
Or the shorthand version
ng g c src/app/dashboard --project=ngmodule-app
```

Let's break this down so that we can understand what's happening here and what we are telling the Angular CLI tooling to do.

- **ng**: This is the A**ng**ular CLI.
- **generate** (g): This is telling the Angular CLI that we want to use the generated schema.
- **component** (c): This is telling the Angular CLI that we want to use the component schema.
- **/dashboard**: This is the directory we want to create the component in.
- **--project**: The name of the project that we want the component to be in.

The Angular CLI will allow us to run the command without writing anything to disk and will show us the results as if it had been executed. To take advantage of this, we can add the **--dry-run** flag to the command. If the results are what we are expecting, then we can run the command again without the **--dry-run** flag, this can save us from creating components (**services**, **directives**, **pipes**, and so on.) in the wrong directory or even the wrong project.

Tip: *There are a few shortcuts we can use to reduce the amount of typing.*

`ng g application [name]`	Generates a new basic application definition in the "**projects**" subfolder of the workspace.	`[aliases: app]`
`ng g class [name]`	Creates a new, generic class definition in the given project.	`[aliases: cl]`
`ng g component [name]`	Creates a new, generic component definition in the given project.	`[aliases: c]`
`ng g directive [name]`	Creates a new, generic directive definition in the given project.	`[aliases: d]`

`ng g interface [name] [type]`	Creates a new, generic interface definition in the given project.	`[aliases: i]`
`ng g library [name]`	Creates a new, generic library project in the current workspace.	`[aliases: lib]`
`ng g module [name]`	Creates a new, generic NgModule definition in the given project.	`[aliases: m]`
`ng g service [name]`	Creates a new, generic service definition in the given project.	`[aliases: s]`

There are other schematics we can use for creating app-shells, guards, pipes, resolvers, service-workers, web-workers, enums, configuration files, and environment files.

Some other shortcuts are:

`--flat` : generates a component without creating a directory for the component.

`--skip-tests` : doesn't create any `spec` files.

`-d` : an alias for the dry run flag.

`--force` : force overwriting of existing files.

If you are coming from an older version these commands are no longer available:

`--inline-styles (-is)` : don't create the CSS file, styles will be applied in the **`ts`** file.

`--inline-templates (-it)` : don't create the HTML file, HTML will be created in the **`ts`** file.

Open VS Code (or whichever IDE you are using). For VS Code from the terminal/ command line, enter:

```
code .
```

Or

```
code-insiders .
```

Your project should now look like the following figure:

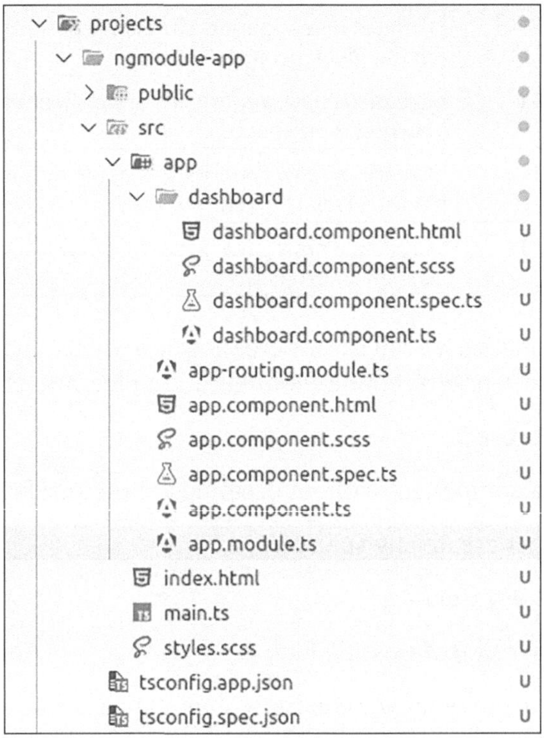

Figure 2.11: *Project structure*

We should now have a new directory called **dashboard** with an **html**, **scss**, **spec**, and a **.ts** file. Now, open the **app.component.html** file and replace the contents of this file with:

```
<div>
  <button [routerLink]="'/dashboard'">Dashboard</button>
</div>
<router-outlet></router-outlet>
```

Here, we are adding a button with the **routerLink** directive for navigating declaratively to a different route, using a relative path to the dashboard component and finally a **router-outlet** directive. This directive will insert the component that matches the browser's URL. For example, when we navigate to the **dashboard**, the **dashboard** component will be inserted into the **router-outlet**.

Next, open the **app-routing.module.ts** and in this file, replace the contents of this file with the following:

```
import { NgModule } from '@angular/core';
import { RouterModule, Routes } from '@angular/router';
```

```
const routes: Routes = [
    { path: 'dashboard', component: DashboardComponent }
];
@NgModule({
  imports: [RouterModule.forRoot(routes)],
exports: [RouterModule]
})
export class AppRoutingModule {}
```

Remember to add any missing imports and save everything.

Back in the terminal/command line, we can now serve and try out our application. At the prompt, enter (if you have set up the shortcuts in the scripts section of the **package.json** file):

```
npm run mod:app
```

Otherwise, enter:

```
ng dev // if inside the ngmodule-app project
Or outside the ngmodule-app (i.e. at the projects level)
ng dev --project=ngmodule-app
```

This will compile the application in memory *shift+click* the link shown in the terminal, this will open a new tab with our application running. It looks a little plain, but should look as follows:

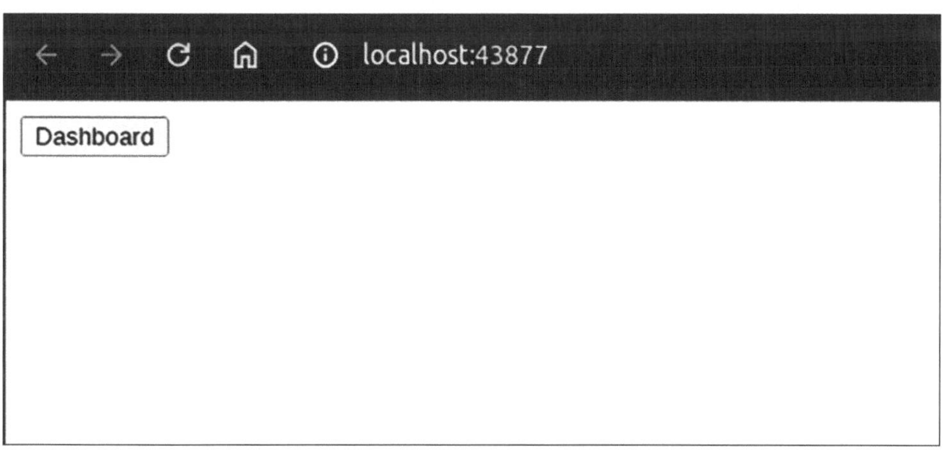

Figure 2.12: *Application routing (home page)*

Clicking the button will now navigate to the **dashboard** component, where we can see that the URL has now changed to **localhost:4200/dashboard** and the content on the page has been updated to show the content from the dashboard component.

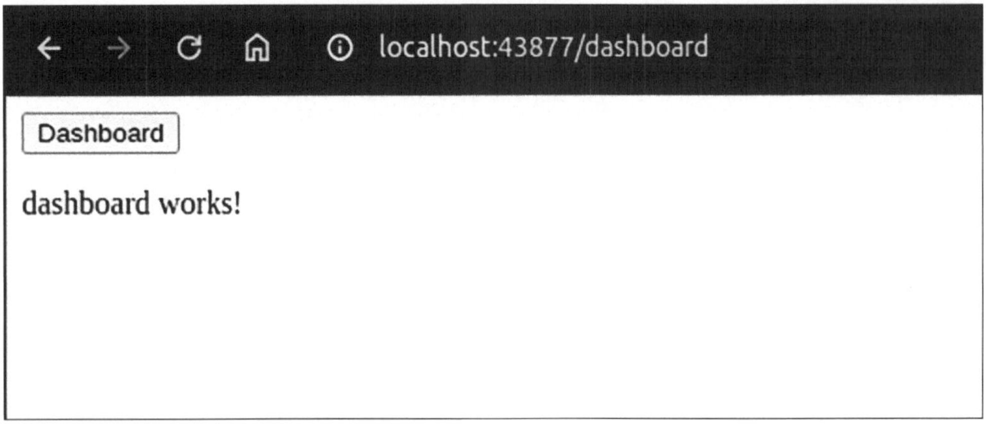

***Figure 2.13**: Application routing (dashboard page)*

Note: *The default port number for an Angular application is 4200, if this port is in use, then another port number will be assigned.*

NgStandalone-app

Let's add the same component to our standalone app. Navigate into the project's directory using the terminal/command line and enter:

```
ng g c src/app/dashboard
```

This will add the **`dashboard`** directory and the four component files (**`.html`**, **`.scss`**, **`.spec.ts`**, and **`.ts`**) respectively. Previously we added a route to the **`app-routing.component.ts`**, but in the standalone version this has been replaced with the **`app.routes.ts`** file, add the following to that file.

```
import { DashboardComponent } from '../app/dashboard/dashboard.
component';

export const routes: Route[] = [

  { path: 'dashboard', component: DashboardComponent },

];
```

All we need to add is the router-outlet and button to the HTML page. Open the `app-`**`component.html`** file and add the following:

```
<div>

  <button [routerLink]="'/dashboard'">Dashboard Standalone</but-
ton>

</div>


<router-outlet></router-outlet>
```

We need to add the **`RouterModule`** to the imports array in the **`app.component.ts`** file. This would have been imported into the **`app-routing.module.ts`** but as this no longer exists, we need to import it into the component instead. Replace the code in the **`app.component.ts`** with:

```
@Component({
  selector: 'app-root',
  standalone: true,
  imports: [RouterOulet, RouterModule],
  templateUrl: './app.component.html',
  styleUrls: ['./app.component.scss'],
})
export class AppComponent {
  title = 'ngstandalone-app';
}
```

We can now serve the application using the shortcut command if you have created one or using a longer command if not.

```
npm run std:app
```

```
Or outside the ngstandalone-app (i.e. at the projects level)
```

```
ng dev --project standalone-app
```

In the browser, we should see the same as in the preceding figure, and clicking the button redirects us to the dashboard component.

Now that we have both applications working, let's compare the two approaches.

NgModule

This application has a few more files, and as the application grows, the number of files (particularly module files) will increase. However, in terms of kilobytes, the overall size may not be significant.

Having **`NgModules`** does add an extra level of complexity to a project, and this is evident when learning Angular, as there are feature modules, routing modules, shared modules, and so on and issues can arise around which module should be importing or exporting files, other issues can include missing imports and duplication, especially on large applications.

Standalone

This application setup will seem strange at first if you have used the **`NgModules`** style previously. However, once you get comfortable with it, you will find it much easier to use smaller project sizes and fewer files and only import what we use. For example, we can import just **`*ngIf`** or **`*ngFor`** rather than the whole of the common module file.

Less issues around which module a file should be imported or exported from, less risk of duplication and immediate feedback if there is a missing import. Though this is becoming more automated with each release of Angular, it's now possible to import a component, for example, from the HTML, we now see the light-bulb above the component that has the issue and (shown here with the red squiggly line) clicking that provides with a **quick-fix** option where we can import our component.

***Figure 2.14**: Importing components from HTML*

If there is an existing **NgModule** project and would like to convert it to **Standalone**, Angular 15.2.0 introduced a schematic that allows existing projects to be converted to use the standalone feature. To use this schematic, your project first needs to build successfully, then type the following in the project's directory:

```
ng g @angular/core:standalone
```

This schematic needs to be run three times, ensuring your project builds each time and with each run, a different option needs to be selected.

First pass: select "**Convert all components, directives and pipes**" to standalone.

Second pass: select "**Remove unnecessary NgModule classes**"

Third pass: select "**Bootstrap the project using standalone API's**"

Finally, run linting and formatting and fix any build errors. It's also likely that the schematic won't remove all **NgModules** so some manual intervention will be required to tidy up.

Note: *We have not introduced linting; this topic is covered in more detail in a later chapter.*

Eager and Lazy Loading

Now that we have routing set up, our applications can navigate to other components. We need to consider when our components (or modules) will get loaded. In Angular, feature modules can be eagerly loaded, which means they are loaded as the application starts, which might not be an issue on a small application. However, this can impact the performance of large applications. To improve performance on larger applications, we only need to load modules when they are used. For this, we can use lazy loading to load on demand. Another option is to pre-load feature modules which means loading modules after the application starts.

NgModule-app

To make our application use lazy loading, we need to add a new module to the dashboard component. From the terminal/command line in the project's directory type the following:

```
ng generate module src/app/dashboard

Or the shorthand version

ng g m src/app/dashboard
```

```
In this file, add the following:
    const routes: Routes = [{path: '', component: DashboardCompo-
    nent}];

    @NgModule({
      imports: [RouterModule.forChild(routes)],
    })
    export class DashboardModule {}
```

This is like what we had in the **app.component.ts** file, with the exception that we are now using **forChild** on the router module instead of **forRoot**.

The **forRoot** and **forChild** both create **NgModules**, including all the directives and the given routes. The forRoot also includes the router service whereas the **forChild** doesn't. The **forRoot** method sets up the router configuration for the global injector. The **forChild** method doesn't have an injector configuration and uses **routerLink** and **routerOutlet** directives.

We now need to update the **app-routing.module.ts** file to make it lazy-loading, open this file in VS Code, and change the routes array to the following:

```
const routes: Routes = [
  {
    path: 'dashboard',
    loadChildren: () =>
      import('./dashboard/dashboard.module').then(
        (dashboard) => dashboard.DashboardModule
      ),title: 'dashboard'
  },
];
```

If we now restart the application and open the Chrome developer tools (or the developer tools for your browser of choice) and switch to the network tab, we can see that there are several JavaScript files with various names, the favicon, and so on (around 15 files in total). If we now clear the **network** tab and hit the **dashboard** button, then we can see our dashboard module load; we have successfully implemented lazy loading!

This shows that the page loads only when we click the button. We can also see that the title of the browser tab changes to **dashboard** using the new title attribute of the router.

Standalone-app

To change the **standalone-app** to lazy, change the **routes.ts** file to load the dashboard component. Open the **routes.ts** file and change the **routes** array to the following:

```
export const routes: Route[] = [
  {
    path: 'dashboard',
    loadComponent: () =>
      import('./dashboard/dashboard.component').then(
        (dashboard) => dashboard.DashboardComponent
      ), title: 'dashboard - standalone'
  },
];
```

The main difference here is that we are now using the **loadComponent** instead of **loadChildren** as we did in the **ngmodule-app**, as we don't have a module to load. One thing you may have noticed between the **NgModule-app** and the **Standalone-app** is the standalone-app now only loads 13 files and only one file once redirected to the dashboard component, where **NgModule-app** loaded two files once redirected to the dashboard and 15 files initially, a small saving, but a saving nonetheless.

Route Preloading

When a user navigates to a given URL, we can download and cache our JavaScript files to improve performance as these are only loaded if required. We are trying to predict where the user might go next and to get the JavaScript ready. There is a configuration property called **preloadingStrategy**, which defines the logic for preloading and lazy loading of modules. We have two types of strategy:

- **PreloadAllModules**: Preloads all lazy loaded routes.
- **QuicklinkStrategy**: Preloads routes that only have links on the current page.
- **Custom**: We can create our own preloading service.

In the **ngmodule-app**

```
import { NgModule } from '@angular/core';
import { RouterModule, Routes, PreloadAllModules} from '@angular/
router';
const routes: Routes = [
  {
    path: 'dashboard',
    loadChildren: () =>
      import('./dashboard/dashboard.module').then(
        (dashboard) => dashboard.DashboardModule
      ),
    title: 'dashboard',
  },
];
@NgModule({
imports: [RouterModule.forRoot(routes, { preloadingStrategy: pre-
loadAllModules })],
exports: [RouterModule]
})
export class AppRoutingModule {}
```

If our sample application had another couple of feature modules when the application starts, then it would load all the modules in the application, and if it was a large application this could bring the performance right down and could potentially affect the user interface and make for a terrible user experience.

The second option is a third-party library from **GoogleChromeLabs** called **quicklink**, this library uses the **intersectionObservable** API to prefetch URLs for links that are visible on the current page. To install **quicklink** at the terminal/command prompt type:

```
npm install --save ngx-quicklink
```

Once installed, we can add it to our project using the **QuicklinkStrategy** and provide the **QuicklinkModule** to the router's **preloadingStrategy**.

```
import { NgModule } from '@angular/core';
import { RouterModule, Routes, PreloadAllModules} from '@angular/
router';

const routes: Routes = [
  {
    path: 'dashboard',
    loadChildren: () =>
      import('./dashboard/dashboard.module').then(
        (dashboard) => dashboard.DashboardModule
      ),
```

```
    title: 'dashboard',
  },
];
@NgModule({
imports: [RouterModule.forRoot(routes, { preloadingStrategy:
QuicklinkModule})],
 exports: [RouterModule]
})
export class AppRoutingModule {}
```

With this approach, modules would only be loaded when they became visible on the page, improving the application performance and load times.

Raw URL: https://github.com/GoogleChromeLabs/quicklink

Note: *This third option is just for reference, and you do not need to add to the project unless you want to practise and discover – which is always encouraged ·.*

The third option is to create our own custom preloading strategy. With this option, we will need to create a service that extends the **`PreloadingStrategy`**. Let's create a new service in the terminal/command line for the **`ngmodule-app.`**:

```
ng g s src/app/preload

// this will add a file called preload.service.ts to the app folder.
```

This will create a service for us, we've not introduced services yet, so we are getting ahead of ourselves a little, but a service is a class that is instantiated when the application starts, services are singletons, meaning there is only one instance of the service in the entire application, this is set by using the **`providedIn: 'root'`**, which refers to the root of the application. Add the following code to the service.

```
import { Injectable } from '@angular/core';
import { PreloadingStrategy, Route } from '@angular/router';
import { EMPTY, Observable } from 'rxjs';

@Injectable({ providedIn: 'root' })
export class CustomLoadingStrategy extends PreloadingStrategy {
  preload(route: Route, fn: () => Observable<any>): Observable<any> {
    return route.data?.['loadInAdvance'] === true ? fn() : EMPTY;
  }
}
```

On the routes array, add a data property and a flag called **`loadInAdvance.`** The service we just created will look for this flag and if it finds it, then it will preload our module.

```
import { CustomLoadingStrategy } from '../../src/app/preload.
service';

const routes: Routes = [
```

```
    {
      path: 'dashboard',
      loadChildren: () =>
        import('./dashboard/dashboard.module').then(
          (dashboard) => dashboard.DashboardModule
        ),
      title: 'dashboard',
      data: { loadInAdvance:true }
    },
  ];
  @NgModule({
  imports: [
  RouterModule.forRoot(routes,
  { preloadingStrategy: CustomLoadingStrategy })],
  exports: [RouterModule],
  })
        export class AppRoutingModule {}
```

With this in place if we re-run the application again, then we have around 19 files loaded, a few more than before, but if we clear the network tab and then hit the dashboard button, we see the dashboard load successfully, but there is no new network traffic as our component has already been loaded.

For the Standalone version of the application, we can add the **`PreloadAllModules`** to the **`provideRouter`**, using the **`withPreloading()`**.

```
import {
  ApplicationConfig,
  provideZoneChangeDetection } from '@angular/core';
import {
  PreloadAllModules,
  provideRouter,
  withPreloading,
} from '@angular/router';
import { routes } from './app.routes';

export const appConfig: ApplicationConfig = {
  providers: [
    provideZoneChangeDetection({ eventCoalescing: true }),
    provideRouter(routes, withPreloading(PreloadAllModules)),
  ],
};
```

Route Ordering

The order in which routes are constructed is important because the router uses a first-match approach and the first route to match wins. So, when building up our route configuration, we need to place specific routes above fewer specific routes, for example:

```
export const routes: Route[] = [
  { path: 'dashboard', component: DashboardComponent },
  { path: 'anotherComponent', component: AnotherComponent },
  { path: '** ', component: 'PageNotFoundComponent'
];
```

The third route in the preceding example is a wildcard route and will display a 404 page if the route doesn't match either of the first two routes.

Redirects

To configure a redirect, we need a path to redirect from, the component to redirect to, and a path match. This is how the router matches the URL.

```
export const routes: Route[] = [
  { path: 'dashboard', component: DashboardComponent },
  { path: 'anotherComponent', component: AnotherComponent },
  { path: '', redirectTo: '/dashboard', pathMatch: 'full' },
  { path: '** ', component: 'PageNotFoundComponent'
];
```

In the preceding example, we placed the redirect above the wildcard route so that it can redirect to the dashboard using the initial relative URL from the path.

Route Information

While configuring routes, we often need to get parameters from the URL. For example, the `id` of a product so that we can pass the `id` to an API and get all the product details related to that `id`. To get this information, we query the **`paramMap`** of the activated route and get the value of the parameter. In this case, the `id` for example on a URL like: **`https://cool-domain-name.com?id=123`**

```
constructor(private route: ActivatedRoute){}

ngOnInit(){
      this.product.id = this.route.snapshot.paramMap.get('id');
}
```

Or using the observable method.

```
constructor(private route: ActivatedRoute){}

ngOnInit(){
      this.route.paramMap.subscribe((params: ParamMap)=> {
      this.product.id = params.get('id');
      }
}
```

One of the cool new features released in Angular 16 is the ability to get the route parameters automatically. To do that when setting up the routing, we supply the **bindToComponentInputs** option of the **RouterModule.forRoot** or using the standalone application, we can supply the **withComponentInputBinding**.

Let's look at an example, starting with the **ngmodule-app**:

```
const routes: Routes = [
  {
    path: 'dashboard',
    loadChildren: () =>
      import('./dashboard/dashboard.module').then(
        (dashboard) => dashboard.DashboardModule
      ),
    title: 'dashboard',
  },
  {
    path: 'dashboard/:id',
    loadChildren: () =>
      import('./dashboard/dashboard.module').then(
        (dashboard) => dashboard.DashboardModule
      ),
    title: 'dashboard',
  },
];
@NgModule({
  imports: [RouterModule.forRoot(routes, {bindToComponent
Inputs:true})],
})
export class AppRoutingModule{}
```

In the component, we can now add an **@Input()** to get the parameter we need. For example, to get the id from the url **https://cool-domain-name.com?id=1234**, we can add the following to a component.

```
@Input() id!: string;
```

Or we can use an **@Input** with a setter.

```
@Input()
set id(productId: string) {
this.product$ = this.service.getProduct(productId);
}
```

This will return the id from the url as a string, also introduced in Angular 16, we can use the transform property on the **@Input** to turn this into a number, so instead we could write:

```
@Input({ transform: numberAttribute }) id!: number;
```

Or again with a setter.

```
@Input({ transform: numberAttribute }) set id(productId: number) {
    this.product$ = this.service.getProduct(productId);
  }
```

Note: *The other transform property is* **booleanAttribute** *for transforming values into booleans.*

For the standalone applications, it's called **withComponentInputBinding**, which makes the change in the **appConfig.ts**.

```
import {
  provideRouter,
  withComponentInputBinding,
} from '@angular/router';

export const appConfig: ApplicationConfig = {
  providers: [provideZoneChangeDetection({ eventCoalescing: true
}),
    provideRouter(routes, withComponentInputBinding()),
  ],
};
```

If your application doesn't have an **app.config.ts** file, then check `main.ts`.

```
bootstrapApplication(AppComponent, {
  providers: [provideRouter(routes, withComponentInputBinding())],
}).catch((err) => console.error(err));
```

And we can use the same **@Inputs** in our code as previously mentioned.

If we have more than one parameter that we need, we can add more **@Inputs**. The name of the input needs to match the parameter. This means that we no longer need to import the **ActivatedRoute** service in our components or set up a subscription to get the parameter values.

Note: *The router inputs are only available to the routed component, if you need to get the parameters at a child component level, then you will need to either pass this in from the parent or use* **activatedRoute** *as previously described.*

Conclusion

In this chapter, we covered creating a new Angular application using the Angular CLI. We set up some initial routing (we will cover this in more detail in a later chapter) and covered the new standalone feature. We created two Angular applications one using the **NgModule** structure, and one using the Standalone structure. We have gone through the differences between applications using **NgModules** and the ones using the new Standalone feature.

We looked at routing and learned how to navigate to another component. We learned about eager loading, lazy loading, and pre-loading.

Next, we looked at the ordering of routes and learned why ordering is important. We then moved on to redirects and the ways to redirect to another component and a "**`404 page not found`**".

Finally, we looked at passing parameters in our URL and how to retrieve the values from the URL. We also learned about a new way to automatically retrieve the parameter values using the new **`componentInputBinding`** and **`withComponentInputBinding`** feature first introduced in Angular 16.

In the next chapter, we will cover an introduction to Typescript. All Angular applications we create will use Typescript, so we need to understand the Typescript language to write our applications.

CHAPTER 3
Introduction to Typescript

Introduction

In this chapter, we'll introduce TypeScript, a programming language that is used extensively in Angular (in fact Angular is built using TypeScript). We'll introduce data types and how specifying a data type for our variables can save us from unexpected errors during development and once the application has been deployed. We'll compare this against JavaScript and discuss the differences and what TypeScript provides to avoid these issues.

Structure

In this chapter, we'll cover the following topics:

- Introduction to Typescript
- Introduction to Data Types
- Introduction to Accessors

Introduction to Typescript

For many years JavaScript was (and still is) the go-to scripting language, so why do we need Typescript? For many years JavaScript went through a period where updates and new features were few and far between. To help with this, in 2014 Microsoft released Typescript not just to fill the gap in the lack of JavaScript updates and new features but also to improve on some of JavaScript's failings.

JavaScript is a dynamically typed language, which means the data type of a variable is based on the value assigned at runtime and this can change as and when we assign different values. This lack of type checking at design time can be a big issue and means errors are only caught at run time when the application may have also been deployed to production.

In this situation, at best, it could fail with an error and either a broken or partially broken web page, and at worst, the application could continue to work with no visible errors allowing inaccurate data to be stored, leading to other issues that may not be found for days, weeks, or months.

What does Typescript have that can help prevent these errors from occurring? Static type checking, this is where data types are checked at design time to ensure that the correct data type is being used; for instance, you cannot assign a number to a type that has already been assigned to a Boolean data type (we'll discuss data types shortly), where this would be possible in JavaScript and errors can creep in and go undetected.

This is one of Typescript's main benefits, but it's not only for type checking. Typescript also offers so much more, for example: classes, interfaces, Enums, types, generics, and a lot more.

Note: *JavaScript has in recent years adopted some of these like classes and others that are being proposed like Signals in JavaScript, though that might be a while before that's available.*

Typescript

Typescript is a Superset of JavaScript. What does that mean? It means Typescript knows about all of JavaScript's syntax and all its capabilities, but it also adds additional features and capabilities on top.

Throughout this chapter, we'll look at these additional capabilities and see how they can improve our development processes and reduce the potential for introducing errors into our applications.

Before we can understand Typescript static syntax checking, we need to understand a little bit of what goes on under the hood. Let's start with how JavaScript handles data types.

JavaScript has several Primitive Data Types built in. But what is a Primitive Data Type? JavaScript's most common Primitive Data Types are string, number, and boolean. These types hold values whereas Non-Primitive Data Types are reference data types, objects, arrays, and functions.

The key difference between these two types is mutability; primitive data types are immutable and can't be changed whereas non-primitive data types are mutable and can be changed. When we store a value in a primitive data type, we are storing just a single value. If we change that value, then we are not updating the value, we are creating a whole new variable leaving the original untouched. With non-primitive data types, we share a reference to that value in memory. The other difference is that non-primitive data types have methods, take the array for example, we can split an array, insert, and remove items.

Note: *JavaScript also comes with String, Number, and Boolean (these start with a capital letter), and are perfectly valid data types, but these are special built-in types, and you'll rarely ever have a need to use, stick to the lowercase versions string, number, and boolean.*

Primitive Data Types

- **`bigint`**: Very large integer numbers
- **`boolean`**: True or false
- **`null`**: Represents no data
- **`number`**: Whole or 64-bit floating point
- **`string`**: Any ASCII characters
- **`symbol`** – Unique symbol
- **`undefined`** – Unassigned variable

Non-Primitive Data Types

- **Object**: Name value pairs
- **Arrays**: A collection of items
- **Date**: A date object
- **Functions**: A set of statements

Data Types

Let's go through each of these data types and find out what they are and what data they can hold for us. A data type describes what data a variable can hold.

String

A **`string`** can be any ASCII character that does need to be wrapped in quotation marks, either single or double.

```
var firstName = "Duncan";
```

Boolean

A **`boolean`** is either `true` or `false` but can also be expressed as either a **`1`** or **`0`** respectfully.

```
var isName = true;
```

Number

The **`number`** data type is a 64-bit floating point, and this means it can be a whole number or a decimal, for example:

```
var x = 8;
or
var x = -10.7;
```

Bigint

The **bigint** data type, introduced to JavaScript in 2020 is for large integer numbers, JavaScript stores all numbers in a 64-bit floating point, up to 9007199254740992 (2^{53}) and down to -9007199254740992 (-2^{53}), integer numbers beyond this start to lose precision. For really large numbers we can use the **bigint** data type by either appending the letter n to the end of the number or to call **Bigint()**.

```
var x = 1234567890123456789012345n;
Or
var x = BigInt(1234567890123456789012345);
```

Undefined

When a variable has yet to be assigned a value, the variable will be assigned **undefined** with the data type of **undefined**.

```
var x;
console.log(x); // undefined
```

Null

Null is very similar to undefined in that it represents no data; if we haven't assigned a value to a variable, then it's undefined, whereas with **null** we are intentionally leaving it empty.

```
var x = null;
// x is currently empty but may have a value later.
```

When checking the type of a variable, **null** will return an `object` where undefined returns undefined.

```
var x = null;
console.log(typeof x);  // object

var x;
console.log(typeof x);  // undefined
```

Symbols

Symbols were introduced to JavaScript as part of es6 (es2015). Creating a Symbol returns a guaranteed unique Symbol. As Symbols are immutable, it's just a reference to the **Symbol**; the value of the **Symbol** remains private and is for internal use. Symbols can be used as a key in an object because they are guaranteed to be unique.

```
const symbol = Symbol();
```

Each time we create a new **Symbol**, we will get a new unique Symbol which will be different from all other Symbols. We can also pass in a parameter when creating a Symbol, this acts as a description and as developers, we can use this to identify a Symbol if we require multiple Symbols.

```
const anotherSymbol = Symbol('name');
```

There are a couple of things to remember about Symbols; they are not enumerable, meaning that they can't be used in **for..of** or **for..in** loops, they are also not part of **Object.keys()** or **Object.getOwnPropertyNames()**, but we can access them from the **Object.getOwnPropertySymbols()**.

Non-Primitive Data Types

Object

The **object** data type is declared using the curly braces **{}**, and the properties used within the curly braces are name value pairs separated with commas.

```
var obj = {id:'1', name: 'product name'};
```

The **Object** data type can also be any one of the following:

- An object – *(as previously discussed)*
- An array
- A date

Array

An **array** is created using the square brackets [] and is a comma-separated list of items. These items can be of type **string**, **number**, **dates**, and **boolean** or any combination; it is also possible to nest arrays.

An example of an array: a list of car names:

```
const name = ['Mustang', 'Corvette', 'Dodge', 'Chrysler']
```

Arrays are zero-based, meaning that the first item in the array is at position zero; this can cause some issues if you are learning arrays for the first time.

Date

The **Date** object is created using the **new Date()** constructor and has nine different parameters that we can pass in.

```
new Date()
new Date(date string)
new Date(year, month)
new Date(year, month, day)
new Date(year, month, day, hours)
new Date(year, month, day, hours, minutes)
new Date(year, month, day, hours, minutes, seconds)
new Date(year, month, day, hours, minutes, seconds, milliseconds)
new Date(milliseconds)
```

When we use **new Date()** without any parameters it will return us the current date, time, and time-zone as a string, for example:

```
console.log(new Date());
```

```
Returns: 'Tue Sep 05 2023 09:01:21 GMT+0100 (British Summer
Time)'
```

We can also pass in a string of a date to the `Date()` function.

```
console.log(new Date('2002-03-10'));
```

Or we specify the date using numbers.

```
console.log(new Date(2022, 11, 25));
```

Note: *The month part of the date runs from 0 to 11 (Jan to Dec) with 0 being January and 11 being December, this can cause issues when starting with dates.*

Functions

Functions are reusable blocks of code that perform a task, this could be to get data from a service or to perform a calculation.

Now that we understand what a data type is, let's look at how JavaScript instantiates a variable. In JavaScript a variable's data type is inferred by the value that it holds, for instance:

```
function someFunction(){
	// this is inferred as a string
	// because it's wrapped in quotes
	var model = 'Mustang';
	console.log(model);
	// A bit later
	// we assign a boolean value
	model = true;
	console.log(model);
}
```

Initially, the variable is inferred as a string and sometime later, in that function, the value changes to a boolean (a true or false value). This would be perfectly acceptable in JavaScript, and this is where some of the issues lie. This is a simple example and obvious to spot the error, but JavaScript makes no attempt to stop this change, this is what makes JavaScript a dynamic language.

As JavaScript doesn't assign a data type to a variable but only infers it at runtime, it cannot check if the data type has changed (based on the new value) from what it was originally set to.

This is where TypeScript can help us.

Benefits of Using TypeScript

Typescript gives us the ability to assign a data type to a variable when declaring it.

```
someFunction() {
      // Declare a variable and assign it to a string data type
      let model: string;
      // assign the variable a string
      model = 'Mustang';
      // and a bit later in the function
      // we assign a boolean value
      model = true; // this will generate an error //
}
```

This now generates a design time error saying a string can't be assigned to a type of boolean and the application will not compile. We now can fix this error before it gets deployed to production.

Declaring Variables in JavaScript

In JavaScript variables were usually declared using the `var` keyword, this keyword tells JavaScript that this is a variable, but it doesn't know what data type to give it until it has been assigned a value; this can be when declaring it or at some point later. It's also possible in JavaScript to assign a variable before it has been declared, and this is possible because variables in JavaScript are hoisted to the top of the function.

This means that variables in a function are visible throughout the function, even if the variable was declared in a code block like an **`if...else`** or a **`for...loop`**, for example.

The variable doesn't physically move in your code but gets hoisted at runtime. This hoisting of variables can cause issues as values can get updated as the scope is not where we expected it to be, for example:

```
function someFunction() {
var models = ['Mustang', 'Dodge', 'GMC', 'Chrysler'];
models.forEach((item)=> {
      var model = item;
      // this will log each name to the
      // browsers console
      console.log({model});
});
model = 'Corvette';
// here we can assign a new
// model to the model's property even
// though the scope of the variable
// was declared within the forEach...loop
console.log(model);
}
```

JavaScript added the **let** and const keywords in 2015 (es2015 / es6) which improves the scoping to a block level. JavaScript still hoists both let and const but only to the top of the block where it's declared, and it can't use it until it is declared. With **let,** you cannot redeclare a variable in the same block.

```
{
        let newModel = 'Mustang';
        // code block like if...else
        {
                let newModel = 'Corvette';
                let spares = 'Tyres';
                console.log(newModel); // this will log Corvette
                console.log(spares); // this will log Tyres
        }
        // this will log out the outer variable
        console.log(newModel); // this logs out 'Mustang'
        console.log(spares); // this will return undefined
}
```

As the variable **newModel** is declared in two different blocks, this will compile without errors.

With const variables, these must be initialized at the time they are declared, for example:

```
const ONE_MILLION = 1,000,000;
ONE_MILLION = 1 // this will error
ONE_MILLION = ONE_MILLION + = 2000000 // this will also error
```

With **const**, variables cannot be redeclared or reassigned. We should use const when we know the value shouldn't change and we should be using const for the following:

- New array
- New function
- New object
- New reg ex

Remember that a const variable's value is not defining a constant value but a reference to a value, and that's why we cannot reassign a const value, array or object, though we can change array elements and object properties.

Declaring Variables in Typescript

As the scoping in JavaScript hoists variables to the top of the function or block, using Typescript gives us a much better scoping of variables for example:

```
someFunction() {
      let models = ['Mustang', 'Chrysler', 'Dodge', 'Ford'];
      // code block
      {
            let model = 'Corvette';
            // add model to models array
            models.push(model);
      }
      // this will generate an error
      console.log(model);
}
```

In this example, the `model` variable is not accessible outside of the code block.

Note: *It is possible to declare a variable in Typescript using the `var` keyword, following best practices it should* **not** *be used as it is not blocked scoped, and variables will be hoisted when compiled to JavaScript.*

As with JavaScript, Typescript also provides the following data types:

Primitive Data Types

- **`string`**: Any ASCII characters
- **`boolean`**: True or false
- **`number`**: 64-bit floating point
- **undefined:** Uninitialized variables
- **`null`**: Absence of object value
- **`void`**: Non-returning functions
- **any**: This is a super type and is a dynamic type, this opts out of typescripts type checking.

Non-Primitive Data Types

- object
- arrays
- Date

The data types given above work the same as they do in JavaScript, so let us not repeat it here. The only data types we've not covered are the `any` and `void` data types.

any

The **any** is a super type and means the type is inferred based on what has been assigned. Using **any** removes Typescript's ability to provide design time data type checking on that variable and anything that uses it, so try and avoid using it as much as possible.

```
let firstname: any;
```

Returning a Value

In TypeScript we can assign a data type to a variable, so it makes sense that we can assign a data type to a function. When a function returns a value, we can set what that data type should be, for example:

Returning a value with a data type:

```
calculate(firstValue: number, secondValue: number): number {
      return firstValue + secondValue;
}
```

The value returned from the calculate function is the sum of the two values and is returned as a number, in this instance, if we wanted to format the return value, we can change the returned data type to be of a string, for example:

```
calculate(firstValue: number, secondValue: number): string {

      return `The total value = ${firstValue} + {secondValue}`;

}
```

Void

Returning a void, this type of function doesn't return a value back to the calling function:

```
private fullname:string;
SomeFunction(firstname: string, lastname: string): void {
      this.fullname = `${firstValue} ${lastname}`;
}
```

Scoping in Typescript

We have looked at scoping in JavaScript. Now, let's have a look at scoping in Typescript. In Typescript we have three types of scope:

- **`Global` scope**: Variables declared in this scope can be accessed from anywhere in the application.
- **`Class`**: Variables declared in this scope are accessible to the class and declared outside of any methods in that class.
- **`Local`**: Variables declared in this scope are declared within methods and code blocks and are only accessible where they are declared.

```
const global_variable: number = 10; // this is a global level
variable
class MyClass {
      let class_variable: string; // this is a class level variable

calculate(val1: number, val2: number): number {
```

```
        const local_variable: number; // this is a local level
        variable.
        }
}
```

When declaring variables in TypeScript, place your variables closest to the scope in which they will be used; class variables at the top of the class, local variables at the top of the method, or within the code block.

User-Defined Data Types

With all the different data types that Typescript has to offer, there are times when we need to create our own. In this section, we'll explore the following items:

- Enums
- Literal Types
- Interfaces
- Classes

Enums

Enums are one of the few data types that is not an extension of JavaScript. As TypeScript is a Superset of JavaScript, it can give us additional features on top of what JavaScript provides. We can create a set of constants with the **enum** data type, making it easier to describe our intent. It's possible to create both `numeric` and string **enums**. We define an **enum** as follows:

```
export enum ButtonState {
        Enabled,
        Disabled,
        Loading
}
```

In our component, we would use the **enum** like:

```
export class ButtonComponent {
buttonState = ButtonState.Enabled;
buttonLabel = "Change button state";

buttonClick() {
        if(this.buttonState === ButtonState.Enabled){
                this.buttonState = ButtonState.Loading;
                // some asynchronous loading operation...
                this.buttonState = ButtonState.Enabled
        }
}
```

In the **buttonClick** event, we check to see if the **buttonState** equals the **enum** state **ButtonState.Enabled**, if it does, then we change the **buttonState** to the **enum** **ButtonState.Loading**, once the loading operation has completed, we change the **buttonState** back to the **enum** state **ButtonState.Enabled**.

The HTML for the button would look as follows:

```
<button
[disable]="buttonState === ButtonState.Disabled
            || buttonState === ButtonState.Loading"
      [class.enabled]="buttonState === ButtonState.Enabled"
      [class.loading]="buttonState === ButtonState.Loading"
      (click)="buttonClick()" ">
{{buttonLabel}}
</button>
```

We disable the button using property binding, so in the preceding code, if the **buttonState** is equal to the enum state of `ButtonState.Disabled` or (||) the enum state of `ButtonState.Loading` then the button is disabled. The click event fires the `buttonClick` event, triggers our event handler, and changes the state. The `class.enabled` and `class.loading` change the appearance of the button depending on the selected state.

The **ButtonState enum** is a numerical enum; if we don't initialize the first item, (that is, '**Enabled**'), then it would start at zero and '**Disabled**' would have the value of one and so on.

The other type of **enum** is a `string`. These are like `numeric` **enums** but behave differently at runtime. With **string** enums, we need to initialize each member with a string literal, for example:

```
export enum ButtonState {
      Enabled = "Enabled",
      Disabled = "Disabled",
      Loading = "Loading"
}
```

Using a string **enum** is the same as the numeric version. String **enums**, for example, don't provide an auto-incrementing option, but they do serialize, which if you need to debug something, then the value of a string **enum** is quite readable. Unlike numeric **enums**, where the value returned is a number which may not provide any meaningful context.

A downside to **enums** comes when our TypeScript code is transpiled to JavaScript. The JavaScript code generates two mappings; one from the name of the **enum** to the value and a reverse mapping. This allows us to either compare or check our enum values by name or number, the **string** enums don't get the reverse mapping.

Example of an enum transpiled into JavaScript:

```
var ButtonState;
(function(ButtonState2) {
    ButtonState2[ButtonState2["Enabled"] = 0] = "Enabled";
    ButtonState2[ButtonState2["Disabled"] = 1] = "Disabled";
    ButtonState2[ButtonState2["Loading"] = 2] = "Loading";
}
)(ButtonState || (ButtonState = {}));
```

Member Enums

Enums allow us to create a set of constants that can have a value (this can be computed, inferred, or literal). A literal **enum** member has no initial value or values that aren't any of the following:

- Any string literal: "Mustang", "Dodge", and so on...
- Any numeric literal: 2, 10, 100, and so on ...
- A negative numeric literal: -2, -10, -100, and so on...

When all **enum** members have literal values, then Enum members can become types for example:

```
export enum Shape {
  Square,
  Circle
}

export interface Circle {
  kind: Shape.Circle,
  radius: number
}

export interface Square {
  kind: Shape.Square,
  length: number
}

// some class
{
let circle: Circle = {
            kind: Shape.Square, // this throws an error
            radius: 50,
      }
}
```

The error thrown is **'Shape.Square'** is not assignable to **'Shape.Circle'**. Using **enums** in this way can help prevent accidental errors from cropping up in our code.

Another benefit we get with **enum** types is that they become a union of each **enum** member because TypeScript knows the values that are in the **enum** and can help catch errors when comparing values, for example:

```
export enum Shape {
  Circle,
  Square
}

private someMethod(myShape: Shape) {
  if( myShape !== Shape.Circle || myShape !== Shape.Square){
     // unintentional comparison, myShape.Circle and
     // myShape.Square have no overlap.
  }
}
```

In this example, we first check to see if **myShape** is not a **Shape.Circle**. If this returns true, then the body of the if statement will run, but if this returns false then **myShape** can only be **Shape.Circle** and doesn't need to check if **myShape** is **Shape.Square**.

Objects

Alternatively, we can use an object with "**as const**", for example:

```
// using an object with "as const"
const Direction = {
  North: 0,
  South: 1,
  East: 2,
  West: 3
} as const;
```

What does the "**as const**" do? Using the direction example above, if we removed the "**as const**" for a moment, and hover over the **Direction** variable name, we see that each direction is of type **number**, but notably, these are mutable, meaning that the values can be changed, for example:

```
export const Direction = {
  NORTH: 0,
  SOUTH: 1,
  EAST: 2,
  WEST: 3,
};

// some class
{
    Direction.EAST = 64;
    console.log(Direction.EAST); // returns 64
}
```

This may not be desirable and could cause unintended results By adding "**as const**" to our object, we can make each item **readonly**.

```
export const Direction = {
  NORTH: 0,
  SOUTH: 1,
  EAST: 2,
  WEST: 3,
} as const;

// some class
{
    Direction.EAST = 64; // error EAST is readonly
}
```

We can also use "**as const**" on arrays as well as objects, for instance, with an array of strings we can pass them into a function.

```
// some class
{
const firstname: string = 'Duncan';
const lastname: string = 'Faulkner';
const args = [firstname, lastname] as const;
const fullname = this.joinNames(...args);
}

joinNames(firstname:string, lastname:string): string {
Return `${firstname} ${lastname}`;
}
```

This would also work if we had an array of numbers.

Literal Types

TypeScript allows us to define string and number literal types; these work in a similar way to **enums** and allow only the values that are declared, any value other than the ones listed will result in an error.

String literal types

```
export type ButtonTypes = 'Enabled' | 'Disabled' | 'Loading';

private buttonType!: ButtonTypes;

// some function
{
    if (this.buttonType === 'Loading') {
      // do something here
```

```
        }

        // this generates an error
        if (this.buttonType === 'Close') {
          // do something here
         }
    }
```

This type accepts only the strings supplied; if you add a string value that isn't in the list, then an error is generated at design time, giving us feedback that we have supplied the wrong value.

We can also use literals for type aliases to make our code a little easier to read for example:

```
type vehicle = 'car' | 'van' | 'lorry';
const mustang: vehicle = 'car';

type priorities = 1 | 2 | 3; // numbers
type facts = true | false; boolean
type containers = {name: 'byAir'} | {name: 'byRail'}; // objects
type func = (()=>number) | (()=>boolean); //function
```

Numeric Literals

We can also use numeric literals that act the same as the string version.

```
export type StatusLevels = 1 | 2 | 3 | 4;
private statusLevel!: StatusLevels;

this.statusLevel = 6; // throws an error
this.statusLevel = 3; // compiler OK
```

Interfaces

Interfaces are another example of TypeScript providing an additional feature that isn't part of native JavaScript. An interface is a way to describe our objects. We create an interface with properties that represent our object along with a data type that includes methods but not the implementation of the method. An interface is a type of contract that a class/object of variable must implement to fulfill the contract.

Interfaces play an important part in designing an application; they make sure our data models follow some rules, so we can use these between various layers of our application. For example, when it comes to sending data to the server (via an API), our application needs to have the data in a shape that matches the API so that by using interfaces we draw up this type of contract that ensures consistency between both parties.

```
export interface Directions {
  position: string;
  description: string;
  // other properties here
}

// to use the interface
const compass: Directions = {
  position: 'North',
  description: 'due north is straight ahead'
}
```

Combine

We can also combine interfaces with other interfaces, for example, we can use the Product interface within the shopping cart interface:

```
export interface ShoppingCart {
id: number;
product: Product;
totalPrice: number;
quantity: number;
}

export interface Product {
id: number;
name: string;
title: string;
description: string;
price: number;
}
```

Extend

We are also able to extend interfaces. Let's imagine we're adding a new feature to an existing application, and we want to add some new properties to our existing interface, but in doing so, this would break our application (or at least create a lot of refactoring to incorporate the change). What we can do though is we can create a brand-new interface that extends our existing interface so that we can add our new properties without breaking the application.

```
export interface OurExistingInterface {
      // existing properties
}

export interface OurNewInterface extends OurExistingInterface {
      // new properties
}
```

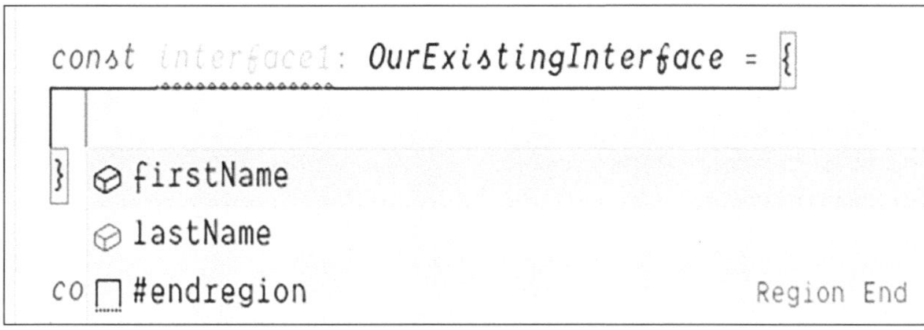

Figure 3.1: *Existing interface*

Figure 3.2: *New interface, extending the original*

In *Figure* 3.2, we can see that our new interface has brought through all the properties from the existing interface, allowing us to extend existing interfaces without breaking the application.

Classes

Classes in TypeScript allow for an object-oriented programming approach called OOP; in this style of programming, we create classes which are user-defined data type objects with members and methods.

```
export class Employee {
  fullname: string;
  constructor (
      public firstName: string,
      public lastName: string
  ) {
    this.fullName = `${firstName} ' ' ${lastName}`;
  }
}
```

In the preceding example, we created a class for an **Employee**; the constructor of the class expects two parameters, the **first** and **last** name of the employee. To create an instance of the **Employee** we use the **new** keyword, for example:

```
const employee = new Employee('Hans', 'Solo');
```

We can also use interfaces with classes, the class must implement the interface, for instance:

```
// interface with properties and a method
export interface Person {
firstName:string;
lastName:string;
fullname(): string;
}

export class Employee implements Person {
  constructor (
       public firstName: string,
       public lastName: string
  ) {}

  fullname(): string {
       return this.fullName = `${firstName}  ${lastName}`;
 }
}

// some other class
{
       const employee = new Employee('Hans', 'Solo');
       employee.fullname(); // returns the first and last name
}
```

Interfaces and classes work well together, the class has a requirement to fulfill the interface and provides design time checking if we forget to implement interface properties or methods. We are not limited to implementing one interface on a class; we can have multiple interfaces:

```
export class Employee implements Person, Expenses {}.
```

The class in this example would need to implement both **Person** and **Expenses**.

Abstract Classes

Classes can also extend other classes by becoming an **abstract** class. This is where a class provides several methods and properties that are common across several classes, for example:

```
export abstract class Base{
  // we can use the base class constructor to provide any
  // dependencies we need for the base class
  constructor() {}
  abstract fullname(): string;
}
```

```
export class Employee extends Base {
  // we can have a constructor in the derived class
  // but we need to call super() to call the base class, passing
in any
  // dependencies the base class needs
  // constructor(public firstName: string, public lastName: string) {
  //   super();
  // }
  override fullname(): string {
    return `${this.firstName} ${this.lastName}`;
  }
}

// in some other class, we create an instance of our derived class
const employee = new Employee('Hans', 'Solo');
employee.fullname();
console.log(employee.fullname());
```

When creating a base class, we can use the constructor for dependency injection, it also means that any derived class also needs to supply the same dependencies, it can be unnecessary as the derived class may not require those dependencies.

```
export abstract class Base {
  constructor(public http: HttpClient){}
  abstract fullname(): string;
}
export class Employee extends Base {
  constructor(public firstName: string, public lastName: string,
  override http: HttpClient) {
    super(http);
  }
  override fullname(): string {
    return `${this.firstName} ${this.lastName}`;
  }
}
```

With the introduction of the `inject` function in Angular 14, we can inject our dependencies in the base class outside of the constructor and any derived class then doesn't need to supply them. We still need to call **`super()`** from the derived class.

```
export abstract class Base {
  http = inject(HttpClient);
  constructor() {}
  abstract fullname(): string;
}

export class Employee extends Base {
```

```
    anotherService = inject(Router);

    constructor(public firstName: string, public lastName: string) {
      super();
    }
    override fullname(): string {
      return `${this.firstName} ${this.lastName}`;
    }
  }
  const employee = new Employee('Hans', 'Solo');
  employee.fullname();
  console.log(employee.fullname());
```

Using this format keeps our base classes dependencies separate from our derived classes, saving us from needlessly injecting dependencies just to fore fill the base class, leaving us to only inject what the derived class needs.

Introduction to Accessors

When developing applications, we need to declare variables, methods, and properties to store and manipulate our data. If we make all our variables public, then our application could have a few issues, data could be inadvertently changed, and methods and properties could be passed the incorrect data, not to mention how difficult it would be to maintain and develop with all these variables in the global namespace.

We need to restrict the scope of variables, methods, and properties within our application to avoid having them all in the global scope. We touched upon scope earlier in this chapter, global, class, and local, but we haven't talked about how we assign a variable, method, or property to one of those scopes.

There are four TypeScript accessors, and these are:

- **`Public`**: This is the default accessor, if no accessor is specified.
- **`Protected`**: Similar to public but exposes the variable to the template and code file and derived classes.
- **`Private`**: This is restricted to the code file, and to the code block it's declared in.
- **`Getters and Setters`**: These allow for properties to be read (**`Getters`**) or properties to be set (**`Setters`**).

JavaScript recently (es6) introduced a new private accessor the hash (#).

- **`#`** - This is JavaScript's new keyword (if you can call it a keyword?) for declaring private variables.

We can use the **`#`** keyword in TypeScript to truly get private variables and methods in our compiled JavaScript code.

Public

By default, all variables, methods, and properties, unless specified with an accessor are `public`, this means that they are available throughout your entire application. There are a few times where this could be intentional, for example, interfaces, enums, services, and so on where we only want these variables, methods or properties to be accessible throughout our application. We should follow best practices, make our intentions clear and add the accessor to the variable, method, or property.

```
// with the accessor
export class Employee {
  public firstName: string;
  public lastName: string;
  public age: number;

  public CalculateAgeFromDateOfBirth(age: number): number {
       // calculation method here
       return ...
  }
}

// the same without the accessor (the default)
export class Employee {
  firstName: string;
  lastName: string;
  age: number;

  CalculateAgeFromDateOfBirth(age: number): number {
       // calculation method here
  }
}
```

Protected

The **`protected`** accessor modifier allows variables, methods, or properties of a class to be accessible within the class or subclasses (this also includes template files).

```
export class Employee {
  protected firstName: string;
  protected lastName: string;
  protected age: number;

  protected CalculateAgeFromDateOfBirth(age: number): number {
       // calculation method here
  }
```

```
  getFullName(firstName: string, lastName: string): string {
// this is public
  }
}
//some other class
{
  const employee = new Employee();
  employee.firstName = 'Hans'; // this would error
  employee.lastName = 'Solo'; // this would error
  employee.age = 34; // this would error
}
```

We get a TypeScript error on the screen that we cannot access the property as it's protected and only accessible in the class that created it or any subclasses.

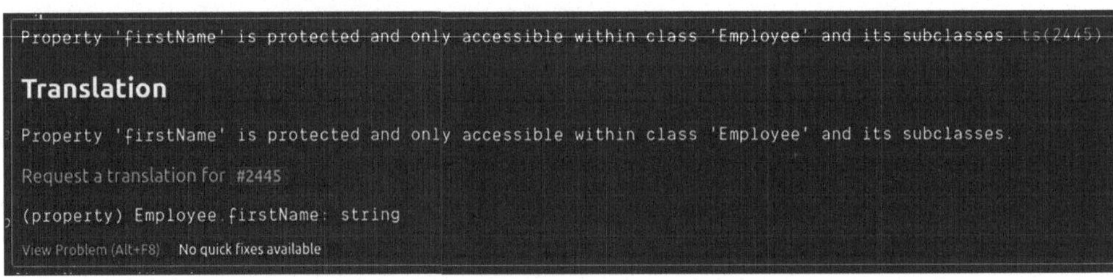

***Figure 3.3**: Protected warning message*

Private

TypeScript has the private accessor for making our variables private, this means variables, methods, and properties won't be visible outside of the class, method or property that it's declared in, for example:

```
// with the accessor
export class Employee {
  // available only to this class
  private firstName: string;
  private lastName: string;
  private age: number;

  private CalculateAgeFromDateOfBirth(age: number): number {
       // calculation method here
       private minimumAge: number = 18;

if (age < minimumAge) {
         // age is below the minimum
       }
  }
```

```
    // this is public
    getFullName(firstName: string, lastName: string): string {
  // this is public
    }
  }
```

The point to remember here is that the **`private`** keyword is part of TypeScript and not a part of JavaScript, so while developing we get instant feedback that we're trying to access a private variable, method or property, but this keyword is stripped out when our application is transpiled into JavaScript, essentially making the variables public, which is probably not what we want. So how do we stop this from happening? JavaScript added the hash(`#`) keyword to make variables, methods, and properties truly private.

(hash)

Up until ES2022, JavaScript didn't have the concept of `private` variables, there was an unwritten convention by developers that if you wanted to indicate that a variable was private, it was a common practice to prefix variables with an underscore, but this didn't make the variable private.

With the inclusion of the hash (**#**) keyword, JavaScript now has a private accessor. To use this accessor, we prefix our variables (methods and properties) with the hash (**#**), for example:

```
export class Employee {
  // available only to this class
  #firstName: string;
  #lastName: string;
  #age: number;

  #CalculateAgeFromDateOfBirth(age: number): number {
       // calculation method here
       #minimumAge: number = 18;

       if (age < #minimumAge) {
         // age is below the minimum
   }
  }
```

Now when our TypeScript gets transpiled to JavaScript our variables will still be private, and unlike before, we will not be able to access them. Let's explore this a little further with an example, where we can see how to access a private variable at run time:

Note: *We'll cover what a service, component, pipe, and directive are in a later chapter; the main point here is the private variable and how it is declared and used.*

Let's start by creating a service.

```
@Injectable({ providedIn: 'root'})
export class DashboardService {
  salesUrl = 'api/sales';
  orders = [];

  logger() {
    console.log('Url:', this.salesUrl);
  }

  constructor() {
    this.logger();
  }
}
```

In our component, let's inject our service.

```
export class DashboardComponent {
  dashboardService = inject(DashboardService);
  constructor() {
    this.dashboardService.salesUrl = 'api/someOtherEndPoint';
    this.dashboardService.logger();
  }
}
```

If we run the application, we would see that we got the **`salesUrl`** but also be able to update it, this is expected as the variables are `public`.

Let's make `salesUrl` private:

```
@Injectable({ providedIn: 'root'})
export class DashboardService {
  private salesUrl = 'api/sales';
  orders = [];

  logger() {
    console.log('Url:', this.salesUrl);
  }

  constructor() {
    this.logger();
  }
}
```

We should see an error in our component that the **`salesUrl`** is private and only accessible within the **`DashboardService`** class.

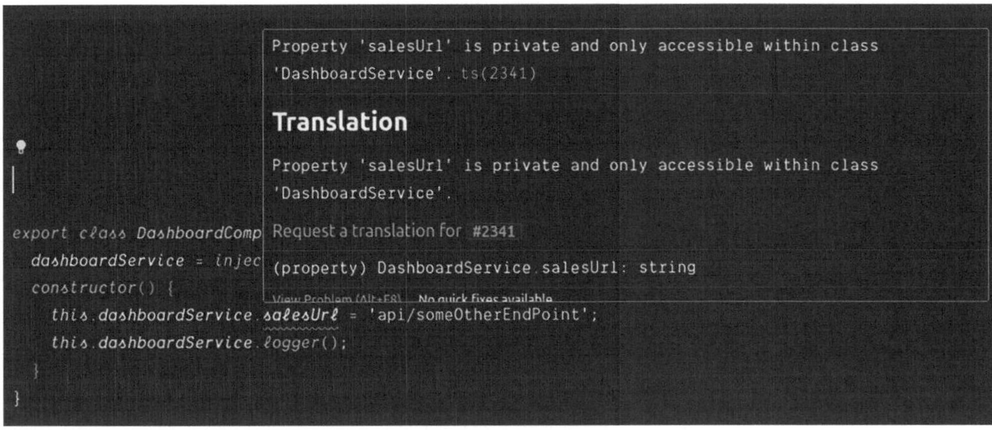

***Figure 3.4**: Variable is not accessible*

To get past this error, we can change it to the following:

```
this.dashboardService['salesUrl'] = 'api/someOtherEndPoint';
```

which allows us to not only see the private variable in the console logs but also, we are still able to change the value, even though it's marked as private. If we add a **`for...in`** loop, then we can see we can list our public and private variables as well.

```
for (let i in this.dashboardService) {
      console.log('properties', i);
}
```

In the service, let's update this to use the hash (#) keyword:

```
#salesUrl = 'api/sales';
  orders = [];
  logger() {
    console.log('Url:', this.#salesUrl);
  }
```

Back in our component, we can see that the code that was updating our end point is no longer able to access this, even if we add the hash (#).

```
this.dashboardService['#salesUrl'] = 'api/someOtherEndPoint';
```

To get our code to compile, we need to comment out this line. In our **`for...in`** loop though, we can see that only the **`public`** variable is now visible and that our `private` variable is truly private. This will take time to be adopted, mainly because it looks different, and developers are used to seeing (and typing) the **`private`** keyword.

Conclusion

In this chapter, we looked at what TypeScript is and where it sits in the JavaScript ecosystem and learnt that TypeScript is a superset of JavaScript. We also looked at the different data types and how to use them. We learnt about scoping our variables, methods, and properties and how TypeScript and JavaScript differ in how they deal with variable scopes.

In the next chapter, we will look at the different types of components that Angular uses to build different components. We will also focus on components, directives, services, and pipes.

CHAPTER 4
Components, Directives, Pipes, and Services

Introduction

In this chapter, we will look at the items we use to build our applications, which will cover components, services, directives and pipes. When building an application, we create these components to perform various tasks and each of these components plays a specific role and together they make our application come to life.

Structure

In this chapter, we will cover the following topics:

- Introduction to Components
- Introduction to Directives
- Introduction to Pipes
- Introduction to Services

When building an Angular application, we create components, directives, pipes and services, for example, **`components`** provide the user interface that allows for interaction, **`services`** provide business logic and connections to external data sources, **`directives`** apply behaviors to our components and `pipes` transform our data. Ideally, we should try to make our components small and reusable, pulling in resources from services, directives and pipes when needed.

Introduction to Components

Before we start digging into components, we will take a quick look at how Angular applications work. We know that Angular creates Single Page Application (SPA), and as the name suggests, there is only one HTML page for the entire application, which is the `index.html` page this consists of the following three sections:

- HTML: This is the Document itself.
- Head: This section is for metadata, titles, and resources like external styles.
- Body: This section is where our application HTML code resides.

An example **`index.html`** file.

```
<html>
  <head>
    <title>My app</title>
    <!-- Links to fonts, external style sheets and JavaScript
    files -->
  </head>
  <body>
    <my-app>Loading...</my-app>
  </body>
</html>
```

The interesting part is in the body tag, in a more traditional web application, this is where we would have all our HTML in this section, but in an Angular application we have a custom element (this can be renamed to something in keeping with your organizations coding guidelines), but the default is:

```
<app-root>Loading...</app-root>
```

There needs to be a matching `selector` in the **`app.component.ts`** file. When this element is called the Angular framework takes control of the application loading the **`app.component.ts`** file, from the main and either loads **`app.component.ts`** directly or via the **`NgModule`** file, depending on whether we are using a **`Standalone`** or **`NgModule`** style application.

Note: *Later, we'll use the* **`routerOutlet,`** *this is where our components will be rendered as we navigate to different components based on our route configuration, we'll look at routing in more detail in an upcoming chapter.*

```
// app.component.ts
@Component({
  selector: 'app-root',
  standalone: true,
  imports: [],
  templateUrl: './app.component.html',
  styleUrl: './app.component.scss',
})
export class AppComponent {}
```

Now we have reminded ourselves of how Angular loads our components into the **`index.html`** page, let's look at the components that make up the user interface.

These components are the building blocks of our application and make up the parts our users will interact with. Components consist of up to four files; these four files are:

- **HTML** (**.html**): Hyper Text Markup Language.
- **TypeScript** (**.ts**): Code behind file.
- **Stylesheet** (**.css**): Cascade Styling Sheet (can also be SCSS or LESS).
- **Unit test** (**.spec**): A TypeScript file that unit tests our code.

With small components we can combine the HTML and CSS all in the TypeScript file.

```
Component({
  selector: 'app-some-component',
  template: `<div>Some template</div>`,
  styles: [``
      .my-class: {
        color: red;
      }
    `, `],
  standalone: true,
  imports: [],
})
export class MyComponent {
// class code here
}
```

Hypertext Markup Language

The **.html** file is the template for the user interface and has the markup for the component. This is where we'll add buttons, text boxes, and images, for example, to allow the user to enter data, upload an image, save data for retrieval later, or navigate to other pages. The markup on this page doesn't require the html, head, or body tag as our components will be rendered in the body section of the main **index.html** file.

Let's create a component using the standalone application we created previously in a chapter. There are a couple of ways we can create a component in Angular, this can be done manually, but this requires us to remember the initial boilerplate code, which will come with practice, but the easiest way is to use the Angular CLI. Open a terminal command line, navigate to the project's directory (**standalone-app**), and type:

```
ng g c src/app/about-us -d
```

This will complete a dry run showing the components it would create. If everything looks correct (as given in the following image) and the components are in the location we are expecting, then we can run the command again without the **-d** flag.

```
● duncan@GAMING-XAX:ngstandalone-app:(main)$ ng g c src/app/about-us
  CREATE projects/ngstandalone-app/src/app/about-us/about-us.component.scss (0 bytes)
  CREATE projects/ngstandalone-app/src/app/about-us/about-us.component.html (23 bytes)
  CREATE projects/ngstandalone-app/src/app/about-us/about-us.component.spec.ts (604 bytes)
  CREATE projects/ngstandalone-app/src/app/about-us/about-us.component.ts (242 bytes)
○ duncan@GAMING-XAX:ngstandalone-app:(main)$ █
```

***Figure 4.1**: Create a component using the dry-run*

When the CLI has created our component, let's add a little bit of code to the HTML file.

```
<h1>About Us</h1>
<p>
  Our company has been successfully producing...
</p>
<div style="display: flex; flex-direction: row; gap: 10px">
  <span>Subscribe to our mailing list</span>
  <input type="text" name="email" />
  <button>Subscribe</button>
</div>
```

The preceding HTML adds a title in the form of an h1 tag; these are heading tags with h1 being the largest and h6 being the smallest in terms of font size. Underneath that we have a paragraph tag this is a block element that takes up the full width of its container, and we finish off with a div element that contains a span tag, an input element and a button. The styling uses Flexbox and sets the contents in a row with a spacing between the components (see *Figure* 4.2).

To get to this page we need to update our routes, so add this to the route file, and place it after the dashboard route.

```
{
    path: 'about-us',
            loadComponent: () =>
           import('./about-us/about-us.component').then(
            (aboutUs) => aboutUs.AboutUsComponent),
},
```

The HMTL describes how a page will look, where controls will be located, and any styling we might want to include. The browser will interpret this document and render the page displaying the elements, positioning the items, and applying the styling. The preceding code example creates an example about-us page, we have some information about the company and the ability to enter an email address to subscribe to a mailing list and we can see how the code looks when the browser renders that information.

```
● duncan@GAMING-XAX:ngstandalone-app:(main)$ ng g c src/app/about-us
  CREATE projects/ngstandalone-app/src/app/about-us/about-us.component.scss (0 bytes)
  CREATE projects/ngstandalone-app/src/app/about-us/about-us.component.html (23 bytes)
  CREATE projects/ngstandalone-app/src/app/about-us/about-us.component.spec.ts (604 bytes)
  CREATE projects/ngstandalone-app/src/app/about-us/about-us.component.ts (242 bytes)
○ duncan@GAMING-XAX:ngstandalone-app:(main)$ ▋
```

***Figure 4.2**: About-us component example*

The **`About Us`** page given here is an example of a typical page that we would create in our applications. But if we just created pages in our applications, we would start to repeat functionality, layouts, and more which would be inefficient and make our application difficult to maintain and add new features. Luckily, we can break our pages down into small reusable components. By breaking our components down into small components, we have the benefit of reusing our components across various pages (or web projects if we create the component as a library), making it easier to test as we are just testing a small part rather than a large page.

Let's look at another example and create our own components. These are usually based on standard HTML components or UI libraries but have some additional or specific functionality that we want to encapsulate into a component.

Here, we will create a component that increments or decrements a value.

***Figure 4.3**: Counter*

Using the CLI, let's create a shared component that we could use in multiple components. Start by using the CLI to generate the component, in the terminal command line type:

```
ng g c src/app/shared/counter
```

Optionally, using the **`dry-run flag (-d)`**, if you want to check where the CLI will create your component, once the CLI completes, we can open the **`counter.component.ts`** file and we'll implement the functionality using Angular's new Signal feature.

```
import { Component, signal } from '@angular/core';
@Component({
  selector: 'app-counter',
  standalone: true,
  templateUrl: './counter.component.html',
  styleUrls: ['./counter.component.scss'],
})
export class CounterComponent  {
  protected count = signal<number>(0);
  protected Increment() {
     this.count.set(this.count() + 1);
  }
  protected Decrement() {
```

```
      if (this.count() > 0) {
       this.count.set(this.count() - 1);
     }
   }}
```

Signals is Angular's new reactivity framework, this new set of APIs changes the way Angular handles updating the UI. Previously Angular would run a change detection cycle which looks at all the components and checks to see if any values have been updated, this can be inefficient as components that hadn't changed were still checked. Improvements were gained by changing the **`changeDetectionStrategy`** to **`onPush`**, though the performance was better, it wasn't perfect.

Signals improves this as it handles change detection and updates the UI, without having to check all the other components in the application. In the preceding code, we are creating a variable called `count` and making it of type **`signal<number>`** and setting the initial value to zero in parentheses **`(0)`**. In the **`increment`** method, we are setting the value of `count` to be the current value of **`count`** and adding one to it, likewise, the **`decrement`** checks to see if the value of **`count`** is greater than zero. If it is, then it subtracts one from the value of **`count`**, but once `count` gets to zero we are not able to go any lower.

Let's add the HTML for the counter:

```
<div style="display: flex; flex-direction: row; gap: 1px">
         <div>
          <button style="background-color: lightgray;
             height: 40px; width: 40px; border: none;
             border-top-left-radius: 6px;
             border-bottom-left-radius: 6px;"
             (click)="decrement()"
             >
             -
             </button>
          </div>
          <div style="display: flex; background-color: lightgray;
             flex-direction: row; justify-content: center;
             align-items: center; height: 40px; width: 40px;">
             <div>
               {{ count() }}
             </div>
          </div>
          <div>
             <button
      style="
        background-color: lightgray;
        height: 40px;
        width: 40px;
        border: none;
```

```
          border-top-right-radius: 6px;
          border-bottom-right-radius: 6px;
        "
        (click)="increment()"
      >
        +
      </button>
    </div>
  </div>
```

We have not covered the CSS part yet so for the moment we'll just inline the styling. This should be self-explanatory, we'll cover CSS in more detail later. For now, it's just making all three elements the same size with a common background color and rounded corners.

We can now use this component in other components, by adding this to a page by using the selector **`app-counter`**, (this is the selector we set when we created the component) for example:

```
<h1>Interest Calculator</h1>
<div>
  <span>
      Use the plus or minus buttons to
      increment or decrement the interest value
  </span>
  <app-counter></app-counter>
</div>
```

The browser will now include our component on the page. We'll look at how to pass data to and from a component in an upcoming chapter.

We can also create this component as a library project, which could be used across many other applications and even hosted on a repository site like NPM, for example, for now creating libraries is out of scope for this book.

TypeScript

The TypeScript (**`.ts`**) file is the code of the file and contains all the variables, methods, properties, and some logic for the component.

Note: *"Some logic", it depends on whether the component is a smart or parent component or a dumb or presentation component, parent components tend to have logic whereas presentational components don't.*

These variables, methods, and properties control how data is passed to the html template, services, directives, pipes and other components.

```
@Component({
  selector: 'app-counter',
  standalone: true,
  imports: [],
  templateUrl: './counter.component.html',
  styleUrl: './counter.component.scss',
})
export class CounterComponent {
  protected count = signal<number>(0);

  protected increment() {
    this.count.set(this.count() + 1);
  }

  protected decrement() {
    if (this.count() > 0) {
      this.count.set(this.count() - 1);
    }
  }
}
```

Our counter component would be considered a parent or smart component as we are not passing data into this component. We have some logic in our component, but we could also call a service to load (or persist) data. For example, when we need a component to display information then we create a dumb/presentation component. In these types of components, we pass in data from the parent/smart component and avoid adding any business logic or making calls to services. We can still update the data in the presentation component and emit the changes back up to the parent/smart component, using an **`@output`** event emitter.

Cascade Styling Sheets

The **`.css`** file contains all the styling for the component. The styling applies color, size, position, typography and depth (in the form of a z-index, which are layers vertically stacked), to the html markup. In a similar manner to JavaScript, CSS also had a slow development process and other styling frameworks started to appear, SCSS, SASS, and LESS these frameworks gave CSS superpowers. These superpowers added features that were not part of CSS (at the time, CSS is catching up now), browsers also didn't provide any support for these frameworks, so to use them, it needed to be converted to CSS first.

The most popular are:

- **SCSS (Sassy Cascading Style Sheets)**: curly braces and semicolons.
- **SASS (Syntactically Awesome Style Sheets)**: strict indentation like YAML and Python.

- **LESS (Leaner Style Sheets)**: a SASS-inspired styling, closely matching CSS syntax but based on JavaScript.

These frameworks helped developers by allowing them to write a much more succinct CSS, by providing variables, nesting of selectors, loops, and calculations that weren't available in CSS. As browsers didn't support these frameworks, they require a build process to convert it into CSS and Angular takes care of that for us.

```
SCSS / LESS:
body {
  background-color: lightgrey;
  color: black;
}

SASS:
body
 background-color: lightgrey
 color: black
```

The main difference between SCSS and SASS is that SASS uses whitespace and strict indentation (like Python), whereas SCSS uses curly braces and semicolons. LESS is very similar in syntax to SCSS, with mixins and variables.

Note: *With the release of level 3 of the CSS specification, variables and functions were added along with several other features.*

As we saw earlier, it is possible to add styles directly to the markup, though as a best practice, we should try to avoid doing that as it duplicates styles throughout the HTML, making the HTML longer and harder to read.

```
Inline styles:
<div style="background-color: lightgrey; color: black; height:
200px; width: 100px;">
  <!-- content here-->
</div>
```

When applying CSS to our components, we must consider the specificity or priority order in which our CSS is applied to elements. Browsers calculate this specificity to determine the weight given to a CSS declaration.

For example, if an element has a class and an inline style, both will be applied, but the inline style takes priority and will override any matching styles present in the class.

The three types of categories that are weighted:

- **`ID`**: selectors like **`#address`**
- **`CLASS`**: selectors **`.address`**, or attribute selectors **`[input="text"]`**, or pseudo-classes **`:hover`**, **`:focus`**

- **TYPE**: selectors **p**, **h1**, **pseudo-elements ::before**, **::after**

```
// using an #id
<div id="content">
  <! -- content here-->
</div>

// css
#content {
  background-color: lightgrey;
  color: black;
  height: 200px;
  width: 100px;
}

// using a class
<input type="text"/>
<div class="content">
  <! -- content here-->
</div>

// css
.content {
  background-color: lightgrey;
  color: black;
  height: 200px;
  width: 100px;
  // pseudo class selector
  & :hover {
   cursor:pointer;
  }
  //attribute selector
  input[type="text"] {
    width: 400px;
    padding: 12px 20px;
    margin: 8px 0;
    border: 2px solid red;
    border-radius: 4px;
  }
}

// using a type selector
<h1>Page Title</h1>
<p>
  Lorem Ipsum is simply dummy text of the printing and typesetting
  industry.
</p>
```

```
// css
h1 {
  color: red;
  font-weight: bold;
  font-size: 24px;
}

p::first-letter {
  color: blue;
  font-size: 48px
}
```

The double colon (::) is the pseudo-element selector, in the preceding example, we change the color and font size of the first letter. The single colon (:) is the pseudo-class selector (hover, checked, and so on).

Unit Tests

When writing our code, it is ideal to test it before we ship it to production. But running tests manually can lead to mistakes and can be slow and tiresome, especially if there are multiple scenarios that need to be covered.

This is where the **.spec** file helps; in this file, we'll contain all our unit tests for the component. Unit tests allow developers to verify that the code works and returns the expected results. If a unit test fails, then we know something has changed in the code and requires investigating and fixing, or we need to update the failing unit test(s).

Note: *Angular currently installs Karma when creating a new project, though this is currently deprecated (as of Angular 16), plans are in place to allow developers to select their preferred unit test runner. Currently suggested options are:*

- Web Test Runner
- Jest

Others may be added later.

When we create a new Angular project, currently the default unit test framework is Karma, some other frameworks and libraries can be used instead. For example, Jest is the community's most popular framework and is likely to be officially supported by Angular in the future (possibly by Angular 19), others include Web Test Runner, and more recently Cypress has added support for unit testing.

We'll use Karma in the following examples, but Jest is very similar in terms of syntax and terminology as they both use Jasmine underneath, and their syntax is almost identical. The main difference between Karma and Jest is that Karma runs in the browser, whereas, Jest runs in a virtual browser called JSDom which is a JavaScript implementation of Web Standards and acts like a browser providing most of the same API calls though there are some limitations, like local storage which must be mocked instead.

Note: *This section on unit testing is very high-level. We will be going in detail in a later chapter.*

Let's look at an example set of unit tests. There is a bit of setting up to do when we create a suite of unit tests. All unit tests must be placed within a `describe block`. This describes the suite of tests and makes it easier to find when the tests are executed.

```
describe('Name describing the suite of tests', () => {
  // unit tests
}
```

When we have a lot of unit tests in a suite there will be times when we have code that needs to be run at the start of every unit test and afterwards. To save repeating ourselves, we can set up a **`beforeEach`** and an **`afterEach`** block, ensuring that our tests are consistent by abstracting the setup and teardown.

```
describe('AppComponent', () => {
  let component: AppComponent;
  let fixture: ComponentFixture<AppComponent>;

  beforeEach(() => {
    TestBed.configureTestingModule({
      declarations: [AppComponent],
    });

    fixture = TestBed.createComponent(AppComponent);
    component = fixture.componentInstance;
  });

  afterEach(() => {
    component = null;
    fixture = null;
  }
});
```

Finally, we can write our unit tests, we write our test using an `it()` method, the first part is just a descriptive title and should describe what the test should do and by convention, it should be written like this: **`it('should...')`**, for example, **`it('should create a component')`**.

```
it('should create a component',() => {
    // unit test code to create a component
    expect(component).toBeTruthy();
}
```

```
it('should have a title My App',() => {
    // unit test to check title
    expect(component.title).toEqual('My App');
}
```

For reference, the complete file looks like:

```
describe('AppComponent', () => {
  let component: AppComponent;
  let fixture: ComponentFixture<AppComponent>;

  beforeEach(() => {
    TestBed.configureTestingModule({
      declarations: [AppComponent],
    });

    fixture = TestBed.createComponent(AppComponent);
    component = fixture.componentInstance;
  });

  afterEach(() => {
    component = null;
    fixture = null;
  }

  it('should create a component',() => {
    // unit test code to create a component
    expect(component).toBeTruthy();
  }

  it(`should have a title 'My App'`,() => {
    // unit test to check title
    expect(component.title).toEqual('My App');
}

});
```

Once we have written our unit tests, we must run them to check if they pass or fail. From the terminal/command line, navigate to the project directory and type:

```
npm run test
```

After a minute or so, a browser will launch, and our tests are executed. We should see our tests either pass or fail. As mentioned previously, we'll go into more detail about unit testing and will be setting up a sample application and writing some unit tests. We'll also look at replacing Karma with Jest and modifying the unit tests to work with Jest.

Introduction to Directives

In this section, we'll look at directives, what they are, and how we can use them. There are four types of directives:

- A component directive: as discussed previously.
- A structural directive: these directives start with an asterisk (*)
- Attribute directive: changes an element's behavior or appearance
- Custom directives: reusable components, interacting with third party libraries.

Component Directives

In the previous section we looked at components. Now, this might come as a surprise but the component we just discussed is a directive, the main difference is that these directives have an HTML template.

Structural Directives

A structural directive is responsible for changing the structure of the Document Object Model (DOM). These directives add, remove, and manipulate the elements that they are attached to.

Note: *The DOM or Document Object Model is the API for documents. It's a programmable version of the document. The DOM converts our HTML into something it can add, edit, or delete elements to and from the DOM. For example, using our Interest Calculator from before:*

HTML

```
<h1>Interest Calculator</h1>
<div>
  <span>Use the plus or minus buttons to
     increment or decrement the interest value
  </span>
  <app-counter></app-counter>
</div>
```

DOM

```
HTML
 HEAD
 BODY
   H1
    #text: Interest Calculator
    #text:
    DIV
```

```
     #text:
     SPAN
      #text: Use the plus or minus buttons to increment or
decrement the interest value
     #text:
     APP-COUNTER
     #text:
   #text:
```

The main three structural directives are:

- ***ngIf**: This adds or removes an element based on a Boolean value (true or false).
- ***ngFor**: This iterates over an object or an array and adds or removes elements dynamically.
- ***ngSwitch**: This selects an element based on a match of criteria.

Structural directives always start with an asterisk, the shorthand version and Angular will transform the directive to a **ng-template** that's attached to the element and any descendants it may have.

ngIf

An ***ngIf** would be added to an HTML container (that is, a **div**), for example:

```
<h1>Interest Calculator</h1>
<div *ngIf="counter">
  <app-counter></app-counter>
</div>
```

In the TypeScript file, there will be a variable called **counter** that is either set to **true** or **false**.

```
@Component({...})
export class MainComponent  {
  protected counter: boolean = false;
}
```

If the value is **false,** then the **app-counter** will not be shown but also won't appear in the DOM at all, likewise if it's **true,** then this component will be added.

As mentioned, the ***ngIf** is shorthand, so what happens when Angular encounters a structural directive? Angular expands the shortened syntax into an **ng-template**. Using the preceding example, the expanded syntax will look like this:

```
<h1>Interest Calculator</h1>
<ng-template [ngIf]="counter">
  <div>
    <app-counter></app-counter>
```

```
    </div>
</ng-template>
```

This happens all internally, the **ng-template** is not added to the DOM, this also shows us that the **ngIf** is using property binding behind the scenes.

Note: *A structural directive can only be added to one element; to add others, additional containers will be required.*

The ***ngIf** has two other options and these are **else** and **then** these are used to provide an alternative option, for example:

```
<h1>Interest Calculator</h1>
<div *ngIf="counter; else loading">
  <app-counter></app-counter>
</div>

<ng-template #loading>
  <div>Loading...</div>
</ng-template>
```

This time we are creating an **ng-template** ourselves and setting up a template variable (loading), we are then using this template variable to display a **loading...** if the **counter** is **false**. The div with the ***ngIf** is slightly different this time, with the additional **[ngIfElse]** property binding.

```
<h1>Interest Calculator</h1>
<ng-template [ngIf]="counter" [ngIfElse]="loading">
  <div>
    <app-counter></app-counter>
  </div>
</ng-template>
```

Note: *When we add an* **ng-template** *to our HTML, it's not included in the DOM until something references it, like a template variable, and then it's only the content of the* **ng-template**.

When using the ***ngIfThen,** we have a little more control over our layout and can switch our layouts dynamically, it's also a bit more readable. This time, we'll create a container and two templates.

```
<ng-container
 *ngIf="counter; then showCounter; else loading">
</ng-container>

<ng-template #showCounter>
 <div>
   <app-counter></app-counter>
 </div>
</ng-template>
```

```
<ng-template #loading>
 <div>
   Loading...
 </div>
</ng-template>
```

The *ngIf is transformed into the following:

```
<ng-template [ngIf]="counter"
  [ngIfThen]="showCounter" [ngIfElse]="loading">
</ng-template>
```

There are some additional benefits to using an ***ngIf** if we wrap this around our components and the result of the **ngIf** is false, then not only does our component not show on the page or even appear in the DOM, but it also will not trigger the component initialization, meaning the component will only initialize when required.

ngFor

The ***ngFor** is for manipulating sections of the DOM by adding or removing items dynamically at runtime. With the ***ngFor** we can iterate over an array or object, for example, and render an item from the array/object. The directive works similarly to the ***ngIf** directive, the longhand version creates an **ng-template** and sets up the property binding.

```
<div *ngFor="let item of items; index as i; trackBy: trackByFn">
    <span> {{ item.id }} </span>
    <span> {{ item.name }} </span>
  </div>
```

This will stamp out an item id and name for each item in the array/object. Angular will convert this to:

```
<ng-template ngFor let-item [ngForOf]="items"; let-i="index";
[ngForTrackBy]="trackByFn" >
  <div>
    <span> {{ item.id }} </span>
    <span> {{ item.name }} </span>
  </div>
</ng-template>
```

The **index** property is the current index value and **trackBy** is an optional function to track insertions and deletions, and by using the **trackBy** function only the items that have changed need to be re-rendered.

Some additional values can be used with the ***ngFor**, we've just used the index, the others are:

- **Count**: The length of the object/array

- **First**: True when it's the first item
- **Last**: True when it's the last item
- **Even**: True when the index is an even number
- **Odd**: True when the index is an odd number

To use these additional properties, we just declare them in the directive.

```
<div *ngFor="let item of items; index as i; first as first">
    <span *ngIf="first">First item</span>
    <span> {{ item.id }} </span>
    <span> {{ item.name }} </span>
  </div>
</div>
```

Note: *We can also use* **let i = index** *instead of* **index as i**.

Some of the benefits of using **odd**, **even**, **first**, or **last**, means we can easily apply a CSS class to the **first** or **last** row or alternate the CSS color based on odd or even.

ngSwitch

The ***ngSwitch** directive is made up of one attribute and two structural directives. The ***ngSwitch** requires an outer container and has an attribute directive applied **[ngSwitch]**, this has the expression to be matched with one or more of the structural directives inside the container **[*ngSwitchCase]**, and the second directive is used in case no match is found, this should also be the last case in the **ngSwitch**.

```
<ng-container [ngSwitch]="expression">
  <div *ngSwitchCase="match_1">...</div>
  <div *ngSwitchCase="match_2">...</div>
  <div *ngSwitchDefault>...</div>
</ng-container>
```

This gets expanded into the following:

```
<ng-container [ngSwitch]="expression">
  <ng-template [ngSwitchCase]="match_1">...</ng-template>
  <ng-template [ngSwitchCase]="match_2">...</ng-template>
  <ng-template [ngSwitchDefault]>...</ng-template>
</ng-container>
```

Since the **[ngSwitch]** is an attribute directive, this doesn't change when expanded, only the structural directives change. If more than one case in the **ngSwitchCase** is matched, then both cases are added to the DOM and if no cases are matched, then the **ngSwitchDefault** is added. There are some downsides to the **ngSwitch**, for instance, multiple results being displayed, but also if there are a lot of cases then this can get pretty big. For most cases the **ngIf** or **ngFor** will (or should) cover most scenarios.

In the Angular 17 release, a new syntax was included in the Angular framework, called the Control, Flow, and Defer syntax. This new syntax is not based on structural directives and is now part of the Angular framework. This was brought about (at least in part) with the upcoming (experimental) changes to make **`zone.js`** optional, but also to make it more intuitive to developers. This means we don't need to import **`CommonModule`** or any of the directives **`NgFor`**, **`NgIf`**. We'll go into this new syntax in a later chapter but wanted to mention it here as an alternative to structural directives and the simplicity it brings to our HTML code. With this new syntax, we don't need to add it to a container, we add it directly to our HTML code. Let's look at some examples:

Control, Flow, and Defer

The new syntax uses the **`@`** symbol followed by the type **`if`**, **`for`**, or **`switch`**.

```
@if(showLoading) {
        // show the loading spinner
}

@for(item of items; track item.id){
   // track is now required, but not as a function
}
```

The **`@for`** block also has an optional **`@empty`**, if there is nothing in the collection to iterate over then the **`empty`** block can display a placeholder.

```
@for(item of items; track item.id){
   // track is now required, but not as a function
} @empty {
    // if nothing display placeholder
}

@switch (age) {
    @case (18) {<h1>You are `${{age}}` years old.</h1>}
    @case (21) {<h1>You are `${{age}}` years old.</h1>}
    @default {<h1>I have no idea how old you are</h1>}
  }
</div>
```

The last one to mention is **`defer`**. This defers the loading of anything wrapped inside the defer block.

```
@defer {
  // code block to defer
}
```

The **`defer`** block has several options to specify when something should be loaded, we'll cover these in more detail in a later chapter, but for now, let's look at a few options.

@placeholder

The **@placeholder** has an optional parameter that specifies the minimum amount of time the placeholder should be displayed. The parameter can be in milliseconds (ms) or seconds (s).

```
@defer {
  // component to defer
} @placeholder (minimum 1s) {
  // placeholder content here
}
```

@loading

The **loading** block has two optional parameters, **minimum** for the duration that this placeholder is to be shown and **after** for the time to wait before displaying the template.

```
@defer {
  // component to defer
} @loading (after 100ms; minimum 1s) {
  // placeholder content here
}
```

@error

The **error** block displays content in the event of an error.

```
@defer {
  // component to defer
} @error {
  // error content here
}
```

There are many more, for example:

- **triggers**: Various triggers.
- **on idle**: Display on idle.
- **on viewport**: Display when the viewport becomes visible.
- **on interaction**: When an interaction has been triggered, i.e., click event.
- **on hover**: When hovering over the deferred block.
- **on immediate**: Loads immediately, after the page has finished rendering.
- **on timer**: Trigger on the duration of a timer.
- **prefetching**: Prefetch in preparation for display.

In addition to timers (**after**, **minimum**, and so on), We also have **when**, **on**, and **hover** that we can use to control when a deferred block should be displayed.

Attribute Directives

Angular has several built-in attribute directives, **NgStyle**, **NgClass**, and **NgModel**. These types of directives can be applied to any element to change the behavior and appearance of the element that the directive is attached to. We can add multiple attribute directives to an element, unlike structural directives, where you can only have one per element. Attribute directives use the CSS style of selector, which makes it flexible, though the majority use the square brackets. The full range of options are:

- **[attribute]**: attribute name
- **[attribute=value]**: attribute name and value
- **.class**: class a name
- **element-name**: elements name
- **selectorA**, **selectorB** : Select either **selectorA** or **selectorB**
- **:not(selector)**: Pseudo selectors, apply this to an element that's not the selector

For a full list of built-in directives, see the references link at the end of this chapter.

NgStyle

This directive can set multiple styles using inline HTML styling and we can apply our styles in a few ways. We can add the CSS styling in the HTML, it can also be provided as a JavaScript object using a ternary operator, or we can create a method that sets a property with one or more CSS styles.

```
// Inline
<div [ngStyle]="{'font-size.px': 48,'font-weight': 'bold',color:
'red' }">
  <span>Interest Calculator</span>
</div>
// JavaScript Object
<div [ngStyle]="{ color: this.anotherAmount >= 0
     ? 'green' : 'red'}">
    <span>Interest Calculator</span>
</div>
// Setting a property
<div [ngStyle]="getStyles">
    <span>Interest Calculator</span>
</div>

calculatorStyles: Record<string, string> = {};
  balanceAmount: number = 12;
  getStyles(): Record<string, string> {
```

```
    return (this.calculatorStyles = {
      'font-size': this.balanceAmount > 0 ? '24px' : '18px',
      'font-weight': this.balanceAmount <= 0 ? 'bold' : 'normal',
      color: this.balanceAmount > 0 ? 'green' : 'red',
    });
  }
```

Note: *It's not considered best practice to apply styles inline, it makes the HTML code harder to read, especially if there are a lot of styles applied. It also has the highest specificity, meaning an inline style will take priority over elements, classes, and IDs, unless, !important has been applied to the later, which is also considered a bad practice.*

For styling to be properly applied to HTML elements, there needs to be some rules to govern when styling can be applied and the order in which it is applied. For this we have specificity. The order in which it is applied is as follows:

1. Inline styles: **`<div style="color: red">`**
2. IDs: **`<div id="menubar">`**, **`#menubar`**
3. Classes, pseudo-classes, and attribute selectors: **`.menubar`**
4. Elements and pseudo-elements: **`ul ::before`**

Inline styles have the highest specificity order and override ID's, classes, and element styling. Next, we have IDs and these need to be unique on a page. If the page has more than one ID of the same name, then the styling is only applied to the first item found (from top down). Classes are designed to be reused, and a page can have the same class applied to multiple elements. Finally elements and pseudo styling are where we target specific elements like **`ul`** (unordered list) or an **`h1`** for example. The pseudo-elements are **`::before`**, or **`::after`**.

Tip: *The double colon (::) is used for pseudo elements like* **`before`**, **`after`**, *whereas the single colon (:) is used when specifying things like* **`hover`**, **`focus`**, *and more.*

NgClass

This attribute directive is like the **`ngStyle`** directive but applies to classes. A CSS class is defined in a SCSS (or SASS, CSS, or LESS) file. The class name is the selector in the file and holds all the appearance properties for the element and any nested elements as CSS classes are inherited.

```
// SCSS class
.plus {
  color: red;
}
.negative {
  color: green;
```

```
}

// html
<div [ngClass]="this.anotherAmount >= 0 ? 'plus' : 'negative'">
  <span>Interest Calculator</span>
</div>
<div [ngClass]="{ plus: this.anotherAmount > 0,
                  negative: this.anotherAmount < 0 }">
  <span>Interest Calculator</span>
</div>
```

In the CSS file, the selector for a class starts with a dot and then the class name, for example, **`.plus`** or **`.negative`**. In CSS, properties are wrapped in curly braces **`{}`** and each line terminates with a semicolon (**`;`**). SCSS also follows the same style using curly braces to wrap properties and semicolons to terminate the line.

SASS (the predecessor to SCSS) is slightly different, it doesn't use curly braces or semicolons, instead uses indentations, which can be spaces or tabs, like how Python or YMAL is structured. As SCSS is like native CSS, this has become somewhat of a standard, though with advances in native CSS development, the need to use SCSS is getting lesser.

Note: *SASS and SCSS were developed to provide additional functionality to CSS, things like variables, nesting, functions, but native CSS is catching up. To convert SCSS or SASS to CSS it needs to be processed first.*

We can also call a method and set our CSS in the TypeScript code; this is the same as we did in the preceding **`ngStyle`** section.

```
// Setting a property
<div [ngClass]="getClasses">
    <span>Interest Calculator</span>
</div>

calculatorStyles: Record<string, string> = {};
  balanceAmount: number = 12;
  getClasses(): Record<string, string> {
    return (this.calculatorStyles = {
      'font-size': this.balanceAmount > 0 ? '24px' : '18px',
      'font-weight': this.balanceAmount <= 0 ? 'bold' : 'normal',
      color: this.balanceAmount > 0 ? 'green' : 'red',
    });
  }
```

NgModel

This attribute directive deals with displaying and updating data when that data changes. This directive is imported from the **`FormsModule`** and is used for data binding, this is sometimes referred to as the banana-in-a-box **[()]** syntax. There are two parts to this directive, event binding using square brackets **[]** and property binding using parentheses **()**. We can use the combined version when setting a data-bound property, and we can split them when we need to respond to changes.

```
// data binding
<label for="data-bound-example">[(ngModel)]</label>
<input [(ngModel)]="someItem.name" id="data-bound-example"/>

// property and event binding
<input [ngModel]="someItem.name" (ngModelChange)="setTitle-
Case($event)" id="property-event-example"/>
```

With **NgModel** we can set up two-way data binding, meaning, we can synchronize our data between our form elements and a matching property in the code behind (**.ts** file). Likewise, if the data changes in the component's properties, then the form is updated.

With two-way data binding we get some advantages and disadvantages, we can implement basic form validation, such as **required**, **minlength**, **maxlength**, which updates the form's validity. Error messages are linked to the invalid form element giving instant feedback. Some of the disadvantages with template-driven forms, the validation logic can become complex and difficult to read/write. We can also find that writing custom validation rules can be challenging with limited flexibility though there are third party libraries that can simplify some of these for us.

Custom Directives

We are also able to create custom attribute directives that we can then apply to elements to change the appearance or behavior. It is like creating a component, but instead of **@Component** we use **@Directive**. Let's create a directive to change the background color of a `div`. There are a couple of ways to do this:

```
import { Directive } from '@angular/core';

@Directive({
  selector: '[change-color]',
  standalone: true,
})
export class ChangeColorDirective {
  constructor(element: ElementRef) {
     element.nativeElement.style.backgroundColor = 'lightblue';
   }
}

HTML
<div change-color> <!-- directive selector -->
  <span>Interest Calculator</span>
</div>
```

The **`ElementRef`** is widely used, but this is not ideal, and we should consider using data bindings instead. Even the Angular team suggests that using this API should only be as a last resort, with data bindings or **`Render2`** being the preferred options.

```
import { Directive, HostBinding } from '@angular/core';

@Directive({
  selector: '[change-color]',
  standalone: true,
})
export class ChangeColorDirective {
   @HostBinding('style.backgroundColor') color = 'lightblue';
}

HTML
<div change-color> <!-- directive selector -->
  <span>Interest Calculator</span>
</div>
```

With the `@HostBinding`, we can set the properties on an element. To listen for events, we use the `@HostListener`.

```
import { Directive, HostBinding, HostListener } from '@angular/
core';

@Directive({
  selector: '[change-color]',
  standalone: true,
})
export class ChangeColorDirective {
   @HostBinding('style.backgroundColor') color = 'lightblue';
   @HostBinding('style.border') borderColor!: string;

  @HostListener('click') borderColor() {
    this.borderColor = 'solid 2px red';
  }
}

HTML
<div change-color> <!-- directive selector -->
  <span>Interest Calculator</span>
</div>
```

In this example, when we click the text, a solid border appears two pixels wide and colored red.

Using **`@Hostbinding`** and **`@Hostlistening`** is preferred over **`elementRef`** (there is currently an ongoing discussion about the future of the **`elementRef`** API, there are ongoing discussions about a new **DOMRef** API that will supersede **elementRef**). While **@Hostbinding** and **@Hostlistener** are better alternatives but these remain in the framework for backwards compatibility. What can we use instead? The **host: {}** decorator option is making a comeback and is preferred, especially with the introduction of Signals this makes things a bit easier.

```
host: {
'[class.isValid]': 'isValid()'
}
```

We can use the new **toSignal** function:

```
isValid = toSignal(some_form_control.statusChanges).pipe(
map((change)=> {return change === 'value_to_compare_against'})));
```

Introduction to Pipes

Pipes transform data from one format to another, for example, a date or upper or lowercase text. A pipe is a TypeScript function that takes an input and returns a transformed output. We call the pipe function in our HTML templates, for example,

```
HTML
<div>
  <span>{{ interestStartDate | date:'long'}}</span>
</div>
```

In this example, the format of the date is returned in long-form. There are several other options available for the date pipe (see the link in the *References* section). Angular comes with several prebuilt pipes, here are just a few of them:

- **DatePipe**: Changes date format
- **UpperCasePipe**: Makes all text UPPERCASE
- **LowerCasePipe**: Makes all text lowercase
- **TitleCasePipe**: Capitalizes the first letter of each word, lowercases the rest of the word
- **CurrencyPipe**: Changes number to a string, includes the currency symbol
- **DecimalPipe**: Changes number to a string, includes a decimal point
- **PercentPipe**: Changes number to a string, includes the percentage symbol

```
HTML
// amount = 2
<div>
    <span>{{ amount | percent: "4.3-5" : "es" }}</span>
</div>
```

Here, we are using the percentage pipe, without the additional parameters we get everything left of the decimal point (everything to the right-hand side including the decimal point is not shown). The first value (4) of the first parameter specifies the number of digits up to where the decimal point would be, the next value (3-5) is the minimum and maximum number placed after the decimal point, and the final parameter specifies the locale.

To call a pipe in the TypeScript code file, we need to inject the pipe into our component and then call the transform method, passing in the value:

```
uppercasepipe = inject(UpperCasePipe);
someFunction(value: string)
{
  this.uppercasepipe.transform(value)
}
```

Note: *All values are formatted using locale rules.*

Now we have seen some of the different pipes available and how to use a pipe. Let's look at writing a custom pipe. Pipes are like components and directives and have a decorator to denote the type, but they must also implement the **`PipeTransform`** interface. This interface states it must have a `transform` method that must return something (this will be specified in the return type).

```
// PIPE
import {Pipe, PipeTransform} from '@angular/core';

const currencyValues: Record<string,number> ={
  USD:25,
  EURO: 34
}

@Pipe({
  name: 'currencyConverter'
})
export class CurrencyConverterPipe implements PipeTransform {
  Transform(value: number, currency:string): number {
   return value / currencyValues[currency];
  }
}

// HTML
<span>{{ salary | conversion : "USD" | currency }}</span>

// TS
salary: number = 144000; // change this number to get a different
value.

// Output
$2,618.18
```

Pure versus Impure

Pipes, by default, are pure functions, what this means is that the function, provided with the same arguments will always return the same output with no side effects. Pure pipes are also more performant as pipes are memoized, which means if the data hasn't changed since the last time, then the cached value is returned, and the pipe won't be called.

Impure pipes, on the other hand, are called on every change detection. This can be useful in situations where data comes from an external source.

Note: *It's considered a best practice to use pure pipes for performance and reduce unnecessary change detection cycles.*

Introduction to Services

Services connect data with the view, they can be used to manage state, call out to APIs and other external sources, and serve to share data throughout our application. The created service can be accessed with Angular's dependency injection. Services are singletons, meaning there will be one instance of your service, and it will be shared across our application.

In this section, we'll look at creating a couple of services and how we access them. We'll start with calling an API endpoint as this will make up most of the services in an application.

Calling an API

```
import { Injectable } from '@angular/core';
import { HttpClient } from '@angular/common/http';

@Injectable({
  providedIn: 'root',
})
export class UserService {
  private http =inject(HttpClient);

  getUser(id: string): Observable<User> {
    return this.http.get<User>(`/api/user/${id});
  }

  getUsers(): Observable<User[]> {
    return this.http.get<User[]>('/api/user');
  }
}
```

This is a typical service for calling API endpoints, additionally, this would also have **POST**, **PUT**, **UPDATE**, and **DELETE** calls. Like all other components we've created in this chapter, the service also has a decorator called `Injectable.` This allows the service to be injected into our components via Angular's dependency injection. The **'root'** part means it will be instantiated when the application starts and will be available throughout the lifetime of the application.

In the preceding example, there are two methods - one returns a specific user and is called **getUser**. We're passing in the user ID and return it as an Observable of type **User**, the second returns an array of all **users**. We use an Observable, so we can subscribe to it and access the data returned. Passing in the type to the `GET` ensures that the data returned is in the correct shape, in our case a user object.

```
// user object
export interface User = {
  id: string;
  firstName: string;
  lastName: string;
  age: number;
}
```

To call the service from our components, we need to inject the service and subscribe to it.

```
export class AppComponent implements OnInit {
  protected users!: Observable<User[]>;
  private userService = inject(UserService);

  ngOnInit(): void {
    this.users = this.userService.getUsers();
  }
}
```

There are two ways to get data from an observable, the first and preferred method is to use the **async** pipe, which will subscribe to the observable when data becomes available. It will update the data when the data changes and unsubscribe when the component is destroyed. We use a structural directive to check when our variable has data. As previously discussed, we could include an **else** block to be displayed while the data loads.

```
// example one
@if(users | async as users){
<div>
      {{ users.firstName }}
      {{ users.lastName }}
      {{ users.age }}
</div>
}
```

```
//example two showing if/else
@if(users | async as users){
  <div>
      {{ users.firstName }}
      {{ users.lastName }}
      {{ users.age }}
  </div>
} @else {
  <span>Loading...</span>
}
```

The second method is to subscribe to the observable manually. To do that, we need to change our code slightly.

```
export class AppComponent implements OnInit{
  protected users!: User[];
  private userService = inject(UserService);
  private destroyRef = inject(DestroyRef);

  ngOnInit(): void {
    this.userService.getUsers()
    .pipe(takeUntilDestroyed(this.destroyRef)
    .subscribe((data)=> {
      this.users = data;
    });
  }
}

//HTML
@if(users){
  <div>
      {{ users.firstName }}
      {{ users.lastName }}
      {{ users.age }}
  </div>
      }
```

When we subscribe manually, we need to call our service and then subscribe to it, if we don't subscribe, it will call the service but won't return anything. Once we have subscribed, we can then package the data ready to be used in our **ts** or template file. The one thing we need to remember is to unsubscribe. There are a few ways to unsubscribe:

- Create a **Subscription**
- Use RxJS Subject and **takeUntil**
- Use RxJS take function
- Use RxJS **takeUntilDestroyed** function – shown above

Using a Subscription:

```
private destroy: Subscription = new Subscription();

ngOnInit(): void {
      this.destroy = this.userService.getUsers()
      .subscribe((data) => {
       this.users = data;
    });
  }

ngOnDestroy(): void {
    if(this.destroy){
      this.destroy.unsubscribe();
    }
  }
```

We can also make the **Subscription** an array and then iterate over them to unsubscribe.

```
private destroy: Subscription[] = new Array<Subscription>();
ngOnDestroy(): void {
    this.destroy.forEach(item=>{
      item.unsubscribe();
    })
  }
  ngOnInit(): void {
    this.destroy.push(this.userService.getUsers()
          .subscribe((data) => {
      this.users = data;
    }));
  }
```

Using an RxJS subject:

```
destroy: Subject<void> = new Subject<void>();
ngOnInit(): void {
        this.userService.getUsers()
          .pipe(takeUntil(this.destroy))
          .subscribe((data) => {
      this.users = data;
    });
  }
ngOnDestroy(): void {
    if(this.destroy){
      this.destroy.next();
      this.destroy.complete();
    }
  }
```

Use the RxJS take function:

```
import { take } from 'rxjs'
ngOnInit(): void {
        this.userService.getUsers()
          .pipe(take(1))
          .subscribe((data) => {
      this.users = data;
    });
  }
```

This works because **take** or **of** automatically completes.

Lastly another example of using the takeUntilDestroyed:

```
private destroyRef = inject(DestroyRef);
  private activatedRoute = inject(ActivatedRoute)
    .firstChild?.paramMap.pipe(takeUntilDestroyed(this.destroyRef))
    .subscribe((res) => {
      // get the results from the first child parameter in the url
    });
```

In this example, we are getting the first child of the route, in the route state tree.

Note: *When using any of the above RxJs methods to unsubscribe, remember to make the* **takeUntil**, **take**, *or* **takeUntilDestroyed** *the last chained option in the pipe, this is especially more critical when flattening observables, "like" when using a* **mergeMap** *for example. As this can lead to some undesirable and hard to debug side-effects as outer subscriptions may unsubscribe before the inner subscription, by making this the last option in the chain avoids this issue.*

Managing State

Another use for services is for sharing state between components and one of the ways to manage this state is to use a **Subject**. We could also use a **BehaviorSubject** if we need to supply an initial default value.

Let's create a new service that allows us to share some simple states.

```
// Service
@Injectable({
  providedIn: 'root',
})
export class userStateService {
  private userStateSubject: Subject<User> = new Subject<User>();
  userState$ = this.userStateSubject.asObservable();

  updateUserState(value: User) {
    this.userStateSubject.next(value);
```

```
    }
}

// Component code behind file
userStateService = inject(stateService);
protected userState$!: Observable<User>;

ngOnInit(): void {
    // get latest value from user state service
    this.userState$ = this.userStateService.userState$;
}

// update user state service
onSave(user: User): void{
    this.userStateService.updateUserState(user);
}
```

With this being a service, we can listen for and update our state anywhere our application requires it.

Conclusion

In this chapter, we've covered the basics of creating a component, directive, pipe, and service and you should have a good foundation of knowledge to build upon. In the next chapter, we'll be discussing reactivity in Angular applications, which include signals, RxJs, observables, and reactive pipelines.

References

- https://angular.io/api/common#directives
- https://angular.io/api/core/ElementRef#properties
- https://angular.io/api/common/DatePipe#pre-defined-format-options

CHAPTER 5
Getting Started with Reactivity

Introduction

In the previous chapters, we saw the technical requirements to get started with Angular. Unlike many other JavaScript frameworks, Angular stands out as a highly opinionated framework, from the technologies it relies on to the paradigms it takes advantage of.

In this chapter, we will delve into Angular's building blocks and the reasons behind choices. We will provide a clear understanding of reactive programming by illustrating it through concrete examples, highlighting its distinctions from alternative coding approaches, and explaining why it is particularly well-suited for front-end development. We will then explore diverse methods of implementing reactive programming using the tools provided by Angular, examining their differences and practical applications.

Structure

In this chapter, we will cover the following topics:

- Understanding Reactive Programming
- Introducing RxJS
- Reactivity with Signals

Understanding Reactive Programming

While writing code, there are many ways to achieve the desired outcome. For instance, you can either rely on *Object Oriented Programming* or *Functional Programming* for a given program. In software development, these ways of approaching coding are also referred to as *paradigms*.

Paradigms represent distinct styles of programming and software design, and, while they all can ultimately help you reach your goal, some may be better suited for specific purposes compared to others.

In Angular, as in many front-end frameworks, code is frequently written by combining declarative and reactive programming approaches.

Imperative and Declarative Programming

To fully understand these paradigms and how they operate, let's have a quick introduction to both of them.

Imperative Programming in a Nutshell

Chances are that most of the code you are used to was written imperatively. Behind this term lies the simple idea that you tell your program *how* do to something. For example, take a look at this TypeScript code:

```
const myArray = [1, 2, 3];
let total = 0;
for (let i = 0; i < myArray.length; ++i) {
  total += myArray[i];
}
```

In this example, we are not writing *what* we want to achieve but rather specifying a set of step-by-step instructions that ultimately lead to the computation of the sum of the values of **`myArray`**.

If we were to be in a kitchen and you would like a cup of tea using an imperative approach, you would have to give detailed directions, one step at a time:

1. Boil some water
2. Put a teabag in a cup
3. Pour the hot water into the cup

While this logic is easy to understand in a short code snippet, imperative coding like this can lead to a challenge: variables are often used as containers for values, rather than as meaningful representations of data.

Let's take a closer look at a TypeScript class to illustrate this issue:

```
class Product {
    quantity = 0;
    canBePurchased = false;

    addStock(quantity: number): void {
      this.quantity += quantity;
      this.canBePurchased = this.quantity > 0;
```

```
        }

        buy(quantity: number): void {
          this.quantity -= quantity;
          this.canBePurchased = this.quantity > 0;
        }
    }
```

In the **`Product`** class, the intentions are clear, but it can be challenging to keep track of how each value evolves over time. Both `quantity` and **`canBePurchased`** are modified in the class methods, and to understand how a value is used and assigned, we must have a look at all the references of the variables inside the class.

Declarative Programming in Simple Terms

In contrast to imperative coding, which defines *how* to do something, declarative coding focuses on *what* we want to achieve. For instance, consider a small snippet of HTML:

```
<button>I'm a button</button>
```

In this example, how the button is rendered is not the primary concern: this HTML instruction just states that there should be a button displayed on the page, the implementation details don't matter.

To draw a parallel with our previous example, let's imagine us back in the kitchen again, wanting another cup of tea, but this time using a declarative approach. In this case, we would simply state what we want without detailing the intermediary steps:

- "I want a hot cup of tea with a teabag"

In programming, declarative coding implies that, for a given variable, we can examine its declaration and understand its whole purpose, knowing that it is self-contained and not modified elsewhere in the code.

In practice, if we were to rewrite the computation of the sum of myArray declaratively, here is how we could do it:

```
const myArray = [1, 2, 3];

const total = myArray.reduce((total, element) => total + element,
0);
```

Note: *Since the `total` is now self-contained, it can now be declared as `const`, emphasizing that it is not altered anywhere else.*

Fundamentally, neither of these paradigms is inherently good or bad; they simply serve different purposes. Imperative programming is well-suited for specific and focused tasks, whereas declarative programming is an excellent choice for abstracting details and concentrating on the desired outcome.

Introducing Reactive Programming

When discussing user interfaces, you will often hear about *reactive programming* as a common coding style. Given that Angular is designed for building efficient web applications, it's no surprise that this approach is widely employed.

Since many of Angular's API revolves around reactivity, let's start by understanding what reactivity means and how to approach our algorithms with this in mind.

Core Concepts

Reactive programming is a concept you might have encountered more often than you think. At its core, it's about the idea that a variable can have its value changed over time, and this change might require other parts of the code to be re-evaluated.

In simple terms, when a value changes, other parts of the code can *react* to that change.

One of the most explicit examples we could think of is a timer. When you set a specific time, you see a countdown, and when it hits zero, an alarm sounds. To put it differently, when the current time changes, the countdown *reacts* by reducing the remaining time. Consequently, when the remaining time reaches zero, a certain condition reacts as well, triggering the alarm.

Another practical example can be found right in your web browser. Think about the name of one of your browser's tabs: as you switch between pages, the tab's title changes too. The tab's name *reacts* to the current page's changes.

These examples illustrate the two primary use cases of reactive programming:

- Values that change over **time**
- Values triggered by an **action**

To understand why this paradigm really shines here, we can try to imagine what the behavior of our examples might have been without it.

In the case of the timer, we would have to recompute each value at the end of a large loop, running every second. Additionally, we would need to make sure that all the side effects are handled imperatively. As a result, the code would not only be tightly entangled but also harder to read and maintain.

For scenarios involving actions, like clicking a link in your browser tab, it would also be more challenging. This is because action's outcomes are unpredictable – users can trigger actions at any time. We would have to rely on event handlers to capture these actions. The end result would be quite similar to the timer example: a complex code base with side effects scattered throughout.

Relationship with Declarative Coding

If you are researching how to write maintainable code, chances are that you will see reactive and declarative coding heavily mentioned together. However, we saw that they are two different paradigms, so why is that?

Reactivity, on one hand, provides the ability to simplify things by listening to variable changes or events triggered by user actions or delays, and then executing code based on those changes.

Declarative code, on the other hand, helps define values based on their behavior, rather than specifying a single value.

By combining both of those concepts, you have a powerful and descriptive way of building your application.

To illustrate this, let's consider writing imperative code in an imaginary language to create a spinner that appears whenever something is loading. The code might look like this:

```
isLoading = false;

loadingWatcher(): void {
  while (true) {
    this.isLoading = LoadingManager.isDownloading();
  }
}

spinnerManager(): void {
  while (true)
    this.isLoading ? showSpinner() : hideSpinner();
  }
}
```

In this code, three distinct blocks emerge:

- The first one declares the **`isLoading`** variable, which acts as a container for the boolean it represents.
- A second one updates the value when something changes.
- The third one consumes the variable to perform a side effect (showing or hiding the spinner).

An equivalent code, combining both reactive and declarative programming in pseudo-code, results in a much more concise and explicit code:

```
isLoading = startWith(false)
  .onChangeOf(LoadingManager.isDownloading(), setValue));
```

```
this.isLoading.onChange(isLoading => {
  isLoading ? showSpinner() : hideSpinner();
});
```

In the rewritten code, we now have only two blocks:

- The declaration of **`isLoading`**, which wraps everything about the variable and how it behaves.
- A side effect that consumes the variable and reacts to it.

By merging these two approaches, we have streamlined the code into two distinct types of logic: either a variable is declared or it is consumed.

This might not seem intuitive at first, but it gradually helps you organize your code by grouping related actions together in separate blocks, rather than scattering the logic across your code base, making it easier to reason about.

Sources and Stream

Working with reactive code can easily be challenging if we are still reasoning imperatively.

Triggered events can lead to new values being emitted from any part of our application at any given time. If we try to access it at a specific moment, we might disrupt the flow of information that moves through our code.

One way to manipulate reactive code more effectively is by representing our application as a stream of data that flows through our application. Like any real stream, it takes its source somewhere, and that somewhere represents the core data that our code will be dealing with.

For instance, let's consider a web page displaying products. We might have a list of products, some of which could be out of stock. The user might also apply filters that change which products are displayed.

In this scenario, either the out-of-stock products or the filters can change independently and in any order. Instead of trying to extract specific values from each of these filters, we can represent them as distinct sources, as shown in *Figure* 5.1.

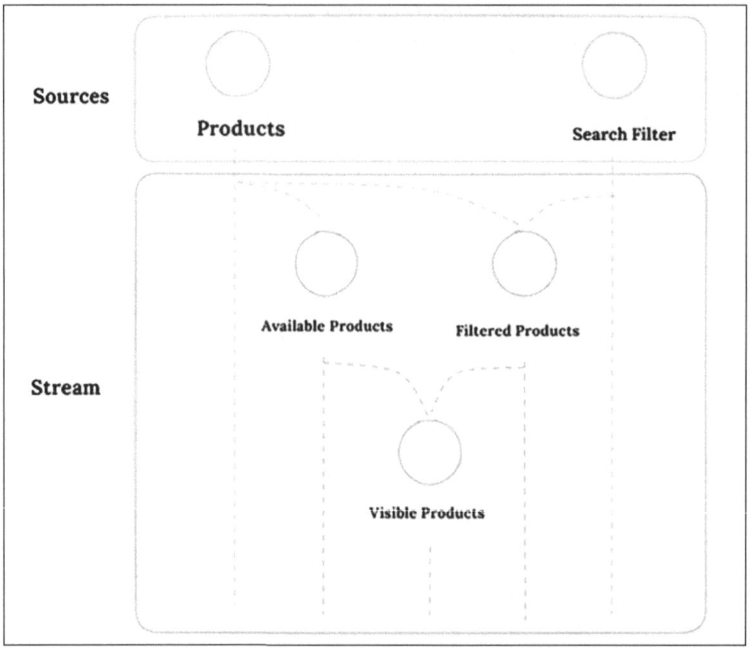

Figure 5.1: *Sources and Stream representation of a flow of data*

Following the sources and stream representation, we can declare our streams independently as reacting from our sources. This approach makes all declarations self-explanatory and eliminates the need to synchronously access values from the source.

Note: *This might sound a bit abstract at the moment, but don't worry! The main goal here is to introduce these concepts so that we can apply them later when working with forms or passing data within our Angular application. Don't hesitate to come back to this chapter later on if needed.*

Introducing RxJS

Angular is designed to create efficient user interfaces, and since web pages involve various events like clicks, image loading completion, HTTP errors, and more, reactivity is at the heart of its design.

This is why one of its core building blocks is RxJS, which stands for *Reactive Extensions for JavaScript*. As the name implies, this library provides many utilities and types for us to work with reactivity, allowing us to easily declare data sources, manipulate the ongoing stream of data, and more.

Note: *RxJS is so deeply rooted in Angular that it is installed by default when creating a new project. You can confirm this by checking the* **package.json** *file of the project you generated in the previous chapter. In future versions, however, this might become optional.*

Observables and Subjects

RxJS introduces an Observable type, which is simply the implementation of the behavioral design pattern known as the Observer.

In this pattern, an object defines a subscription mechanism that allows other objects to listen for any changes that occur. The object being observed is called an Observable because it can be observed, and the entities listening to the changes are referred to as Observers since they observe those changes.

You can think of it in a similar way to subscribing to a newspaper. Once you subscribe to a newspaper, you receive a new edition every time it is printed, and you are free to do whatever you want with it. You can subscribe at any time, regardless of the previous issues, and unsubscribe in the same way.

RxJS defines two main types for emitting and consuming data: Observables and Subjects. Let's explore together what they are and how to use them.

Observables

`Observables` are the implementation of the pattern we mentioned earlier. While it's possible to create one ourselves, RxJS comes with a lot of methods that return new **`Observables`** with various behaviors, saving us a lot of code and potential mistakes.

For instance, the `of` method creates a new `Observable` from a single value and emits it:

```
import { of } from 'rxjs';

const luckyNumber$ = of(13);
```

Note: *Did you notice the $ sign after the* **`Observable`**? *By convention, any variable that can be observed ends with an $. This naming helps to identify what is an observable and what is not.*

`of` is just one of the many functions we can use to create an **`Observable`**. For example, **`interval(period)`** creates an **`Observable`** that will emit a number after a specified period, but others can create observables from events like a click, and much more. The full list can be accessed on the RxJS website at https://rxjs.dev/guide/operators.

Subjects

`Subjects` have the unique ability to function as both an observable (emitting new values) and an observer (having a subscription to the values it emits).

One distinctive feature of a `Subject` is that when it emits a new value, all the code subscribed to it will receive that value. This property makes it a powerful tool for propagating changes pragmatically throughout an application.

Creating a **Subject** is straightforward: you just need to invoke its constructor. Afterward, you can use the **next**, **error**, and **complete** methods to emit a new value, notify listeners of an error, and conclude the emission of values, respectively.

For instance, we could use a **Subject** to keep track of the price of the stock market:

```
import { Subject } from 'rxjs';

const stockPrice = new Subject<number>();

stockPrice.next(0.754);
stockPrice.next(0.749);

// In case of an issue with the broker
stockPrice.error('broker unreachable!');

// The market is closed, we stop the emission
stockPrice.complete();
```

Subjects can come in different "*flavors*" that make them behave differently when listened to. Let's review the most common ones.

Simple Subject

A simple **Subject** is created by calling its constructor with a type parameter, specifying the type of the values it will emit:

```
import { Subject } from 'rxjs';

const employeeCheckIn = new Subject<string>();

// A new employee entered the office!
employeeCheckIn.next('John');

// And now a new one!
employeeCheckIn.next('Doe');
```

All the other types of subjects we will see are derived from this implementation. This kind of subject is useful to pass a value as a notification to your application.

BehaviorSubject

The **BehaviorSubject** is slightly different from the **Subject** because it starts with an initial value:

```
import { BehaviorSubject } from 'rxjs';
```

```
// We know from the start how many spots are free
const remainingParkingSpots = new BehaviorSubject<number>(42);

// The parking is getting filled, we still know how many spots
remain
remainingParkingSpots.next(41);
remainingParkingSpots.next(40);
```

This kind of subject is best suited to keep track of a value over time.

Void Subject

A void subject is not a type on its own but a way to express the fact that something happens when the value itself does not have any interest.

This is materialized by a subject with the type void or none:

```
import { Subject } from 'rxjs';

const userLoggedOut = new Subject();  // same as new
Subject<void>()

// What matters is the action, not the content of the event
userLoggedOut.next();
```

Working with Observables

So far, we have learned how to create observables and have them emit new values. However, this is of no use if we cannot manipulate them.

In this section, we will see how to consume the emitted values and modify them on the fly by adding logic to the observables.

Consuming Observables

Having values emitted is great, but being able to manipulate them would be even better!

As you have seen in the previous chapters, Angular components have two parts where they can interact with the values they manipulate: their logic and the template.

Depending on where the value is used, the syntax to consume an `Observable` varies. Let's see how.

In the Component

We mentioned that an **`Observable`** exposes a subscription to its value. In RxJS, any `Observable` has a `subscribe` method that can be used to get this subscription.

This method accepts an object that can handle the three types of outcomes the `Observable` can send:

- **`next(value)`** : Handles the value emitted by the `Observable`
- **`error(error)`**: Handles an error notification
- **`complete()`**: Handles the notification that the `Observable` has finished emitting new values

Note: *Each one of these methods is optional. You can specify all or none of them if you would like to. For example, If you are only interested in the value, you can only define a value for* **`next`**.

In practice, here is an example of how we could react to an `Observable` that emits whenever a new order is placed in a restaurant:

```
@Component({
  ...
})
export class KitchenComponent implements OnDestroy {
  orderPlaced$: Observable<Order> = ...;
  orderPlacedSubscription: Subscription;

  constructor() {
    this.orderPlacedSubscription = this.orderPlaced$.subscribe({
      next: (order: Order) => alert('A new order has been
placed'),
      error: error => console.error(error),
      complete: () => console.log('Kitchen is closed'),
    });
  }

  ngOnDestroy() {
    this.orderPlacedSubscription.unsubscribe();
  }
}
```

Note: *Since `Subjects` are `Observables`, you can also subscribe to them and they also will emit the values they are holding with some nuances: a* **`BehaviorSubject`** *will immediately emit its value and a* **`ReplaySubject`** *will emit the ones it already had.*

In this example, we can consume the values emitted over time by **`orderPlaced$`**. When a new one arrives, we can handle the new order.

This code will be executed every time **`orderPlaced$`** emits a new value. As you might have guessed, this might not always be necessary: if the user navigates to a page where **`KitchenComponent`** is not displayed, we won't need to manipulate the new Order.

To prevent this logic from running unnecessarily, we manually unsubscribe from the `Observable` once the component is destroyed.

Note: *This step is not to be overlooked! Forgetting to unsubscribe from an* **`Observable`** *may result in memory leaks in your application, as you might still be processing values you are not interested in. As a rule of thumb, whenever you are calling* **`subscribe`**, *call* **`unsubscribe`** *as well.*

In the Template

Sometimes, we don't want to manipulate the data to perform some sort of computation, but simply display them in the interface.

We could reuse the subscribe logic we previously saw:

```
@Component({
  template: '<p>Welcome {{ currentUser }}</p>',
})
export class HomeComponent implements OnDestroy {
  currentUser$: Observable<string> = ...;
  currentUserSubscription: Subscription;

  currentUser: string = ...;

  constructor() {
    this.currentUserSubscription = this.currentUser$.subscribe({
      next: (currentUser: string) => this.currentUser = currentUser,
    });
  }

  ngOnDestroy() {
    this.currentUserSubscription.unsubscribe();
  }
}
```

Even if this works, we lose the benefit of reactivity: we need to actively subscribe to the values to observe them.

Fortunately, Angular has got us covered; since values come asynchronously in Observables, we can ask Angular to display them for us, and the framework will handle all the associated boilerplate.

If you remember the previous chapter, the best way to format a value in a template in Angular is by using a pipe. This is why, to use an `Observable` in that part of the component, Angular exposes an **`AsyncPipe`** out of the box that will greatly reduce the code of the previous example:

```
@Component({
  template: '<p>Welcome {{ currentUser$ | async }}</p>',
```

```
})
export class HomeComponent {
  currentUser$: Observable<string> = ...;
}
```

Since Angular is now taking care of displaying the value and listening to the **Observable**, we no longer have to clean the subscription and keep track of the latest value emitted.

For complex values, we can also use this pipe in an **ngIf** expression so that we only use the observable once:

```
@Component({
  template: `
    <div *ngIf="currentUser$ | async as currentUser">
      <p>Welcome {{ currentUser.name }}</p>
      <p>You are {{ currentUser.age }} years old</p>
    </div>
  `,
})
export class HomeComponent {
  currentUser$: Observable<CurrentUser> = ...;
}
```

Similarly, the aliases also work using the **@if** block (since Angular 17):

```
@Component({
  template: `
    @if (currentUser$ | async; as currentUser) {
      <div>
        <p>Welcome {{ currentUser.name }}</p>
        <p>You are {{ currentUser.age }} years old</p>
      </div>
    }
  `,
})
export class HomeComponent {
  currentUser$: Observable<CurrentUser> = ...;
}
```

Across these examples, we saw how to actively get a value from an **Observable**, either in the logic or the template. However, we won't always get the value we want out of the box. Sometimes, additional computations are required before the value can actually be used. Fortunately, this is a common scenario in many applications and RxJS provides a mechanism to do so. Let's explore it!

Operators

You might have seen on your IDE that when calling a method on an **Observable**, the intelliSense also suggests a method named **`pipe`**. We previously compared an **`Observable`** to a stream of data. As for water, a pipe will allow us to control that flowing stream.

The pipe operator allows us to create a sequence of changes that will operate on the values emitted by the Observable by composing functions together:

```
const positiveOddNumbers$ = numbers$.pipe(
  // Skip values lesser than 0
  filter((number) => number > 0),
  // Wait 500 ms before emitting
  debounceTime(500),
  // Multiply each emitted value by 2
  map((number) => number * 2)
);
```

There are many sorts of operators: some will change the value, others will delay them, others will skip them, and more. All of them are listed on RxJS's website (https://rxjs.dev/guide/operators). We highly recommend you have a look at those to know what your possibilities are when working with Observables.

Reactivity with Signals

Since version 16, Angular (and many other frameworks as well) introduced a new reactive primitive: signals.

The main goal of signals is to make it easier to use reactivity without requiring RxJS and all its operators since they are quite complex.

The idea behind signals is to have a value that can change over time, and other signals can react to it. So far this looks familiar! The change is that signals, as of the time of writing, only work synchronously. This means that any notion of time does not exist in signals.

For a majority of use cases, this is not an issue. However, if you need to have some kind of asynchronous operation or if you need to wait for something, RxJS is still the solution here. The main point is that it is no longer the *only* solution.

Another advantage of signals is that they are much simpler to use than RxJS `Subjects`.

Creating a Signal

At its core, a signal is just a wrapper that holds a value. This value can be of any type, but it needs to be defined on creation:

```
import { signal, type Signal } from "@angular/core";

// Create a signal of type `number`
```

```
const age = signal(42);

// Create a signal `string` or `undefined`
const themePreference: Signal<string | undefined> = signal
(undefined);
```

Upon creation, it is possible to change the value either by computing a new value based on the previous one using **`update`** or by passing in a new one using **`set`**:

```
// Add one the current age
age.update(current => current + 1);

// Change the theme
themePreference.set('dark');
```

To read the value that is currently wrapped by the signal, we can call its getter:

```
console.log(`I am ${age()} years old`);
```

Note: *Notice that there is no concept of subscription here. We don't need any additional code just to read the value the signal currently has.*

Deriving a Signal from Others

We mentioned that one of the strengths of signals is to be derived from others.

Using **`computed`**, it is possible for a signal to be created based on the current value of one or several others. This means that if any signal depends on changes, its value will also be updated:

```
import { signal, computed } from "@angular/core";

const age = signal(18);
const isAnAdult = computed(() => age() > 18);

console.log('Are you an adult? ' + isAnAdult());
// Outputs: Are you an adult? false

age.update(value => value + 1);

console.log('Are you an adult? ' + isAnAdult());
// Outputs: Are you an adult? true
```

Since the value of this signal is computed based on others, it is not possible to update it ourselves directly. This means that `set` and `update` are not callable for it. The only way to modify the value is to update the ones it depends on.

Working with Side Effects

Sometimes, we may want to perform a side effect when a signal changes. For example, if the age of the user changes, we may want to wish them on their birthday. In that case, there is no value to be derived from the age, but an event we would like to react to.

For those cases, the `effect` method can be of great use:

```
@Component({
  ...
})
export class BirthdayComponent {
  readonly age = signal(18);

  constructor() {
    // Will run each time `age` changes
    effect(() => {
      console.log(`Happy ${this.age()} anniversary!`);
    });
  }
}
```

Effects run at least once and will be re-executed each time one of the signals that are called inside it changes.

This can be especially useful if you would like to react to a change, but as a rule of thumb, prefer composing signals using computed instead of creating them from an **`effect`**, as it may result in strange errors.

Choosing the Right Reactive Primitive

Signals and Observables might be confusing primitives at first. Depending on the use case, a value can be reactive but best suited for Observables instead of signals and vice versa.

When choosing which reactive primitive should be used for a variable, it is important to remember the core difference between signals and Observables: they don't have a concept of time and should always have a value.

If the data you are working with must wait for something at any point (a debounce, the response of an HTTP call, and more), then chances are that Observables will be what you want. As an example, manipulating a value of a form field with a debounce of 250ms on it will be best represented by an Observable.

On the contrary, if you don't have anything to wait for, and know upfront that you will always have a value - including on creating your variable - then signals seem to be a better fit for your use case. For instance, the shopping cart of a user is something that is always known and directly updated, and fits the description of a signal.

However, if the choice seems to be impossible to make with certainty, you can still rely on the primitive of your choice and convert it later on using **`toSignal(observable)`** or **`toObservable(signal)`** to convert the type if needed.

Note: *Converting an* **`Observable`** *to a signal will eagerly subscribe to the observable and execute whatever logic it holds. Be sure to properly read the documentation before relying on these methods.*

Conclusion

In this chapter, we provided an overview of reactive programming and how it serves front-end development by offering a powerful way to work with asynchronous events and streams of data. We explored this concept through concrete examples and highlighted its distinctions from other coding approaches.

We also explored how reactivity is integrated into Angular, the reactive blocks of RxJS, and their newer counterparts, known as Signals, designed for managing synchronous operations. For both of them, we learned how to efficiently work with them in components and templates.

In the next chapter, we will explore how to harness these concepts to facilitate efficient data communication between components, enabling the creation of robust communication strategies.

Exercise

In this chapter, we learned about declarative programming, reactivity, and how to use both of these paradigms through observables and RxJS.

In this exercise, we will attempt to refactor a component that has been initially developed using imperative code into a component based on reactivity.

Our component will be a simple gambling game: the current user will start with a fixed amount of coins and will be able to bet some of them in order to play. During each round, they will either receive their coins back along with a bonus or lose everything. As long as the player has sufficient funds, they can continue to play:

```
@Component({
  selector: 'app-gambling-game',
  standalone: true,
  template: `
    <h1>My gambling app</h1>
```

```
    <p>Current Wallet: {{ wallet }}</p>

    <button [disabled]="!canPlay" (click)="play()">
      Play
    </button>
  `,
})
export class GamblingGameComponent {
  wallet = 10;
  canPlay = true;

  play(): void {
    const hasWon = Math.random() >= 0.6;

    this.wallet += hasWon ? 1 : -2;
    this.canPlay = this.wallet > 0;
  }
}
```

Note: *You may have noticed the parentheses and brackets used in the buttons' attributes. For now, simply understand that the expression inside the parentheses will be executed on click, and the* `disabled` *attribute will be set to* `true` *if the* `boolean` *after the equals sign evaluates to true. We will explore these concepts further in Chapter 6, Component Communication and Data Flow.*

Try refactoring this component **using signals** and **using RxJS**.

Hint 1: Try to convert the properties to reactive values.

Hint 2: All the magic happens when you click a button, so let's use this click event as a trigger for the other actions.

Hint 3: `canPlay` doesn't need to have its value explicitly set, but can be derived from the wallet. Declare it once and let it automatically update without changing it elsewhere in your code.

Hint 4: Try to think about `canPlay` as a consequence of the value of `wallet`. Similarly, visualize the wallet as a number that changes in the event of a click on the button.

References

- https://gist.github.com/staltz/868e7e9bc2a7b8c1f754
- https://www.youtube.com/playlist?list=PLvLBrJpVwC7oDMei6JYcySgH1hMBZti_a
- https://angular.io/guide/rx-library
- https://refactoring.guru/design-patterns/observer
- https://angular.io/guide/rx-library#operators

CHAPTER 6
Component Communication and Data Flow

Introduction

Components are the core building block of an Angular application, but, on their own, they can't achieve much and can quickly become challenging to work with.

Fortunately, creating and composing components is one of the core features of the framework, making it easy to break the application into smaller parts with their own set of responsibilities.

However, components will often need to perform some kind of logic based on others, which highlights the necessity of passing values from one to another. Depending on the complexity of the data and operations, several solutions and patterns exist in Angular.

In this chapter, we will see how to logically partition a component and explore efficient strategies for passing data between them.

Structure

In this chapter, we will cover the following topics:

- Component Communication
- Smart and Dumb Components
- Advanced Communication Strategies

Component Communication

The simplest form of communication for any system involves inputs and outputs: you provide data to a system and await the results it returns.

In the case of a function, you would use parameters as inputs, and the returned data as output. Similarly, for Angular components, the principle is essentially the same, with some differences still.

Reactively Set a Value

To set a value to an element from the HTML, Angular uses the concept of *binding*. Simply put, this is the ability of the framework to assign a value to an element.

There are different kinds of elements that lie in a template: native HTML elements (such as buttons, links, and more) and directives (such as Components).

Assigning Properties

Setting the value of an HTML element is done by enclosing the targeted attribute between square brackets **[]**. This syntax indicates to the framework what the targeted DOM property is.

The right-hand side of the attribute is a TypeScript expression to evaluate. This means that if you want to assign a string, you will have to either pass the variable holding that string or use single quotes to wrap the value.

For example, consider the following links where we dynamically assign the URL of the Angular documentation website, either from its value or from a **documentationUrl** variable containing it:

```
@Component({
  // ...
  template: `
    <!– This will dynamically set the attribute value –>
    <a href="https://angular.dev">Browse the docs</a>
    <a [href]="'https://angular.dev'">Browse the docs</a>
    <a [href]="documentationUrl">Browse the docs</a>

    <!– This will not –>
    <a [href]="https://angular.dev">Browse the docs</a>
    <a href="documentationUrl">Browse the docs</a>
  `,
})
export class Component {
  documentationUrl = 'https://angular.dev';
}
```

Using this reactive evaluation, it is possible to dynamically change the behavior of your HTML elements, such as conditionally disabling a button based on the value of a property:

```
@Component({
  // ...
  template: `<button [disabled]="canClick">Button</button>`,
})
export class Component {
  canClick = false;
}
```

Assigning Attributes

While Angular knows about most HTML properties, sometimes you might need to specify other kinds of attributes, such as ARIA or custom ones.

For these use cases, we need to add the **`attr.`** prefix to its name. For instance, to specify the ARIA label of a button or set a custom property, we need to write the binding like this to make it reactive:

```
@Component({
  // ...
  template: `
    <button
      [attr.aria-label]="actionName"
      [attr.my-custom-attribute]="5"
    >Button</button>
  `,
})
export class Component {
  actionName = "Some button";
}
```

However, be careful, there can sometimes be mismatches between the name of the property and the name of an attribute! For example, to set the **`colspan`** attribute, you need to write **`[colSpan]`** with a capital **`S`**.

Assigning Components Inputs

Using the syntax previously mentioned, setting an HTML attribute is fairly straightforward: excluding some exceptions, all we need to do is more or less wrap the attribute with square brackets (**`[]`**).

However, if this is practical for HTML attributes, it would be even better if we could do the same for our components.

For instance, let's consider a **`LoginComponent`** that will display either a login button or a logout button:

```
@Component({
  selector: 'app-login',
```

```
  standalone: true,
  template: `
    @if (currentUser === null) {
      <button>Login</button>
    } @else {
      <button>Logout</button>
    }
  `,
})
export class LoginComponent {
  currentUser: User | null = null;
}
```

And an additional `NavbarComponent` using it:

```
@Component({
  selector: 'app-navbar',
  standalone: true,
  imports: [LoginComponent],
  template: `
    <nav>
      <app-login />
    </nav>
  `,
})
export class NavbarComponent {}
```

If the login component manages the **`currentUser`** by itself and no other component depends on its value, this approach is fine.

However, most components don't work with only their own data but instead rely on some provided on a higher level.

In our example, the navbar might not only show a different button depending on the status of the current user but also show a link to their profile if they are connected, additional tabs depending on their rights, and more.

In that case, the **`LoginComponent`** can no longer be the one owning the value of **`currentUser`** but should rather have it as input from the navbar itself.

To pass down data from a component to a child component in the template, we can use the square brackets in the same way we did to set attributes. To set the value of **`currentUser`** in the login component, we can write the following code:

```
@Component({
  selector: 'app-navbar',
  standalone: true,
  imports: [LoginComponent],
  template: `
```

```
    <nav>
      <app-login [currentUser]="currentUser" />
    </nav>
  `,
})
export class NavbarComponent {
  currentUser: User | null = null;
}
```

Unfortunately, without any further modification, the Angular compiler will notify you of an error:

```
Can't bind to 'currentUser' since it isn't a known property of
'app-login'
```

Indeed, Angular is not aware of any attribute that the **LoginComponent** might have of the same name. We need to specify it from our component.

In Angular, we can define the values a component accepts as input with the **@Input** decorator to make a property part of the component's API:

```
@Component({
  selector: 'app-login',
  standalone: true,
  template: `
    @if (currentUser === null) {
      <button>Login</button>
    } @else {
      <button>Logout</button>
    }
  `,
})
export class LoginComponent {
  @Input() currentUser: User | null = null;
}
```

With that change, Angular is now aware that the **LoginComponent** accepts an input named **currentUser** of type `User` or `null` and will assign the value that a parent component provides whenever specified.

Note: *Angular will also show errors if the value passed as input is not of the same type as the property in the child component. To modify this behavior, you can check the* **strictTemplates** *flag in the* **angularCompilerOptions** *of the* **tsconfig.json**.

Exploring Input Options

The **Input** decorator can do much more than just expose a property as an attribute for our component. Two kinds of parameters can be passed to it to alter its native behavior.

Aliasing the Input

The first type of parameter that can be provided is an alias as a string.

If we would like to name the input differently for any caller, we can specify an alias on the decorator.

Let's reconsider our previous example. If we would like to receive the input as `user` instead of **`currentUser`**, we can do the following:

```
@Component({
  selector: 'app-login',
  standalone: true,
  template: `
    @if (currentUser === null) {
      <button>Login</button>
    } @else {
      <button>Logout</button>
    }
  `,
})
export class LoginComponent {
  @Input('user') currentUser: User | null = null;
}
```

Inside the `NavbarComponent` template, we now have to use the new attribute name:

```
@Component({
  // ...
  imports: [LoginComponent],
  template: `
    <nav>
      <app-login [user]="currentUser" />
    </nav>
  `,
})
export class NavbarComponent {
  currentUser: User | null = null;
}
```

Note: *Changing the attribute name is mandatory as Angular will no longer accept the unaliased name for the input.*

Specifying Additional Options

As for many other libraries, objects are favored rather than primitives to specify options. The Input decorator also accepts an object composed of three optional properties:

```
class Input {
  alias?: string;
```

```
    required?: boolean;
    transform?: (value: any) => any;
  }
```

Let's take a closer look at each of those options.

The `alias` field allows us to achieve the same behavior we previously saw, namely setting up an alias for the input. If it is not set, the name of the property itself will be used.

Using the alias, our previous example can also be written this way:

```
@Component({
  // ...
})
export class LoginComponent {
  @Input({ alias: 'user' }) currentUser: User | null = null;
}
```

The **`required`** field helps us to specify if this property is mandatory for the parent to provide. The default value is `false`, meaning that the caller is free not to specify it, but toggling it to true will throw an error if the value is not set.

The updated code will result in the following:

```
@Component({
  // ...
})
export class LoginComponent {
  @Input({ required: true }) currentUser: User | null = null;
}
```

Angular will effectively throw a compile-time error if the attribute is not set, as shown in *Figure* 6.1:

```
> ng build

✔ Browser application bundle generation complete.

Error: src/app/app.component.ts:29:7 - error NG8008: Required input 'currentUser' from component
LoginComponent must be specified.

29       <app-login />
         ~~~~~~~~~~~~~
```

Figure 6.1: *Screenshot of the build output*

Along with an error within your editor:

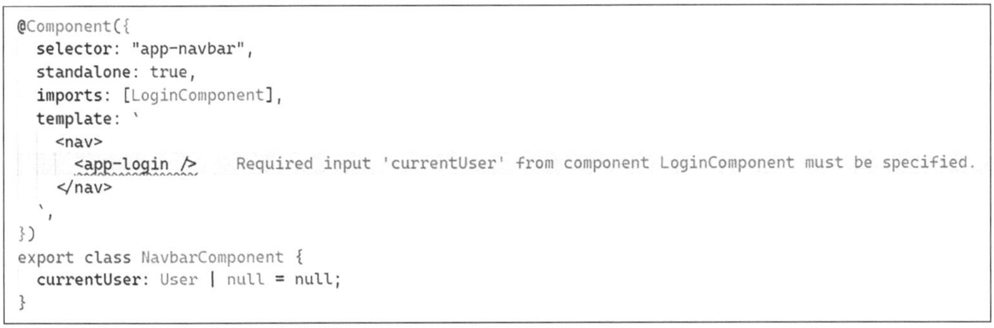

Figure 6.2: *Screenshot of the editor's error*

Finally, the last `transform` field allows us to specify a function to dynamically transform the input value before using it.

If set, the provided value will go through the function before being assigned to the attribute. If this option is not provided, no changes will be made to the value.

In our **`LoginComponent`**, we might not need the whole `User` but rather know if one is provided or not. By combining the **`alias`** and the `transform` property, we can still ask for the current user for the parent, but only effectively check whether the provided user is **`null`** or not:

```
@Component({
  selector: "app-login",
  standalone: true,
  template: `
    @if (isSet) {
      <button>Logout</button>
    } @else {
      <button>Login</button>
    }
  `,
})
export class LoginComponent {
  @Input({
    alias: "currentUser",
    transform: (currentUser: unknown | null) => currentUser !==
null,
  })
  isSet: boolean = false;
}
```

Notice that the property is now a **`boolean`** but the value the input accepts in the transform matches the one provided by the parent. With this change, our component can now only deal with the value if needed rather than the provided ones, without impacting its exposed properties names and types.

Input as Setter

Another way to approach inputs is to use them as setters.

Imagine we would like to log that the user status has changed in the component. By adding the **set** keyword, we can tell Angular to use this input as a setter of our property:

```
@Component({
  // ...
})
export class LoginComponent {
  #currentUser: User | null = null;

  @Input()
  set currentUser(value: User | null) {
    if (this.#currentUser !== value) {
      console.log("Something changed!");
    }

    this.#currentUser = value;
  }
}
```

While the usage stays the same, the behavior can now be customized to execute some code when assigning this property.

There are many use cases when this is useful, such as performing side effects, initializing more than just the field itself or even logging. However, use them sparingly as it may make your component harder to reason about. If you need a lot of side effects, consider using a reactive value instead, as seen in the previous chapter.

Since this is a common use case, you might see a lot of code bases using setters as a way to dynamically update a reactive value, following this pattern:

```
@Component({
  // ...
})
export class FooComponent {
  #foo = signal<Bar | null>(null);

  @Input() set foo(value: Bar | null) {
    this.#foo.set(value);
  }
}
```

By assigning the new value in the setter, the component can use the `#foo` signal like any other reactive value and perform side effects on it.

Signal Input

Fortunately, the Angular development team was well aware of the benefits of this pattern, combining setters and a reactive primitive and introduced a dedicated method to define a new signal as an input:

```
@Component({
  // ...
})
export class FooComponent {
  readonly foo = input<Bar | null>(null);
}
```

This syntax makes it possible to have a reactive input without dealing with the extra boilerplate we used to have. As for the **@Input** decorator, the input function accepts a set of options after the initial value. The main difference is that the required input doesn't accept an initial value and is defined using **input.required**.

For instance, here is how to use an input signal where we used the input decorator:

```
@Component({
  selector: "app-login",
  standalone: true,
  template: `
    @if (isSet()) {
      <button>Logout</button>
    } @else {
      <button>Login</button>
    }
  `,
})
export class LoginComponent {
  readonly isSet = input(false, {
    alias: 'currentUser',
    transform: (currentUser: unknown | null) => currentUser !== null
  });
}
```

From the Routes

In some scenarios, there is no direct relationship between a component and the data it takes as a parameter. It exists a third way to pass a value as an input by binding data from the router to the component's inputs.

If the names of both the input and the value match, since Angular 16, it is possible to configure the router to use **withComponentInputBinding**:

```
bootstrapApplication(AppComponent,
  {
```

```
    providers: [
      provideRouter(appRoutes, withComponentInputBinding()),
    ],
});
```

With this configuration enabled, it is possible to pass data from the router to the component, whether it is in the query parameters, route parameters, or route data.

For instance, instead of passing down the ID of a product from component to component, you can simply retrieve it from the route parameter if the input has the same name:

```
const routes: Routes = [
    // ...
    {
      path: ':productId/details',
      component: ProductDetailsComponent,
    },
  ];

@Component({...})
export class ProductDetailsComponent {
  productId = input.required({ transform: numberAttribute });
}
```

This method really helps to split components into multiple pages, as we will see in *Chapter 9, Routing* later on.

Event Binding

Being able to pass in a value is only one side of any communication and we might still want to communicate back to the caller. Since this is a common use case, Angular also provides the tools to easily do so.

For HTML Elements

To listen for events, the syntax Angular uses is parentheses. We can see this as square brackets to pass values in a component, and parenthesis to pass them out.

As for inputs, HTML elements expose some events by default. Namely, the button element exposes a `click` event, the input element an `input` event, and so on.

Note: *There are a lot of events that exist natively: one raised when leaving a field, when pressing a key, when moving the mouse, and more. Checking the reference before writing your own can spare you a lot of time.*

Binding an event requires specifying two things: the first one being the name of the event itself and the second part is the TypeScript code you would like to call whenever an event is raised.

For example, here is how we could listen for the click event of a button to toggle a flag:

```
@Component({
  selector: "app-light-switch",
  standalone: true,
  template: `
    <button (click)="isOn = true">On</button>
    <button (click)="isOn = false">Off</button>
  `,
})
export class LightSwitchComponent {
  isOn = false;
}
```

In the preceding code, whenever a button is clicked, a **`click`** event will be emitted and the code bound to that event will be executed, toggling the **`isOn`** flag accordingly.

However, since the code inside the quotes can be any TypeScript code, we can call methods instead of writing the logic directly in the template:

```
@Component({
  selector: "app-light-switch",
  standalone: true,
  template: `
    <button (click)="onToggle(true)">On</button>
    <button (click)="onToggle(false)">Off</button>
  `,
})
export class LightSwitchComponent {
  isOn = false;

  onToggle(isOn: boolean): void {
    this.isOn = isOn;
  }
}
```

By calling methods, we can keep the component's logic out of the template, making it easier to find and organize its behavior.

For Components

Native events are useful when manipulating basic HTML events, but our custom components can also emit special handcrafted events.

Just as there is an `Input` directive to receive values, there is also an `Output` directive that can be used to emit events.

As for the input, an output is an attribute bound to the **@Output** decorator. However, this attribute should be of the specific **EventEmitter<TValue>** type, where `TValue` is the value that will be emitted. If none, we can use the type `void`.

Let's reconsider our **LoginComponent** so that it emits the details of the user when logged in, and an event without any value when he logs out. We would first need to create the associated outputs:

```
@Component({
  // ...
})
export class LoginComponent {
  @Input() currentUser: User | null = null;

  @Output() loggedIn = new EventEmitter<User | null>();
  @Output() loggedOut = new EventEmitter<void>();
}
```

Note: *An additional parameter of type string can be provided to* **@Output()** *in order to specify an alias, exactly like* **@Input()** *does.*

We will then need to bind the click on each of the buttons to emit the appropriate event.

An **EventEmitter** has a method called **emit** that allows us to emit the value passed as a parameter, which must be of the same generic type as the one passed to the **EventEmitter**. In our case, here is how we could do that:

```
@Component({
  selector: "app-login",
  standalone: true,
  template: `
    @if (currentUser === null) {
    <button (click)="loggedIn.emit({ name: 'John' })">Login</
button>
    } @else {
    <button (click)="loggedOut.emit()">Logout</button>
    }
  `,
})
export class LoginComponent {
  // ...
}
```

Note: *Notice that the* **EventEmitter<void>** *does not take any value as a parameter when emitting.*

From the **NavbarComponent**, consuming these events is done in the same way as we did for HTML events like **`(click)`:** by wrapping the event name between parentheses and specifying the code to execute when an event is raised.

Here is how we can listen to the events emitted by the **`LoginComponent`** to update the **`currentUser`**:

```
@Component({
  selector: "app-navbar",
  standalone: true,
  imports: [LoginComponent],
  template: `
    <nav>
      <app-login
        [currentUser]="currentUser"
        (loggedIn)="onLoggedIn($event)"
        (loggedOut)="onLoggedOut()"
      />
    </nav>
  `,
})
export class NavbarComponent {
  currentUser: User | null = null;

  onLoggedIn(user: User | null): void {
    this.currentUser = user;
  }

  onLoggedOut(): void {
    this.currentUser = null;
  }
}
```

Note: *Did you notice that the* **`onLoggedIn`** *method is called with a parameter named* **`$event`?** *This parameter is a special one that Angular provides and its value is the one emitted by the event bound to this expression, in our case, a value of type* **`User`** *or* **`null`**.

We saw in the previous section that the Angular team introduced signal inputs as an alternative to the input decorators. Similarly, there is an output method that can be used in the same way as the **`EventEmitter`**:

```
@Component({
  // ...
  template: `
    @if (currentUser === null) {
      <button (click)="loggedIn.emit({ name: 'John' })">Login</
button>
    } @else {
      <button (click)="loggedOut.emit()">Logout</button>
```

```
    }
  `,
})
export class LoginComponent {
  readonly currentUser = input<User | null>(null);

  readonly loggedIn = output<User | null>();
  readonly loggedOut = output<void>();
}
```

Two-Way Binding

In some scenarios, we might want to both set and read a value. For instance, let's assume that we are building a control panel in which a user can toggle the developer mode. Having seen how to use inputs and outputs, we could write the following component with Input and Output decorators:

```
  @Component({
  selector: 'app-dev-mode',
  standalone: true,
  template: `
    <button (click)="onToggle()">
      {{ isDevModeEnabled ? 'Disable' : 'Enable' }} developer
mode
    </button>
  `,
})
export class DevModePanelComponent {
  @Input() isDevModeEnabled = false;
  @Output() isDevModeEnabledChange = new EventEmitter<boolean>();

  onToggle(): void {
    this.isDevModeEnabledChange.emit(!this.isDevModeEnabled);
  }
}
```

Using this component, we could change the value of **isDevMode** on the fly and react to it:

```
@Component({
  selector: 'app-root',
  standalone: true,
  imports: [DevModePanelWithInputOutputComponent],
  template: `
    <app-dev-mode
      [isEnabled]="isDevModeEnabled"
```

```
      (isEnabledChange)="setIsDevModeEnabled($event)"
    />

    <p>Is developer mode enabled? {{ isDevModeEnabled }}</p>
  `,
})
export class AppComponent {
  isDevModeEnabled = false;

  setIsDevModeEnabled(isDevModeEnabled: boolean): void {
    this.isDevModeEnabled = isDevModeEnabled;
  }
}
```

In this example, **AppComponent** is responsible for both updating and assigning the value of **isDevModeEnabled** to the child component **DevModePanelComponent**. While this code works, it also introduces an extra overhead by both providing the flag and handling its update.

Note: *In the example we are using decorators for inputs and outputs, but the same logic and overhead would be present if we were to use signals as well.*

Fortunately, Angular has a powerful built-in mechanism known as two-way binding to synchronize a value between parent and a child component that solves exactly this type of problem.

The Banana In a Box

Two-way binding allows you to listen for the update of a value and simultaneously update it. The syntax for Angular's two-way binding is known as "*banana in a box*" as it consists of wrapping the input between square brackets and parentheses:

```
@Component({
  selector: 'app-root',
  standalone: true,
  imports: [DevModePanelWithInputOutputComponent],
  template: `
    <app-dev-mode [(isEnabled)]="isDevModeEnabled" />
    <p>Is developer mode enabled? {{ isDevModeEnabled }}</p>
  `,
})
export class AppComponent {
  isDevModeEnabled = false;
}
```

Doing so will tell Angular that **isDevModeEnabled** is passed as the **isEnabled** input but also must change according to the value emitted by **isEnableChange**.

Under the hood, in order to make it work, the targeted input/output couple **must** follow a specific naming convention: the output having the same name as the input, suffixed with **-Change**. For instance, to bind **[(size)]**, a component must have a **size** input and a **sizeChange** output.

Using Model Input

Since the first release of signals, the Angular team has put a lot of effort into making Angular components and their input/output API reactive. As a result of these efforts, since Angular 17.2, we can use the `model` input as a replacement for combining input and output to control a value.

When using model to define an input, Angular automatically creates the associated output for it, allowing you to use two-way binding in its parent. Here is what our previous example will look like with model:

```
@Component({
  selector: 'app-dev-mode',
  standalone: true,
  template: `
    <button (click)="onToggle()">
      {{ isDevModeEnabled() ? 'Disable' : 'Enable' }} developer
mode
    </button>
  `,
})
export class DevModePanelComponent {
  isDevModeEnabled = model(false);

  onToggle(): void {
    this.isDevModeEnabled.update((isEnabled) => !isEnabled);
  }
}
```

Notice that **isDevModeEnabled** is now exposed as a `signal`, as it would be if we were using a signal input. However, unlike signal input, this value can be set or updated as we did in **onToggle**. The difference is that whenever the value of a model is updated, the associated event is emitted. In practice, the preceding code is similar to:

```
@Component({
  selector: 'app-dev-mode',
  standalone: true,
  template: `
    <button (click)="onToggle()">
      {{ isDevModeEnabled() ? 'Disable' : 'Enable' }} developer mode
    </button>
  `,
```

```
})
export class DevModePanelComponent {
  isDevModeEnabled = input(false);
  isDevModeEnabledChange = output<boolean>();

  onToggle(): void {
    this.isDevModeEnabledChange.emit(!this.isDevModeEnabled());
  }
}
```

In short, by leveraging two-way data binding, you can easily synchronize value between a parent component and its child with a minimal amount of code, thanks to Angular built-in utilities.

Smart and Dumb Components

With the ability to communicate data back and forth from components, it is possible to propagate data across your application.

Unfortunately, if each component represents a specific business case, you might end up with a lot of components, each tied up to a dedicated logic that is not reusable, losing the opportunity to think about components as reusable blocks for your application.

One way to reason about your components in order to increase their reusability is to consider them as smart and dumb components, also called container and presentational components. Let's see what this is about.

Core Principles

Creating a component allows us to divide an interface into chunks of reusable code and logic. Usually, a new component is created for each scope it can have on a web page.

Consider, for example, in a TODO list, you might have a **`TodoListComponent`** in charge of managing several **`TodoItemComponents`** that display a specific TODO item. Both those components might have their own logic and occasionally interact with each other.

In our example, a **`TodoItemComponent`** might be in charge of the completion status of the item:

```
@Component({
  selector: "app-todo-item",
  standalone: true,
  template: `
    <span (click)="toggleCompletion()">
      <input type="checkbox" [checked]="todoItem.isDone" />
```

```
      <span>{{ todoItem.name }}</span>
    </span>
  `,
})
export class TodoItemComponent {
  @Input({ required: true }) todoItem!: TodoItem;

  toggleCompletion(): void {
    this.todoItem.isDone = !this.todoItem.isDone;
  }
}
```

While the **`TodoListComponent`** manages the list itself:

```
@Component({
  selector: "app-todo-list",
  standalone: true,
  imports: [TodoItemComponent],
  template: `
    <ul>
      @for (todo of todoItems; track todo.id) {
      <li>
        <app-todo-item [todoItem]="todo" />
        <button (click)="deleteItem(todo.id)">Delete</button>
      </li>
      }
    </ul>
  `,
})
export class TodoListComponent {
  todoItems: TodoItem[] = [
    { id: 1, name: "Get groceries", isDone: true },
    { id: 2, name: "Do the dishes", isDone: false },
  ];

  deleteItem(id: number): void {
    this.todoItems = this.todoItems.filter((item) => item.id !==
id);
  }
}
```

This is working at the scale of the example, but this can be quickly unmanageable since it can be harder to locate where the value is actually changed. In our example, one component can change its completion status while the other can delete some. If more features were to be implemented, the edition would probably be located in one component, and in another the addition of a new one.

To regroup the logic and reason more easily about components, a pattern known as smart and dumb components, or container and presentational components, has emerged among JavaScript frameworks.

It consists of lifting all the logic in a higher component that will then handle the operations on the entities it manages while delegating the emission of the events, triggering the actions to smaller ("**dumber**") components.

By structuring your code this way, you will get two benefits out of the box: first, all the actions performed on an entity will be collocated instead of split across several components; second, dumb components will be easier to maintain since they won't deal with business logic anymore.

Refactor Existing Logic

Our previous example still contains logic in multiple components instead of grouping in a single place. Let's see how to rework it so that the **TodoItemComponent** acts as a dumb component and the **TodoListComponent** handles all the logic.

First, we need to identify the action handled by the **TodoItemComponent**. In our case, it reacts to a click to toggle the completion status. Since this component should no longer handle business logic, we will transform that into a named event instead:

```
@Component({
  selector: "app-todo-item",
  standalone: true,
  template: `
    <span (click)="toggleCompletion.emit()">
      <input type="checkbox" [checked]="todoItem.isDone" />
      <span>{{ todoItem.name }}</span>
    </span>
  `,
})
export class TodoItemComponent {
  @Input({ required: true }) todoItem!: TodoItem;
  @Output() toggleCompletion = new EventEmitter<void>();
}
```

With the event being raised, we can react to it from the **TodoListComponent** by updating the associated **TodoItem**:

```
@Component({
  selector: "app-todo-list",
  standalone: true,
  imports: [TodoItemComponent],
  template: `
    <ul>
      @for (todo of todoItems; track todo.id) {
```

```
        <li>
          <app-todo-item
            [todoItem]="todo"
            (toggleCompletion)="onToggleCompletion(todo.id)"
          />
          <button (click)="deleteItem(todo.id)">Delete</button>
        </li>
        }
      </ul>
    `,
})
export class TodoListComponent {
  todoItems: TodoItem[] = [
    { id: 1, name: "Get groceries", isDone: true },
    { id: 2, name: "Do the dishes", isDone: false },
  ];

  deleteItem(id: number): void {
    this.todoItems = this.todoItems.filter((item) => item.id !==
id);
  }

  onToggleCompletion(id: number): void {
    this.todoItems = this.todoItems.map((item) =>
      item.id === id ? { ...item, isDone: !item.isDone } : item
    );
  }
}
```

And we're done!

With this change, we lifted the logic from one component to another to group the logic related to the same data we manipulated: an array of **TodoItems**. To perform this change, the steps remain the same:

1. Locate what event is handled internally
2. Create an output to emit that event instead
3. Listen for that event in the parent component
4. If the data is in the child component, move it to the parent component, and pass it as input to the child component
5. Perform the logic on the entity from the parent component whenever the event is raised

Commonly, the piece of data manipulated in an application is also called *state*. By using the dumb and smart component pattern, our state is now managed in a single place, the smart component, making it easier to explore and enhance.

Advanced Communication Strategies

Emitting and receiving events from your component and being able to structure your architecture around guidelines such as smart and dumb components is a step in the right direction to ensure that an application can grow while still being maintainable, but, as your application grows, so will the data it manages. In that sense, managing the state will become harder as it is split across your components.

Fortunately, every team faces that challenge, and several solutions exist in order to keep this under control.

State Management

Strategies and patterns around the structure of the state of an application are commonly called *state management*.

Imagine if your bank account was split into several places where you commonly spend your money: one small account at your favorite grocery store, another one just for your loan, another one for special expenses for your family, and so on. This can be hard to think about your money in terms of "*How much money do you currently have*", since each account should be checked.

For this scenario, if your account is only in a specific bank (your state), each place where you need to spend money interacts with the method exposed by your bank (credit card, and more), and you can easily get an overview of everything that happens to your money and where to do some operations since everything is under the responsibility of your bank account.

The idea remains globally the same for web applications, even if the methods employed might differ: the state is the data your application manages, and it is only manipulated by itself, while letting consumers access its information but not directly modify it.

Service-based Communication

As our bank does, the most straightforward way to manage our state is to expose a service that will handle the data.

Fundamentally, all we have is a wrapper around a piece of data and expose it as read-only:

```
@Injectable({ providedIn: "root" })
export class BankAccountService {
  #state = signal({ money: 5723 });
  state = this.#state.asReadonly();
}
```

Components can now use that piece of data for their own logic, for example, displaying the current amount, or if we still have money:

```
@Component({
  selector: "app-bank-account",
  standalone: true,
  template: `
    <p>You have {{ state().money }} € in your bank account</p>
  `,
})
export class BankAccountComponent {
  #bankAccountService = inject(BankAccountService);
  state = this.#bankAccountService.state;
}
```

Exposing data is simple, but how can we act on it? All we have to do is expose the methods we want in the service managing our state because it's the only place where our data can be updated. If we would like to be able to withdraw money, here is how we could do it:

```
@Injectable({ providedIn: "root" })
export class BankAccountService {
  #state = signal({ money: 5723 });
  state = this.#state.asReadonly();

  withdrawMoney(amount: number): void {
    this.#state.update((state) => ({
      ...state,
      money: state.money - amount,
    }));
  }
}
```

Since the method is public, another component can call it:

```
@Component({
  selector: "app-bank-account",
  standalone: true,
  template: `
    <p>You have {{ state().money }} € in your bank account</p>
    <button (click)="withdrawTenEuros()">Withdraw 10 €</button>
  `,
})
export class BankAccountComponent {
  #bankAccountService = inject(BankAccountService);
  state = this.#bankAccountService.state;

  withdrawTenEuros(): void {
```

```
        this.#bankAccountService.withdrawMoney(10);
      }
    }
```

When the button is clicked, the component will ask the service to withdraw the specified amount and the service itself will update the state. Since it is also the one exposing the data, all components that listen to that state will also have the new updated value and won't need to recompute it on their side.

To summarize, keeping your state in a service allows you to define what methods you would like to expose to consumers and provides a unique place where you can manage it, preventing the state from being split across your application and having the same value everywhere.

Redux

Service-based state management is good enough until it no longer is.

For huge applications or massive amounts of data and/or events, you might end up with a very large service doing a lot of things.

To keep this manageable, another pattern called Redux emerged in 2015.

Core Principles

Redux was originally a library but has evolved as a set of principles applied in many different libraries in various frameworks such as Angular, React, and so on.

At its core, the idea remains the same: structuring the state of an application in a predictable and centralized manner. However, the realization revolves around the following principles.

Single Source of Truth

As for our service-based state management system, the goal is to have a unique place where your data - your state - is.

It allows us to consider it as the single source of truth of our application, where it will always be up to date and without the need to synchronize it among several components.

By having that single place where everything is defined, it is also easier to debug, store, or act on the state since it will require significantly less effort than it being split among different parts of our application.

Read-Only State

Having a centralized source of truth is great for keeping things in sync across your application, but if every piece of code can update it, it might be challenging to understand where the state is updated and by whom.

In Redux, the state can be read but not modified by the callers.

This way, you can work with the assertion that no modification can be done externally and consider it only as a source of data while working with your state from your components.

Changes with Pure Functions

Redux embraces the principle of immutability, where we don't modify data but replace it with its newer value.

Since modifying the state is forbidden, each action replaces the state with its new value.

For instance, in a TODO list, adding an item should not be pushing a new TODO in an array, but providing a whole new array with the item.

By doing so, you can write functions that don't cause any side effects and create a new state based on the input parameters. These functions act as *reducers*: they take an intention and transform it into a new piece of state.

For instance, when the intention is "*add this TODO item*", the resulting output is a new state, with the TODO item added.

Implementation Using NgRx

Several libraries implement the Redux pattern in Angular: StateAdapt, Akita, Elf, Ngxs, and so on. However, the most popular one at the time of writing is NgRx.

NgRx is a state management library based on Redux and RxJS. It manages the state from a *reducer*, exposes it through read-only *selectors*, updates it using the pure functions called *reducers*, and manages events through *actions*.

Let's break that down by rewriting the bank account example!

Modeling the State

Before managing the state, we need to define what it will be. In our case, it is just the amount of money in our bank account. This can be represented as an interface:

```
interface BankAccountState {
  money: number;
}
```

Defining the Actions

In this state, we need to define which actions will happen and in what context.

In our example, we only have one action, occurring in the context of the bank account, which will be withdrawing a specified amount of money.

To create the actions in NgRx, we can use the **`createActionGroup`** method:

```
import { createActionGroup, props } from "@ngrx/store";

const BankAccountActions = createActionGroup({
  source: "Bank Account",
  events: {
    "Withdraw Money": props<{ amount: number }>(),
  },
});
```

This allows us to create a new action by calling the generated code like this:

```
BankAccountActions.withdrawMoney({ amount: 50 });
```

This action will symbolize what our intentions are towards the state, with the necessary payload for it to update it.

Creating the Reducer

Now that we know what the state is and what actions it should support, we can write the reducer that will manage it.

In NgRx, a reducer is an object that can *reduce* actions and replace the state accordingly. It takes an initial state of the type of our state and a sequence of pure functions that will output a new state for each *action* that is listened to.

For the bank account, here is what our reducer will be:

```
import { createReducer, on } from "@ngrx/store";

const initialState: BankAccountState = {
  money: 5723,
};

const bankAccountReducer = createReducer(
  initialState,
  on(BankAccountActions.withdrawMoney, (state, {amount}) => ({
    ...state,
    money: state.money - amount,
  }))
);
```

Selecting Parts of the State

For now, we can model and act on our state but still can't read it.

In NgRx, it is possible to read parts of the state using *selectors*, which are functions that will expose the state's content in an efficient and read-only way. What makes selectors powerful is their ability to be combined and only recomputed when needed.

To create a selector, we must first define what state we would like to read using **createFeatureSelector** and then select parts of this selector by calling **createSelector** on it.

A selector is created by calling **createSelector** with the selectors we want to query as parameters, and a final function that will return the result of what we want to select:

```
Const selectorD = createSelector(
  selectorA,
  selectorB,
  selectorC,
  (a, b, c) => /* do something with the values of the selectors
*/
);
```

For instance, here is how we could access the amount of money in the bank account and derive this value to know if there is still money on it:

```
import { createFeatureSelector, createSelector } from "@ngrx/
store";

const selectBankAccount = createFeatureSelector<BankAccount-
State>("bankAccount");

const selectMoney = createSelector(
  selectBankAccount,
  (bankAccount) => bankAccount.money
);

const selectIsAccountInPositive = createSelector(
  selectMoney,
  (money) => money > 0
);
```

Plugging-in Into Angular Dependency Injection

Before using the reducer, we must register it in our application so that Angular knows that it exists. To do so, we need to specify what reducers compose our store from the main configuration in **main.ts**:

```
import { provideStore } from "@ngrx/store";
import { AppComponent, bankAccountReducer } from "./app/app.com-
ponent";

bootstrapApplication(AppComponent, {
  providers: [provideStore({ bankAccount: bankAccountReducer })],
}).catch((err) => console.error(err));
```

Or in your **app.module.ts**, if you are using NgModules:

```
import { StoreModule} from "@ngrx/store";
import { AppComponent, bankAccountReducer } from "./app/app.
component";

@NgModule({
    imports: [
      BrowserModule,
      StoreModule.forRoot({ bankAccount: bankAccountReducer }),
    ],
    declarations: [AppComponent],
    bootstrap: [AppComponent],
  })
  export class AppModule {}
```

With the reducer plugged into the Angular dependency injection container, we can update our component to use the store.

Consuming the Store

Now that we can read and update the state, all that is left is to plug it into our application and consume it from our components.

We will be able to use the three blocks we defined previously:

1. Inject the store that manages our state-of-type **BankAccountState**
2. Select from the state the money on the bank account
3. Emit an action to the state to update it with the withdrawn money

```
@Component({
  selector: "app-bank-account",
  standalone: true,
  template: `
    <p>You have {{ money() }} € in your bank account</p>
    <button (click)="withdrawTenEuros()">Withdraw 10 €</button>
  `,
})
export class BankAccountComponent {
  // 1.
  #store = inject(Store<BankAccountState>);

  // 2.
  money = this.#store.selectSignal(selectMoney);  // 2.

  withdrawTenEuros(): void {
    // 3.
    this.#store.dispatch(BankAccountActions.withdrawMoney({
```

```
amount: 10 }));
  }
}
```

Takeaways

As you can see, leveraging Redux and using NgRx require significantly more code, but each of its parts has a clear scope.

This introduction only showcases how to manage a simple state; however, this library is much more powerful and comes with additional tools like an integration to Redux Devtools to log and debug the events, effects to perform side effects, local state management, and much more. If you are interested in learning more about NgRx, head out to their documentation at https://ngrx.io.

However, NgRx should not be a default choice for state management, but rather an evolution. As a rule of thumb, start small when managing the state and, if it grows, upgrade your state management solution too. If you use NgRx upfront, you might introduce too much complexity in your code, but if you don't with a large state, you will have a hard time keeping the state coherent and consistent using only services.

Conclusion

In this chapter, we saw how to communicate data to and from components by using `Input` and `Output` decorators and how to leverage this to orchestrate communication between our components by considering them as a container and a presentational component (or smart and dumb components).

We also pushed the management of our state further by extracting it into a single source of truth using an Angular service and introduced Redux for advanced state management strategies.

Through a simple example, we saw how to manage that state using one of the most popular implementations of Redux in Angular named NgRx.

In the next chapter, we will see various ways to manipulate forms to build interactive web applications.

Exercise

Now that you are familiar with the various ways of propagating data between components, it's time to put this knowledge into practice.

In this exercise, we will create a TODO list.

First, create the following interface:

```
export interface TodoItem {
  id: number;
  name: string;
  isDone: boolean;
}
```

Then, incrementally build the application by doing the following steps:

1. Create a **`TodoItemComponent`** that takes a **`TodoItem`** as input. The component should display a button or a checkbox to change the completion status of the **`TodoItem`**.
2. Define an output that is emitting the ID of the **`TodoItem`** when the completion status changes. It should only emit the ID, not change the **`TodoItem`** itself.
3. Write a **`TodoListComponent`** that lists several **`TodoItem`** and displays them using the **`TodoItemComponent`**. This component should be in charge of modifying the completion status of a **`TodoItem`**.
4. Move the **`TodoItems`** you defined in the **`TodoListComponent`** from the component to a service named **`TodoItemService`**. The service should now be in charge of handling the **`TodoItems`** and their modification.
5. Create a store using NgRx. Completing a **`TodoItem`** should dispatch a new action and handle it in the reducer.
6. Try to add a new functionality to your example. What about creating a new **`TodoItem`**? If you have trouble doing it, go through each one of the previous steps to build this new feature.

References

- https://angular.dev/guide/templates/property-binding
- https://angular.dev/guide/templates/event-binding
- https://ngrx.io/guide/store
- https://en.wikipedia.org/wiki/Redux_(JavaScript_library)
- https://redux.js.org/understanding/thinking-in-redux/three-principles

Kcy Terms

- Smart/Dumb components
- Refactoring
- @Input/@Output
- Service-based communication
- Redux
- State management libraries

CHAPTER 7
Reactive and Template-driven Forms

Introduction

In a previous chapter, we looked at how components were created and their structure. In this chapter, we'll look at creating forms. Forms provide a way to allow users to enter data into our applications. We will also look at the two ways we can create forms in our applications:

- Template-driven
- Reactive-driven

In Angular, we can build forms using either Template-driven forms. This is where we build the form using HTML elements and use directives like **`NgModal`** for data binding and manipulating the object model, with Template-driven forms we have implicit access to the object model.

The other type is Reactive forms, where we build our form using TypeScript. We still must add HTML elements to the page, we don't need to apply the directives to control data binding. With Reactive forms we have explicit access to the object model.

Reactive forms are more robust, scalable, reusable, and testable, but anything you can do in Reactive forms you can do in Template forms; one has more HTML and directives and the other has more TypeScript.

Structure

We will look at how the two types of forms work, ultimately, they both produce the same result and work similarly under the hood.

In this chapter, we will build up a small user entry form using both Template and

Reactive-driven forms, using the standalone application we created in *Chapter 2, Angular Application*. Following screenshot is the application we'll be building.

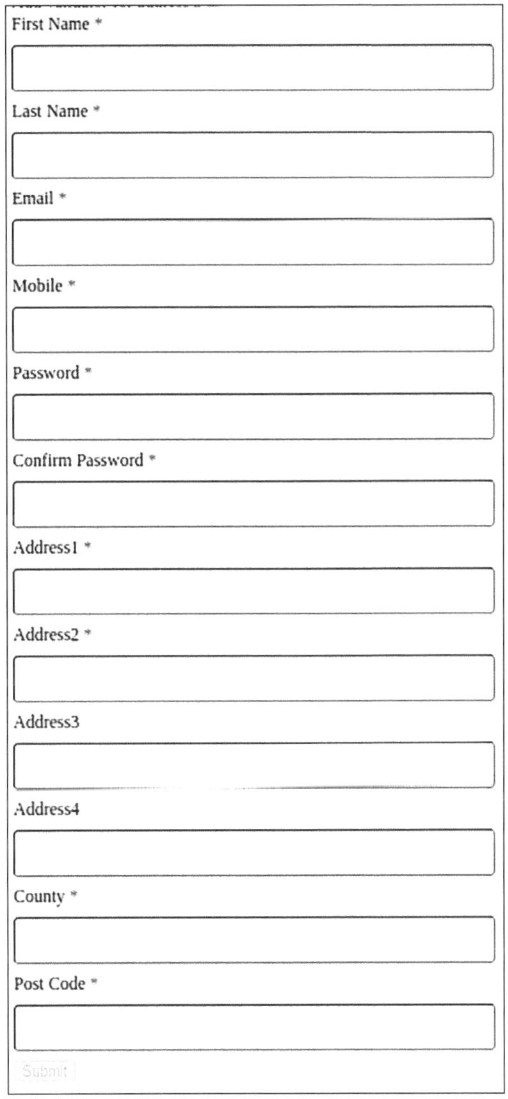

***Figure 7.1**: Application preview*

Note: *We won't go through the* **ngmodule** *application we created in Chapter 2, Angular Application as the changes are identical, the only difference being that the imports will be in the* **dashboard.module.ts** *file rather than in the component imports.*

Template-driven Forms

Template-driven form creation uses HTML elements to build up the form's layout and the directives handle the behavior. Open the terminal and navigate to **projects/standalone-app/** we created in *Chapter 2, Angular Application* and type the following:

```
ng g c /src/app/form-templates/template-driven
```

Tip: *If you want to check that the files will be created in the location you are expecting them, then you can use the* **--dry-run** *flag.*

This should now create a set of four files in a directory called **template-driven**, we also need to update our route config, so open the **routes.ts** file and add the following route:

```
export const routes: Route[] = [
// dashboard path here
{
    path: 'template-driven',
    loadComponent: () =>
      import('./form-templates/template-driven/template-driven.
component').then(
        (formTemplate) => formTemplate.TemplateDrivenComponent
      ),
    title: 'Template Driven - Standalone',
  },
]
```

And lastly, add a button on the **app.component.html** page using a **routerLink** to navigate to the **template-driven** component.

```
<button [routerLink]="'/template-driven'">Template Driven</button>
```

Now we can create the User Entry form in the **template-driven.component.html**, open the file, and replace any HTML with the following:

```
<form>
  <div>
    <label for="firstName">First Name</label>
    <input type="text" id="firstName" />
  </div>
  <div>
    <label for="lastName">Last Name</label>
    <input type="text" id="lastName" />
  </div>
  <div>
    <button>Submit</button>
  </div>
</form>
```

If we now run the application and go to the dashboard page and click the **Template Driven**, then we should now see the user entry form and a **submit** button and see the whole page refresh (which is correct as we've not added any Angular directives).

If we open the **template-driven.component.ts** file and in the **imports** array add the **FormsModule,** then we need to add the import as well at the top of the file; **FormsModule** is imported from **@angular/forms**. Save the changes, rerun the project, and click on the submit button again. This time the page doesn't refresh.

At first, that might appear a little strange, since all we have done is add an import and not done anything with it. The answer becomes clearer when we look at what happens when we include **FormsModule** in the imports array. We can use the browser's console to see what's happening, open the dev tools, then right-click one of the inputs, and then in the open elements tab locate the **form** element in the HTML and now, switch to the console tab.

We have access to all the elements on our form; to access them, we call the **window** function, then ng (this is shorthand for A**ng**ular). As we are interested in the directives for the form element we'll call **getDirectives** function passing in $0 (the selected item):

```
window.ng.getDirectives($0)
```

This function then returns an array of three directives, and it just so happens that the three directives are what the **FormsModule** import applied and is the reason why the form now doesn't refresh when we click the button:

```
NgNoValidate
NgControlStatusGroup
NgForm
```

Note: *There are many other functions that we can use to get information about our elements. These can help when we are debugging an issue.*

If we look at the Angular source code for **NgForm**, we can see that the directive has three selectors separated by commas, the last two don't apply to us in this instance, but the first selector does.

```
@Directive({
  selector: 'form:not([ngNoForm]):not([formGroup]),ng-form,[ngForm]',
  providers: [formDirectiveProvider],
  host: {'(submit)': 'onSubmit($event)', '(reset)': 'onReset()'},
  outputs: ['ngSubmit'],
  exportAs: 'ngForm'
})
export class NgForm ... {
  // code omitted for brevity
}
```

Tip: *Try selecting the form element without the* **FormsModule** *imported, this will be an empty array.*

The first selector is applying the directive to HTML **form** elements, where that form element does not have **ngNoForm** or **formGroup** on it. The host section of the directive applies events that get emitted when the submit is clicked, this is equivalent to writing a host directive and the output array is the same as an **@Output** decorator.

Before we can set up template binding, we need an object model to bind to, so let's create that now. In the **standalone** application, create a new directory under **apps** called **models** and create a new file called **user.model.ts**. In this file, we'll add the following interface.

```
export interface UserModel {
  firstName: string;
  lastName: string;
  email: string;
  mobile: string;
  address: {
    address1: string;
    address2: string;
    address3: string;
    address4: string;
    county: string;
    postcode: string;
  };
}
```

Here we have the **UserModel** with a few properties, the **UserModel's** address property is an object. In a real-world scenario, the user could have multiple addresses (Billing, Delivery, and so on) and we'll separate the address into its own component.

We can now bind our model to the form in the **template-driven.component.ts** file. We need to create a property that references the **UserModel**.

```
export class TemplateDrivenComponent {
user: UserModel = {
    firstName: '',
    lastName: '',
    email: '',
    mobile: '',
    address: {
      address1: '',
      address2: '',
      address3: '',
      address4: '',
      county: '',
      postcode: '',
    };
  };
}
```

We'll just set them to empty strings for the moment. In the HTML page on the **firstName** input element, we need to bind our model to this input. There is a directive called **ngModel** that connects the model to the form but doesn't give us any data binding.

```
<div>
    <label for="firstName">First Name</label>
    <input ngModel type="text" id="firstName"/>
</div>
```

To get one-way data binding, we can use the **@Input('ngModel')** on the directive to pass in data to our form.

```
<div>
    <label for="firstName">First Name</label>
    <input type="text" ngModel [ngModel]="user.firstName" id="first-
Name"/>
</div>
```

If we look at the console of our browser, we can see that we have the following error message:

```
Error: NG01352: If ngModel is used within a form tag, either the
name attribute must be set, or the form control must be defined as
'standalone' in ngModelOptions.
```

To fix this error, we need to add the **name** attribute to the input element. This gives the element a unique name and links the model property to the correct element.

```
<div>
    <label for="firstName">First Name</label>
    <input type="text" ngModel
      [ngModel]="user.firstName"
      name="user.firstName"
      id="firstName"
    />
</div>
```

We can also now remove the **ngModel**, the one that's not in square brackets because if the input and a directive selector have the same name, we can remove the selector. With this, we now have one-way data binding. If we replace the **firstName's** empty string in the user model with a name, then we should see the **firstName** input populated with that name.

```
user: UserModel = {
  firstName: 'Fred',
  lastName: '',
  email: '',
  mobile: '',
  address: {
  address1: '',
```

```
        address2: '',
        address3: '',
        address4: '',
        county: '',
        postcode: '',
    };
    };
```

Refreshing the browser, we should now see the **firstName** input has been updated that looks like the following image.

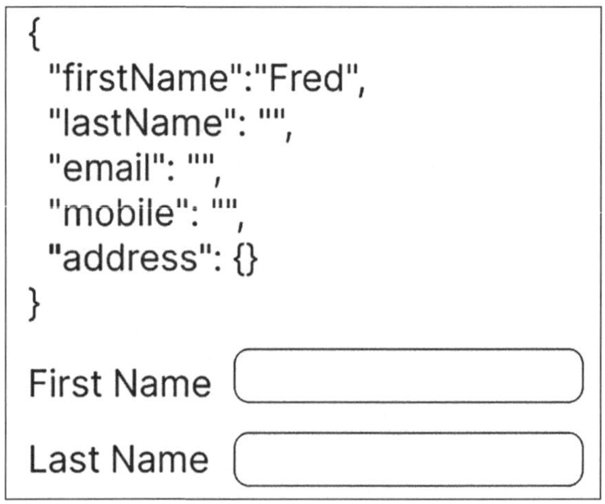

***Figure 7.2**: UserModel*

The section at the top of the image in curly braces is the output of the **UserModel**. To see this in your browser, add the following line to your HTML.

```
<form>
  <pre>{{ user | json }}</pre>
  ...
</form>
```

When the page loads our **firstName** property has a name in both the input and the user model (section in curly braces), but if we change the **firstName** [via the input] to something else, the change isn't reflected in the top section. In other words, the user model is not being updated, for this, we need to set up two-way data binding. For that, we need to change from an input property to an input property that includes event binding, this is sometimes referred to as the "*banana in a box*" "[()]" and is the shorthand syntax. So, now when we update the **firstName**, it is immediately reflected in the user model.

```
<div>
    <label for="firstName">First Name</label>
    <input type="text" ngModel
      [(ngModel)]="user.firstName" name="user.firstName"
```

```
        id="firstName"
    />
</div>
```

There may be times when you want or need to handle events separately. In this scenario, we can use the **ngModelChange** event instead.

```
<div>
    <label for="firstName">First Name</label>
    <input type="text" ngModel
      [ngModel]="user.firstName"
      (ngModelChange)="modelChangeFn($event)" name="user.firstName"
      id="firstName"
    />
</div>

// in the ts file you would add
modelChangeFn (firstName: string) {
    // manipulate the data here before updating
    // the object model
    this.user.firstName = firstName;
}
```

It is possible to only use the standard **change** event, the most notable difference here would be that the object model would only be updated after the input has lost focus, whereas using the **ngModelChange** or the banana in a box syntax, the object model is updated immediately.

Tip: *Using the* **[(ngModel)]** *will cover most scenarios and is a preferred method.*

In this section, we'll complete the form so that we can see all the data coming through when submitting our form. We'll also cover grouping as the address is a nested object.

```
<form>
  <!-- for displaying the user model -->
  <pre>{{ user | json }}</pre>
  <div>
    <label for="firstName">First Name</label>
    <input
      type="text"
      [(ngModel)]="user.firstName"
      name="user.firstName"
      id="firstName"
      autocomplete="off"
    />
  </div>
  <div>
    <label for="lastName">Last Name</label>
    <input
```

```
      type="text"
      [(ngModel)]="user.lastName"
      name="user.lastName"
      id="lastName"
      autocomplete="off"
    />
  </div>
  <div>
    <label for="email">Email</label>
    <input
      type="text"
      [(ngModel)]="user.email"
      name="user.email"
      id="email"
      autocomplete="off"
    />
  </div>
  <div>
    <label for="mobile">Mobile</label>
    <input
      type="text"
      [(ngModel)]="user.mobile"
      name="user.mobile"
      id="mobile"
      autocomplete="off"
    />
  </div>
  <!-- insert address section here -->

  <div><button>Submit</button></div>
</form>
```

This completes the first part of the user model and now we need to add the address section. We can add the address section the same way as we have done with the user section, and it will work fine. But the chances are in a real-world application, the address is likely to be a separate component and used in multiple places. We'll start by creating the address as a separate component.

In the **standalone** application, under the **src** directory create a new directory called **shared** and within that directory create an **address** directory. In the newly created address directory, create a new file called **address.component.ts** and add the following:

```
// add imports here
@Component({
  selector: 'app-address',
  standalone: true,
```

```
    imports: [CommonModule, FormsModule],
    template: `<ng-container>
      <div>
        <label for="address1">Address1</label>
        <input
          type="text"
          [(ngModel)]="user.address.address1"
          name="user.address.address1"
          id="address1"
          autocomplete="off"
        />
      </div>
      <div>
        <label for="address2">Address2</label>
        <input
          type="text"
          [(ngModel)]="user.address.address2"
          name="user.address.address2"
          id="address2"
          autocomplete="off"
        />
      </div>
      <div>
        <label for="address3">Address3</label>
        <input
          type="text"
          [(ngModel)]="user.address.address3"
          name="user.address.address3"
          id="address3"
          autocomplete="off"
        />
      </div>
      <div>
        <label for="address4">Address4</label>
        <input
          type="text"
          [(ngModel)]="user.address.address4"
          name="user.address.address4"
          id="address4"
          autocomplete="off"
        />
      </div>
      <div>
        <label for="county">County</label>
        <input
          type="text"
          [(ngModel)]="user.address.county"
```

```
          name="user.address.county"
          id="county"
          autocomplete="off"
        />
      </div>
      <div>
        <label for="postcode">Post Code</label>
        <input
          type="text"
          [(ngModel)]="user.address.postcode"
          name="user.address.postcode"
          id="postcode"
          autocomplete="off"
        />
      </div>
    </ng-container>`,
  })
export class AddressComponent {
  @Input() user!: UserModel;
}
```

In the template-driven component, we need to add this component, open the **template-driven.component.html** file, and add this just above the **submit** button.

```
<app-address [user]="user"></app-address>
```

And in this **template-driven.component.ts** file import the **AddressComponent** in the imports array.

```
@Component({
  selector: 'app-dashboard',
  standalone: true,
  imports: [CommonModule, FormsModule, AddressComponent],
  templateUrl: './template-driven.component.html',
  styleUrls: ['./template-driven.component.scss'],
})
export class TemplateDrivenComponent {
  …
}
```

If we run the application at this stage, with the developer tools open, and complete our form, we can see at least one-way data binding as the top section in curly brackets is updating. If we click the submit button and look at the console, we can also see our user model, but when we expand it we can see that the address part didn't come through.

There are two parts to fixing this; first, we need to add the **ngModelGroup** to the **ng-**

`container` element of the address component, so the **`address.component`** can link up with the parents **`ngForm`**. With this added, we now have an error saying:

```
No provider for the ControlContainer found in NodeInjector
```

If we look at the source code for the **`NgModelGroup`,** then we can see that it stops looking for a **`ControlContainer`** when it reaches the Host element of the current component.

```
@Directive({selector: '[ngModelGroup]', providers: [modelGroupProvider], exportAs: 'ngModelGroup'})
export class NgModelGroup extends AbstractFormGroupDirective implements OnInit, OnDestroy {
 /**
  * @description
  * Tracks the name of the `NgModelGroup` bound to the directive. The name corresponds
  * to a key in the parent `NgForm`.
  */
 @Input('ngModelGroup') override name: string = '';

 constructor(
  @Host() @SkipSelf() parent: ControlContainer,
  @Optional() @Self() @Inject(NG_VALIDATORS) validators: (Validator | ValidatorFn)[],
  @Optional()
  @Self()
  @Inject(NG_ASYNC_VALIDATORS)
  asyncValidators: (AsyncValidator | AsyncValidatorFn)[],
 ) {
  super();
  this._parent = parent;
  this._setValidators(validators);
  this._setAsyncValidators(asyncValidators);
 }
```

Figure 7.3: *Angular Source Code (Note: Source code from the Angular project)*

We are able to access the provider from **`viewProviders`** that are declared on the Host element, thanks to the power of Angulars' Dependency Injection. Let's add a **`viewProviders`** array after the **`ng-container`** element:

```
  // template details omitted for brevity.
  </ng-container>`,
  viewProviders: [{ provide: ControlContainer, useExisting: Ng-
Form }],
})
export class AddressComponent {
  @Input() user!: UserModel;
```

If we run the page, then we can see that the page loads and the error has been fixed and the user and address input boxes on the page, all that is left to do now is to connect the submit button.

To be able to submit data for storage to a database for example, we need to collect all the data. Luckily for us, this is in our **`UserModel`** object we created earlier.

If we remember the **ngForm** directive from the Angular source code, then we can see that the host is listening for the **submit** (and **reset**) events.

```
@Directive({
  selector: 'form:not([ngNoForm]):not([formGroup]),ng-form,
[ngForm]',
  providers: [formDirectiveProvider],
  host: {'(submit)': 'onSubmit($event)', '(reset)': 'onReset()'},
  outputs: ['ngSubmit'],
  exportAs: 'ngForm'
})
export class NgForm extends ControlContainer …
```

If we go back to our HTML form, then we can see we have the **form** element wrapping our layout. We need to add two things to this element: a template variable and the **ngSubmit** event, the template variable allows us to pass the model associated with the form.

```
<form #form="ngForm" (ngSubmit)="onSubmit(form)">
  <div>
    <label for="firstName">First Name</label>
    <input type="text" id="firstName" />
  </div>
  <div>
    <label for="lastName">Last Name</label>
    <input type="text" id="lastName" />
  </div>
  // other details omitted for brevity.
  <div>
    <button>Submit</button>
  </div>
</form>
```

Next, open the **template-driven.component.ts** file and add the **onSubmit()** event:

```
onSubmit(form: NgForm) {
    console.log(form.value);
}
```

If we run the application again, open the developer tools and fill in all the values and then, click the **submit** button. We should now see our **userModel** in the console of the developer tools, and if we expand it, we should now see a full object.

```
{
  "user.firstName": "Fred",
  "user.lastName": "Bloggs",
  "user.email": "fred@gmail.com",
  "user.mobile": "0123456789",
  "address": {
   "user.address.address1": "Acme Ltd",
   "user.address.address2": "The Hight Street",
   "user.address.address3": "Downtown" ,
   "user.address.address4:" "Outer District",
   "user.address.county": "London",
   "user.address.postcode": "W1 4QW",
}
```

Figure 7.4: *UserModel Object*

In this section, we have covered creating a user entry form using template-driven forms. We have learned about how to set up one-way and two-way data binding, submitting the form with a child component.

Coming up in the next section is Reactive forms, we'll build the same user entry form using Reactive forms.

Reactive-driven Forms

Reactive-driven forms use TypeScript to handle the construction and data binding of our form. We still need to place HTML elements on the page to allow the user to interact with the form, but TypeScript creates all the form controls, groups, and arrays.

Open the terminal and navigate to **`projects/standalone-app/`** we created in *Chapter 3, Angular Applications* and type the following:

```
ng g c /src/app/form-templates/reactive-driven
```

Tip: *If you want to check that the files will be created in the location you are expecting them, then you can use the* **`--dry-run (-d)`** *flag first.*

This should now create a set of four files in a directory called **`reactive-driven`**, we also need to update our route config, so open the **`routes.ts`** file and add the following route:

```
export const routes: Route[] = [
// dashboard path here
{
    path: 'reactive-driven',
```

```
    loadComponent: () =>
      import('./form-templates/reactive-driven/reactive-driven.
component').then(
        (formTemplate) => formTemplate.TemplateDrivenComponent
      ),
    title: 'Reactive Driven - Standalone',
  },
]
```

And lastly, add a button on the **app.component.html** page using a **routerLink** to navigate to the **reactive-driven** component.

```
<button [routerLink]="'/reactive-driven'">Reactive Driven</button>
```

We'll start with the same HTML for the user entry form as for the Template-Driven form with all the directives removed (we'll add the address component later). Open the **reactive-driven.component.html** file and add the following HTML.

```
<form>
  <div>
    <label for="firstName">First Name</label>
    <input type="text" id="firstName" />
  </div>
  <div>
    <label for="lastName">Last Name</label>
    <input type="text" id="lastName" />
  </div>
  <div>
    <label for="email">Email</label>
    <input type="text" id="email" />
  </div>
  <div>
    <label for="mobile">Mobile</label>
    <input type="text" id="mobile" />
  </div>
  <div><button>Submit</button></div>
</form>
```

Just like we did with the template-driven form, we'll add the **ReactiveFormsModule** to the imports array on the **reactive-driven.component.ts** file, then in the browser, right-click to inspect the page and select the form element and switch over to the console tab. In the console tab type:

```
window.ng.getDirectives($0)
```

This time we only get two directives:

- NgNoValidate
- NgControlStatusGroup

Note: *There is no* **NgForm** *directive this time, as controlling the form is now our responsibility.*

As we saw in the last section, these directives are applied because of the **form** element on the page. If we look at the Angular source code again, we can see that this directive has six selectors, and this time, it's the fifth selector that is applying the directive to our form.

```
@Directive ({
  selector:
      '[formGroupName],[formArrayName],[ngModelGroup],
[formGroup],form:not([ngNoForm]),[ngForm]',
  host: ngGroupStatusHost
})
export class NgControlStatusGroup extends AbstractControlStatus {
  constructor(@Optional() @Self() cd: ControlContainer) {
    super(cd);
  }
}
```

This selector is applying this directive to our form element as there is not a **ngNoForm** directive on the element.

Let's start to build our form. If we look at the layout, we have a collection of inputs, these are our **FormControls** and wrapping all the **FormControls** (invisibly) is the **FormGroup**.

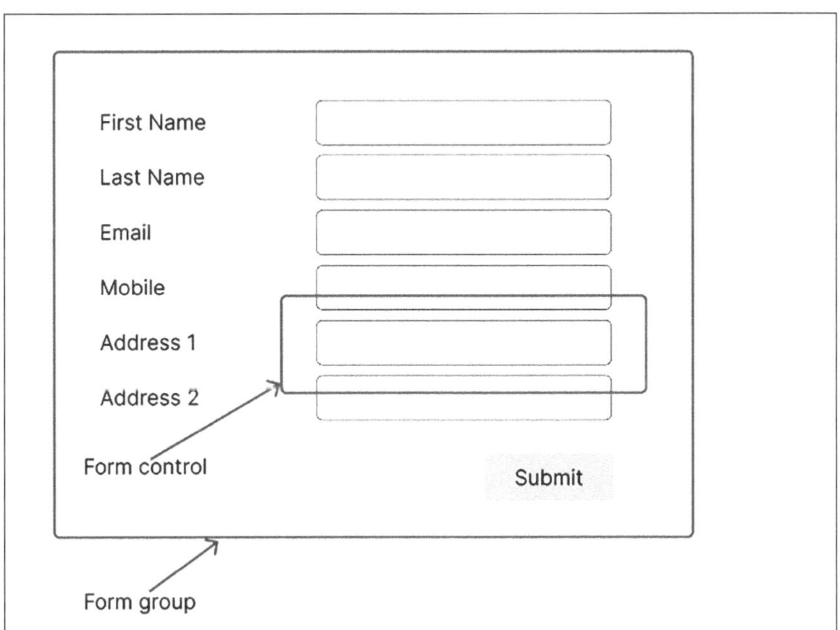

***Figure 7.5**: Reactive form layout*

Form Controls

In the **reactive-driven.component.ts** file, we need to create a variable to contain our **FormGroup** and within this **FormGroup**, let's add the **firstName** input.

```
form = new FormGroup({
  firstName: new FormControl('');
});
```

On the HTML we need to add a reference to the **formGroup** and we do that by passing our **form** variable to the **[formGroup]** directive.

Note: *This time we don't need to create a template variable, the form variable is the* **FormGroup** *we created in the TypeScript file.*

```
<form [formGroup]="form" >
  <div>
    <label for="firstName">First Name</label>
    <input
      formControlName="firstName"
      type="text"
      id="firstName"
    />
  </div>
...
</form>
```

We also need to link our input to the **firstName** using the **formControlName**.

Let's now link up the other inputs and add the remaining **FormControls** to our form group.

```
form = new FormGroup({
    firstName: new FormControl(''),
    lastName: new FormControl(''),
    email: new FormControl(''),
    mobile: new FormControl(''),
    address: new FormGroup({}),
  });
```

You will notice that the address field is of type **FormGroup** rather than **FormControl**. This is because the address section is part of the address component, which we will create shortly.

The **firstName**, **lastName**, **email**, and **mobile** are all the same and all we need is to add the **formControlName.**<form>

```
  <!-- previous sections removed -->
  <app-address2 formGroupName="address" ></app-address2>
```

```
    <div><button>Submit</button></div>
  </form>
```

The address section is a little different. Here, we're adding the **formGroupName** to the **address2** element, the name of this matches the name we set in the **FormGroup**.

Now let's create our address component, at the terminal window type:

```
ng g c /src/app/shared/address/address2
```

This will now create the usual four files (**.html**, **.ts**, **.spec**, and **.scss**), open the HTML file, and add the following markup.

```
<ng-container>
    <div>
      <label for="address1">Address1</label>
      <input
        type="text"
        id="address1"
      />
    </div>
    <div>
      <label for="address2">Address2</label>
      <input
        type="text"
        id="address2"
      />
    </div>
    <div>
      <label for="address3">Address3</label>
      <input
        type="text"
        id="address3"
      />
    </div>
    <div>
      <label for="adddress4">Address4</label>
      <input
        type="text"
        id-"address4"
      />
    </div>
    <div>
      <label for="county">County</label>
      <input
        type="text"
        id="county"
      />
    </div>
```

```
      <div>
        <label for="postcode">Post Code</label>
        <input
          type="text"
          id="postcode"
        />
      </div>
    </ng-container>
```

Like we did earlier, we just need to add the **formControlName** to each input field.

```
<div>
   <label for="address1">Address1</label>
   <input
   formControlName="address1"
   type="text"
   id="address1"
   />
</div>
```

We added the **FormGroup** for the address section on the **reactive-driven.component.ts** file and left it as an empty object.

Next, we need to add the **FormGroup** to the TypeScript file, in the **address2.component.ts** file add the following:

```
@Component({
  selector: 'app-address2',
  standalone: true,
  imports: [CommonModule, ReactiveFormsModule],
  stylesUrl: ['./address2.component.scss'],
  templateUrl: './address2.component.html',
  viewProviders: [{ provide: ControlContainer,
   useExisting: FormGroupName }],
})
export class Address2Component implements OnInit {
constructor(private parent: FormGroupName) {}

  ngOnInit(): void {
    this.parent.control.addControl(
      'address',
      new FormGroup({
        address1: new FormControl(''),
        address2: new FormControl(''),
        address3: new FormControl(''),
        address4: new FormControl(''),
        county: new FormControl(''),
        postcode: new FormControl(''),
      })
```

```
    );
  }
}
```

There are two parts to this, the first one is the **FormGroup**, for each input we add a new **FormControl**, that is attached to a parent variable, which is of **FormGroupName** and we get this from the **viewProviders**. We also used this in the template-driven section, this time though we are using the **FormGroupName** from the **ControlContainer**.

Save everything and rerun the application, select the Reactive-Driven button and our form should look like this:

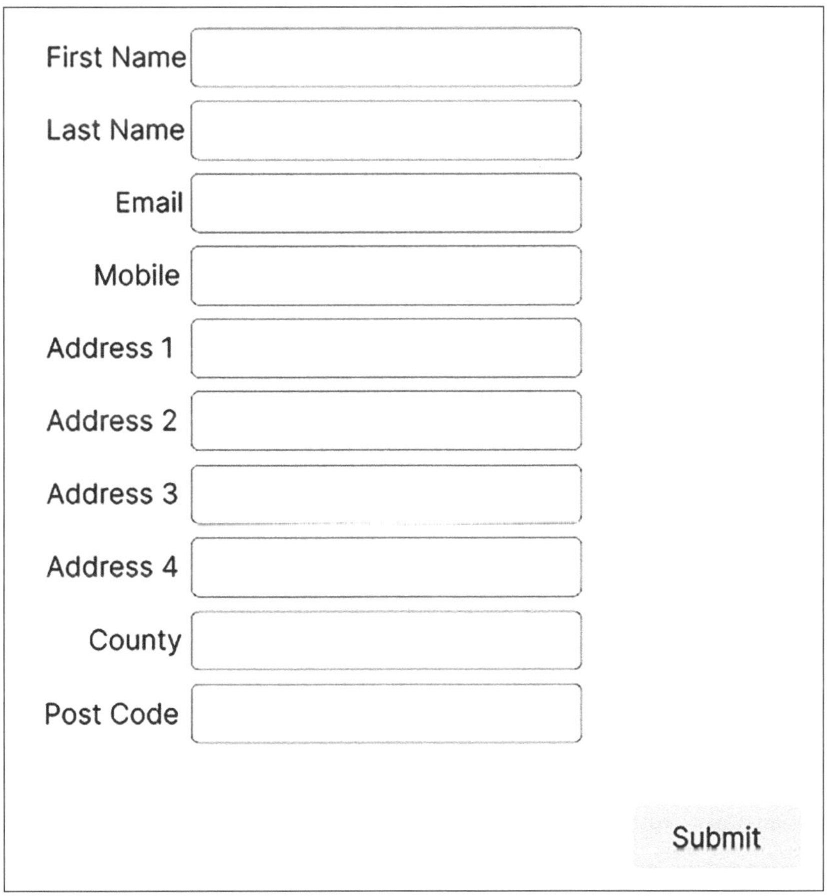

Figure 7.6: *Form layout*

Before we can submit our data, we need to create our **onSubmit** event, in the **reactive-driven.component.ts** and add a call to **console.log**, passing in the form's value.

```
onSubmit() {
  console.log(this.form.value);
}
```

Filling in all the fields and hitting the submit button we should now see the following in the console of the browser.

```
{
  "address"
   "address": {
     "address1": "Acme Ltd",
     "address2": "The Hight Street",
     "address3": "Downtown" ,
     "address4:" "Outer District",
     "county": "London",
     "postcode": "W1 4QW",
   "firstName": "Fred",
   "lastName": "Bloggs",
   "email": "fred@gmail.com",
   "mobile": "0123456789",
}
```

***Figure** 7.7: Usermodel results*

With reactive forms, there is some shorthand syntax that will make building with reactive forms a lot easier. In the following section, we'll go through the same form, this time using the shorthand syntax.

Form Groups

Rather than specifying all the **formControls** individually, we can use the **FormBuilder** from **@angular/forms**. We need to inject the **FormBuilder** into our component, we'll use the newer inject function instead of passing the dependency in the constructor.

```
private formBuilder = inject(FormBuilder);
form!: FormGroup;
form = this.formBuilder.group({
      firstName: [''],
      lastName: [''],
      email: [''],
      mobile: [''],
      address: new FormGroup({}),
    });
```

In the **address2** component, we need to update that to the following:

```
private parent = inject(FormGroupName);
private formBuilder = inject(FormBuilder);

ngOnInit(): void {
    this.parent.control.addControl(
      'address',
      this.formBuilder.group({
        address1: [''],
        address2: [''],
        address3: [''],
        address4: [''],
        county: [''],
        postcode: [''],
      })
    );
}
```

Loading Data

There is one part that we've not covered and it's the same for both Template-driven and Reactive-driven forms, as we can see in all the examples we've created so far, the model or **formControl/Group** properties all start with empty strings. In a real-world application, we would be loading data from a database or some other external source and populating these properties, so let's add this to our example.

In this example, we'll just use a local Json server to act as an API server. First we need to install the JSON server. In the terminal for the standalone application project type:

```
npm install -g json-server
```

Note: *remove the* **-g** *flag if you don't want to install json-server globally.*

Next, we need to create a json file in the project's **src** directory called **db.json** and add our **userModel**.

```
{
  "userModel": {
    "firstName": "Fred",
    "lastName": "Blogs",
    "email": "fred@gmail.com",
    "mobile": "0123456789",
    "address": {
      "address1": "Acme Inc",
      "address2": "The High Street",
      "address3": "Downtown",
      "address4": "Outer District",
```

```
        "county": "London",
        "postcode": "W14 5QW"
      }
    }
  }
```

Finally, we need to open a new terminal in the standalone applications project directory and start the **json-server**.

```
json-server --watch db.json
```

This will run the server on **https://localhost:3000** by default, to change the port to a different port add the **--port** flag.

```
json-server -watch --port 9000 db.json
```

Open a new browser tab and go to **https://localhost:3000** and you should see the **userModel** being displayed.

To populate the model or the **formControl/formGroup**, we need to load that data first. As mentioned in a previous chapter, the service component is what we need to use to make calls to external resources, let's add a service to our application.

From the terminal let's use the CLI to create our service:

```
ng g service src/app/form-templates/data.service
```

Don't forget to use the **--dry-run** flag if you want to check the location first. Next, add the following to the service.

```
import { HttpClient } from '@angular/common/http';
import { Injectable, inject } from '@angular/core';
import { Observable, map } from 'rxjs';
import { UserModel } from '../models/user.model';

@Injectable({
  providedIn: 'root',
})
export class DataService {
  private http = inject(HttpClient);
  getUser(): Observable<UserModel> {
    return this.http.get<UserModel>  ('http://localhost:3000/us-
erModel').pipe(
      map((data: UserModel) => data)
          );
  }
}
```

With the **json-server** running, we will now be able to make a call to the API and get our **userModel** data back, to get this we need to subscribe to the service in our reactive-**driven.component.ts** file. In the **ngOnInit** life cycle, we created a new form group and assigned empty strings to each of the values.

```
// inject the DataService
private dataService = inject(DataService);

form = this.formBuilder.group({
      firstName: [''],
      lastName: [''],
      email: [''],
      mobile: [''],
      address: new FormGroup({}),
});
```

We'll subscribe to the **getUser** method from the **DataService**, here, we have a couple of options for setting the value: **setValue** and **patchValue** and they do pretty much the same thing, except **setValue** requires all properties (even if they are optional), whereas **patchValue** will except one or more properties. To use the **setValue**. we use the model (called **form** in our example) and pass in an object of all properties in our model.

```
this.dataService.getUser().subscribe({ next: (data) => {(this.
user = data),
this.form.setValue({
      firstName: this.user.firstName,
      lastName: this.user.lastName,
      email: this.user.email,
      mobile: this.user.mobile,
      password: this.user.password,
      confirmPassword: this.user.confirmPassword,
      validate: true,
      address: {
        address1: this.user.address.address1,
        address2: this.user.address.address2,
        address3: this.user.address.address3,
        address4: this.user.address.address4,
        county: this.user.address.county,
        postcode: this.user.address.postcode,
      },
    });
});
  }
```

And we can use the **patchValue** to update some of the field values.

```
    this.data.getUser().subscribe({
      next: (data) => {
        (this.user = data),
```

```
            this.form.patchValue({
                firstName: this.user.firstName,
                lastName: this.user.lastName,
                email: this.user.email,
                mobile: this.user.mobile,
    },
        });
      }
```

We need to make a similar change to the **address2.component.ts** file, but before we move on to that we need to add an input binding to the **app-address2** element.

```
<app-address2 formGroupName="address" [user]="user"></app-address2>
```

Let's open the **address2.component.ts** file, this time we'll set up some getters to provide the form controls to remove some of the repetitiveness' of the code.

```
get address1(): FormControl {
  return this.form.get('address1') as FormControl;
}
get address2(): FormControl {
  return this.form.get('address2') as FormControl;
}
get address3(): FormControl {
  return this.form.get('address3') as FormControl;
}
get address4(): FormControl {
  return this.form.get('address4') as FormControl;
}
get county(): FormControl {
  return this.form.get('county') as FormControl;
}
get postcode(): FormControl {
  return this.form.get('postcode') as FormControl;
}

@Input() set user(userModel: UserModel) {
    this.address1?.patchValue({ address1: userModel?.address.
    address1});
    this.address2?.patchValue({ address2: userModel?.address.
    address2});
    this.address3?.patchValue({ address3: userModel?.address.
    address3});
    this.address4?.patchValue({ address4: userModel?.address.
    address4});
    this.county?.patchValue({ county: userModel?.address.county
    });
```

```
      this.postcode?.patchValue({ postcode: userModel?.address.
      postcode});
    }
  };
```

Here we have created a set of getters, these return the **formControl** and it is a good habit to get into as it means you have an easy way to access each **formControl** and helps improve the readability of our code. Once we have the **formControl**, we can call the **patchValue**.

Now when the page loads it will populate the fields with the data from the **db.json**. For the template-driven form, it's a little bit simpler, all we need to add is a call to the DataService's **getUser** method and populate the **userModel**.

```
ngOnInit(): void {
  this.data.getUser().subscribe({
    next: (data) => {
      this.user = data;
    },
  });
}
```

Dynamic Forms

There are times when we want to allow the user to enter multiple entries, such as phone numbers, email addresses, or as in our preceding example, the address property could have multiple addresses, (one for billing, one for deliveries, and so on). But as developers, we don't know how many our users we'll need and we don't want to provide multiple controls when they may or may not be required. Ideally, we need to let the user decide how many they need, and to do this we can use the **FormArray**.

Let's change our phone input to allow the user to add multiple phone numbers, we'll replace the mobile input with this new section, we'll start with the **userModel**, comment out the mobile property, and add the following:

```
// mobile: string;
Telephone: [
{
  phoneNumber: string;
}
]
```

Next, let's change the **reactive-driven.component.ts** file, comment out **mobile,** and add **telephone**:

```
form = this.formBuilder.group({
      // mobile: [''], // comment out this property
      telephone: this.formBuilder.array([
        this.formBuilder.group({
```

```
          phoneNumber: new formControl(''),
            }),
          ]),
          address: new formGroup({});
    });
```

We also need to be able to **Add** and **Remove** a control.

```
addPhone() {
    this.form.controls.telephone.insert(
      0,
      new FormGroup({
        phoneNumber: new FormControl(''),
      })
    );
  }
```

We'll use the insert method to add a new item to our form controls array, we can specify where the item comes in the array, and zero will insert the new control into first place, effectively pushing everything down to 1. Likewise, we could have added it to the end by getting the length of the controls array and adding 1 to the end.

```
addPhone() {
    this.form.controls.telephone.insert(
      this.form.controls.telephone.length + 1,
      new FormGroup({
        phoneNumber: new FormControl(''),
      })
    );
  }
We'll pass in the index of the item to be deleted and remove that
control from the controls array.
  removePhone(index: number) {
    this.form.controls.telephone.removeAt(index);
  }
```

To populate the controls when the page loads, first, we need to update the **db.json** file with our telephone array and some fake data:

```
// mobile - remove this field.
"telephone": [
      {
        "phoneNumber": "07954042620"
      },
      {
        "phoneNumber": "01528875796"
      },
      {
        "phoneNumber": "03032115872"
```

```
        },
        {
          "phoneNumber": "01458279927"
        }
      ],
```

Lastly, we need to update the **ngOnInit** life cycle hook. Previously, we just called the **patchValue** method to update the value of the control. To update our telephone array, we need to loop through the telephone array from our **db.json**, creating a new control and patching the value.

First, we check to see if the telephone array has any items by checking the length of the array. We then create a variable of type **FormArray** and ensure that it's empty by calling the **clear()** method. Next, we iterate over our telephone data array, within this loop we create a **formGroup** with a **formControl** for our phone numbers. We use **Object.keys** to iterate over the controls pulling out the key, in our case, this is **phoneNumber** we can use this key in the call to **patchValue** and set the value, and we finish up by pushing our **formGroup** to the **formArray**.

```
if (data.telephone.length > 0) {
    const arr = this.form.get('telephone') as FormArray;
    arr.clear();

    data.telephone.forEach((item) => {
      const grp = this.buildPhoneFormGroup();
      Object.keys(grp.controls).forEach((key) => {
      grp.patchValue({
        [key]: item.phoneNumber,
     });
    });
    arr.controls.push(grp);
  });
}
```

Create a private function to create a new **FormGroup** with **FormControl**.

```
buildPhoneFormGroup(): FormGroup {
    return this.formBuilder.group({
      phoneNumber: new FormControl(''),
    });
  }
```

Lastly, we need to add HTML to display the array of controls.

```
<div formArrayName="telephone">
    <label>Phone Number</label>
    <button (click)="addPhone()" type="button">Add</button>
    <div
```

```
      *ngFor="let phone of form.controls.telephone.controls;
      index as i"
      [formGroupName]="i"
    >
      <label>Phone {{ i }}</label>
      <input
        type="text"
        formControlName="phoneNumber"
        placeholder="Enter Phone number"
        id="phone-{{ i }}"
      />
      <button (click)="removePhone(i)" type="button">Remove</button>
    </div>
  </div>
```

We added the directive **formArrayName** and assigned it **telephone** to match what we set up in the accompanying **ts** file earlier. We add a label and an **add** button to allow the user to add more phone numbers. Next, we iterate over the telephone controls array and stamp out each phone number stored in the **db.json** file. We set a variable to the index, so that on each iteration, we get a unique index number. We also add the **formGroupName** and set this to the same index number. We add another label with the index number, the input for the phone number itself, and lastly, another button to remove the phone number.

Note: *Removing a phone number will not delete it from the* **db.json** *as we're not performing an actual delete, in a real-world scenario we would call a delete API and remove the selected item from the database.*

FormRecord

FormRecord is very similar to **FormGroup**. With **FormGroup**, we know at design time what the keys will be, we don't know how many controls will be created, for example:

```
// FormGroup
address: new FormGroup<{ [key: string]: FormControl<string>
}>({})
// full example
addressGrp: new FormGroup({
  nameOrNumber: new FormControl(''),
  street: new FormControl(''),
  district: new FormControl(''),
  county: new FormControl(''),
  postcode: new FormControl(''),
})
```

And here is the **FormRecord** version

```
// FormRecord
address: new FormRecord<FormControl<string>>({})
```

With **FormRecord**, it's a little more open-ended, the keys can be dynamic if not known ahead of time, and like **FormGroup**, we don't know how many controls there will be either.

Summary

In this section of the chapter, we've covered Reactive-driven forms and setting up a reactive form. We also looked at **FormControl**, **FormGroup**, **FormArray**, and **FormRecord**.

Conclusion

We covered quite a lot in this chapter and should now have a solid understanding of how we can build up our forms in both Template-driven and Reactive-driven along with the different types of controls and groups we can use.

CHAPTER 8
Form Validation

Introduction

In this chapter, we're going to investigate form validation. In the previous chapter, we learned about Reactive and Template driven forms and how to set these forms up with data binding. Being able to have our applications accept input from a user and to display that data back later is all well and good, but we need to ensure that the data entered is correct and conforms to our models and to any database we may be using to store our data.

Our applications won't be well received if we can add incorrect data, for example, an invalid email address or telephone number. We need to ensure what a user can enter is of the correct data type and is valid data (that is, a properly formatted email address). We also need to inform the user if something has been entered in the correct format, for example, an email address or a telephone number, or whether a field is mandatory.

To achieve this, we need to be able to validate the data that has been entered and to display any errors to the user if there is an issue, for this we have Validators.

Structure

In this chapter, we'll look at the validation model and cover the following sections:

- Built-in validation types
- Template form validation
- Reactive form validation
- Creating custom validators
- Alternative options for long template-driven forms

By the end of this chapter, we should be able to apply different types of validation to our applications and display any validation messages in the event of an error. We'll cover the built-in validation types and follow this up by creating custom validators. We'll also look at different ways we can set up and display our error messages in our applications.

When building an application there is usually a lot of planning around how the pages of our application will look, how users will interact with it, and how our application will communicate with back-end services to fetch and store our data. We also need to prepare our application when a user enters incorrect or incomplete data, to inform the user that some have not worked as expected, and how the user must proceed to rectify this issue. This is where Validation comes to the rescue.

Built-in Validation Types

Angular comes with several built-in validation types. These built-in types make it quick and easy to apply validation to a control, without having to write your own validation types. It is also possible to create your own validation types, and we'll investigate that later in this chapter. The built-in validation types are:

- **`min`** : Validates to ensure the control's value is equal to or above the minimum value specified.
- **`max`** : Validates to ensure the control's value doesn't exceed the maximum value specified.
- **`required`** : Validates to ensure a control has had a value entered
- **`requiredTrue`** : Validates to make a control value true, this is often used in checkboxes.
- **`email`** : Validates to ensure a control value is a valid email address.
- **`minLength`** : Validates to ensure a control value is equal to or greater than the minimum length.
- **`maxLength`** : Validates to ensure a control value is equal or less than the maximum length.
- **`pattern`** : Validates to ensure a control's value matches a regular expression pattern.
- **`nullValidator`** : Validates nothing and performs no operation.
- **`compose`** : Use this to put multiple validators into a single function, this returns a union of individual errors.
- **`composeAsync`** : This is the same as compose but for Async validation.

We'll cover some of these validators in detail in the coming sections. Built-in types can be used in both Template and Reactive forms. Most of these validators should be self-explanatory, but let's go over them to understand them better.

`Min`

This validator validates that the value the user entered in the form control meets the required minimum value, for example, the minimum number of characters in an input field.

Max

This validator validates that the value the user entered in the form control doesn't exceed the maximum, for example, the maximum number of characters in an input field.

Required/RequiredTrue

These validators validate that the user has entered a value into the form control, if no value entered the form remains invalid.

Email

This validator validates that the value passes an email validation test, this typically involves the use of a regular expression pattern.

MinLength

This validator validates that the length of the value entered into the form control is greater than or equal to the value provided, for example, the comments section of a form could have a minLength forcing the user to add a minimum number of characters or words.

MaxLength

This validator validates that the length of the value entered into the form control is less than or equal to the value provided, for example, the comments section of a form could have a **maxLength** forcing the user to limit their response to a maximum number of characters or words.

Pattern

This validator validates that the value entered in the form control matches a particular pattern; this pattern can be either a string or a regular expression. If the value doesn't match the pattern, then the control becomes invalid.

Null Validator

This validator performs no operation, this might seem a bit strange to have a validator that performs no operation, but it could be useful if we need to return a null, we can instead return a **nullValidator**.

```
mobileValidator:validationFn = v => {
      return some_value === some_other_value ?
      Validators.required(v):
      Validators.nullValidator(v);
}
```

Compose/ComposeAsync

With this validator, we can compose multiple validators into one function which returns a union of errors for the provided control.

Template Form Validation

In this section, we'll set up our standalone application with a form that the user needs to enter information into various fields, and we'll add validation to ensure the data entered is correct and/or present. In a previous chapter, we discussed Template-driven forms and that almost all of the logic is in the template, so we must add our validation to our templates too.

Let's start by creating the form that we are going to be using. Open the Angular project we created in a previous chapter, and also open a terminal in the **`standalone-app`** directory. We'll use the template-driven component from a previous chapter and the user model code we created in that chapter, but feel free to create a new directory for this if you prefer. In the template**`.component.html`** file let's add the following html:

```
<form #form="ngForm" (ngSubmit)="onSubmit(form)">
  <div>
      <label for="firstName">First Name</label>
      <input [(ngModel)]="user.firstName" type="text"
        name="user.firstName" id="firstName"
      />
  </div>
  <div>
      <label for="lastName">Last Name</label>
      <input [(ngModel)]="user.lastName" type="text"
        name="user.lastName" id="lastName"
      />
  </div>
  <div>
      <label for="email">Email</label>
      <input type="text" [(ngModel)]="user.email"
        name="user.email" id="email" autocomplete="off"
      />
  </div>
  <div>
      <label for="mobile">Mobile</label>
      <input type="text" [(ngModel)]="user.mobile"
        name="user.mobile" id="mobile" autocomplete="off"
      />
  </div>
  <ng-container ngModelGroup="address" #address="ngModelGroup">
    <div>
      <label for="address1">Address1</label>
      <input type="text" [(ngModel)]="user.address.address1"
        name="user.address.address1" id="address1" autocomplete="off"
    />
    </div>
```

```
      <div>
        <label for="address2">Address2</label>
        <input type="text" [(ngModel)]="user.address.address2"
          name="user.address.address2" id="address2" autocomplete="off"
        />
     </div>
     <div>
       <label for="address3">Address3</label>
       <input type="text" [(ngModel)]="user.address.address3"
         name="user.address.address3" id="address3" autocomplete="off"
       />
     </div>
  <div>
    <label for="address4">Address4</label>
    <input type="text" [(ngModel)]="user.address.address4"
    name="user.address.address4" id="address4" autocomplete="off"
    />
  </div>
  <div>
       <label for="county">County</label>
       <input type="text" [(ngModel)]="user.address.county"
         name="user.address.county" id="county" autocomplete="off"
       />
  </div>
  <div>
       <label for="postcode">Post Code</label>
       <input type="text" [(ngModel)]="user.address.postcode"
         name="user.address.postcode" id="postcode" autocomplete="off"
       />
  </div>
</ng-container>
<div>
       <button>Submit</button>
</div>
</form>
<form>
       <pre>{{ user | json }}</pre>
</form>
```

There is nothing new here, this creates a user details entry form with two-way data binding. Let's now add the code to the **`template-driven.component.ts`** file:

```
export interface UserModel {
       firstName: string;
       lastName: string;
       email: string;
       mobile: string;
       address: {
```

```
        address1: string;
        address2: string;
        address3: string;
        address4: string;
        county: string;
        postcode: string;
       };
}
@Component({
 selector: 'app-template-driven',
 standalone: true,
 templateUrl: './template-driven.component.html',
 styleUrl: './template-driven.component.scss',
 imports: [FormsModule, JsonPipe]})
export class TemplateDrivenComponent {
       user: UserModel = {
       firstName: '',
       lastName: '',
       email: '',
       mobile: '',
       address: {
        address1: '',
        address2: '',
        address3: '',
        address4: '',
        county: '',
        postcode: ''
       },
};
onSubmit(form: NgForm) {
       console.log(form.value);
 }
// scss to tidy everything up
  input[type="text"] {
       width: 400px;
       padding: 12px 20px;
       margin: 8px 0;
       border-radius: 4px;
       display: flex;
       flex-direction: column;
  }
```

Before we add any validation, build and run the application to ensure it is all working. You should be able to see the data you enter at the bottom of the page, and by clicking submit you should be able to see the model in the console.

We'll add the following validation to the following fields:

- **`FirstName/LastName`**: Required, Minimum length.
- **`Email`** : Required, Valid email address contains '@' and a top-level domain, for example .com or /co.uk.
- **`Mobile`** : Required and make sure it's numeric only, with a Maximum length of 12 digits.
- **`Postcode`** : Validate it is between 5 and 8 characters, with spacing and letters being uppercased.

Let's start with the **`firstName`** field. We require two validations. The first makes the field required, so the user must add a **`firstName`** and the second that name must reach a minimum number of characters.

```
<input
      [(ngModel)]="user.firstName"
       type="text"
       name="user.firstName"
       id="firstName"
       #firstname="ngModel"
       required
       minlength="2"
  />
```

On the **`firstName`** input, we add the `required` and **`minlength`** properties, providing a value for the **`minlength`**. Using the new Control Flow Syntax, let's add the code blocks that will display our error messages. We've also added a template variable **`#firstname`** and set it to the **`ngModel`** value, we can use this variable to get a reference to our form control.

```
@if (firstname?.invalid && (firstname?.dirty || firstname?.touched)) {
      @if (firstname.hasError("required")) {
        <span class="error">First name is a required field.</span>
      }
}
```

We use the template variable to check if the control is invalid and whether the control has changed (made dirty) or has been touched (interacted with and lost focus) and whether the control's validation object contains any errors; if it does, then we display the error message. We need to repeat this for the **`minlength`** and each subsequent validation we apply to our control.

```
@if (firstname?.invalid && (firstname?.dirty || firstname?.touched)) {
      @if (firstname.hasError("required")) {
       <span class="error">First name is a required field.</span>
      }
      @if (firstname.hasError('minlength')) {
```

```
        <span class="error">Firstname must be two or characters
long</span>
    }
}
```

Next, let's look at the email validation. We know how to apply the **required** validation property, so we'll skip this and go straight to the email address. The **required** and **minlength** are built-in validation types; to validate the email address we need to use a pattern validator, as email addresses follow a pattern **some-name@some-domain.some-top-level-tier**, for example, coyote@acme.com.

```
<div>
    <label class="asterisk" for="email">Email</label>
    <input type="text"
      [(ngModel)]="user.email"
      name="user.email"
      id="email"
      autocomplete="off"
      pattern="^[a-z0-9._%+-]+@[a-z0-9.-]+\\.[a-z]{2,4}$"
      required
      email
      #email="ngModel"
      />
@if (email?.invalid && (email?.dirty || email?.touched)) {
      @if (email.hasError("required")) {
        <span class="error">Email is a required field.</span>
      }
      @if (email.errors?.["email"]) {
        <span class="error">Email address must be properly qualified</
span>
      }
    }
  </div>
```

With pattern validation, we use a regular expression (or regex) syntax to validate whether the email address contains an @ symbol and a top-level domain (i.e. **.com**, **.co.uk**, and so on.). Crafting a regular expression can be quite tricky and is outside the scope of this book, we will add some resources where you can learn more about creating regular expressions at the end of this chapter.

There are a couple of changes to our `input` when using pattern validation. Firstly, we add the **email** property, which is like the **required** property, except this is for email validation. The next change is the addition of the pattern and the regular expression that we are going to use to validate our email addresses. The last change is to the validation check, this time we are checking the errors object of the email form control, a simple regular expression and checks to see if the address has an **@** and a **top-level domain.** There are more complex regular expressions that can check for a lot more.

With the validation for mobile numbers, we'll use the **maxlength**, a pattern that only allows for numbers.

```
<input
      type="text"
      [(ngModel)]="user.mobile"
      name="user.mobile"
      id="mobile"
      required
      #mobile="ngModel"
      autocomplete="off"
      maxlength="11"
      pattern="^[0-9]*$"
  />
@if (mobile?.invalid && (mobile?.dirty || mobile?.touched)) {
     @if (mobile.hasError("required")) {
       <span class="error">Mobile is a required field.</span>
     }
     @if (mobile.hasError("maxlength")) {
       <span class="error">Mobile number can't be more than 11 dig-
its.</span>
     }
     @if (mobile.errors?.["pattern"]) {
      <span class="error">Mobile can only be digits.</span>
     }
 }
```

We could have just changed our input to type number, but let's see how to validate it instead. We also used another regular expression and pattern to check for digits and set a **maxlength** for a total number of characters; if we try and type more than 11, nothing happens.

In this section, we looked at using validation with template-driven forms; it is also possible to create validators using directives and custom validators, which we'll cover next in the reactive forms section.

Note: *You may notice with template-driven form validation the* HTML *could get a bit long, especially for forms that have a lot of controls or controls that require multiple validations, we'll look at alternatives at the end of this chapter.*

Reactive Form Validation

In this section, we'll create the same form. This time we'll use the Reactive form approach and then add the Validation. In Reactive forms, we create the form controls in the TypeScript file rather than the HTML file. With Reactive forms, we must create the controls in code and set up the data binding ourselves. Let's start with the HTML. In our project, open the terminal and using the CLI, generate a new component:

```
ng g c standalone-app/src/app/reactive-forms -d
```

Remove the **-d** (the **dry run** flag) once you're happy this component will be created in the correct location. Open the new component in VS Code and open the html file.

```
<form [formGroup]="form" (ngSubmit)="onSubmit()">
      <div>
        <label class="asterisk" for="firstName">First Name</label>
        <input type="text" id="firstName" formControlName="firstName" />
      </div>
      <div>
        <label class="asterisk" for="lastName">Last Name</label>
       <input type="text" formControlName="lastName" id="lastName" />
      </div>
      <div>
         <label class="asterisk" for="email">Email</label>
         <input type="text" formControlName="email" id="email" />
      </div>
      <div>
         <label class="asterisk" for="mobile">Mobile</label>
         <input type="text" formControlName="mobile" id="mobile" />
      </div>
      <ng-container formGroupName="address">
      <div>
         <label for="address1">Address1</label>
         <input type="text"
              formControlName="address1"
              id="address1"
              autocomplete="off"
         />
      </div>
      <div>
         <label for="address2">Address2</label>
         <input type="text"
              formControlName="address2"
              id="address2"
              autocomplete="off"
          />
      </div>
      <div>
         <label for="address3">Address3</label>
         <input type="text"
              formControlName="address3"
              id="address3"
              autocomplete="off"
```

```
          />
        </div>
        <div>
          <label for="address4">Address4</label>
          <input type="text"
               formControlName="address4"
               id="address4"
               autocomplete="off"
          />
        </div>
        <div>
          <label class="asterisk" for="county">County</label>
               <input type="text"
               formControlName="county"
               id="county"
               autocomplete="off"
               />
          </div>
          <div>
               <label class="asterisk" for="postcode">Post Code</label>
               <input type="text" formControlName="postcode" id="postcode" />
         </div>
        </ng-container>
        <div>
               <button type="submit" [disabled]="!form.valid">Submit</button>
        </div>
  </form>
```

We start with a form control and assign a **formGroup** called form and set up the **ngSubmit()** event. We can't use the **[(ngModel])** on our controls this time so instead, we add a **formControlName**, this name is the name of the component we'll create in the TypeScript code shortly and is a way we can get access to our controls.

The next big difference is the creation of another **formGroup** for the address section, in the template-driven section we were able to reference the address using dot notation.

```
name="user.address.address1"
```

Here we need to create another group to handle the address:

```
<ng-container formGroupName="address">
...
</ng-container>
```

We'll use the same interface and model as before.

```
user: UserModel = {
    firstName: '',
    lastName: '',
    email: '',
```

```
      mobile: '',
    address: {
        address1: '',
        address2: '',
        address3: '',
        address4: '',
        county: '',
        postcode: '',
    },
  };
```

Now let's add the code to create the controls:

```
formBuilder = inject(FormBuilder);
form!: FormGroup;
ngOnInit(): void {
      this.form = this.formBuilder.group({
        firstName: [this.user.firstName],
        lastName: [this.user.lastName],
        email: [this.user.email],
        mobile: [this.user.mobile],
        address: this.formBuilder.group({
         address1: [this.user.address.address1],
         address2: [this.user.address.address2],
         address3: [this.user.address.address3],
         address4: [this.user.address.address4],
         county: [this.user.address.county],
         postcode: [this.user.address.postcode],
        }),
     });
 }
```

And finally, the **onSubmit()** event handler:

```
onSubmit() {
      console.log(this.form);
}
```

Here we are using the **FormBuilder** to create our controls, we could have created the groups and controls ourselves but that generates a lot of repetitive code, for example:

```
this.form = new FormGroup({
      firstName: new FormControl(this.user.firstName),
      lastName: new FormControl(this.user.lastName)
      ...
});
```

If we run the application and fill in the form, we should see the **FormGroup** output in the browsers console, and in the value section, we should see the controls populated with the values entered. To get two-way data binding, we need to update the model in the submit event.

```
        this.user = {
        firstName: this.form.get('firstName')?.value,
        lastName: this.form.get('lastName')?.value,
        email: this.form.get('email')?.value,
        mobile: this.form.get('mobile')?.value,
        address: {
          address1: this.form.get('address.address1')?.value,
          address2: this.form.get('address.address2')?.value,
          address3: this.form.get('address.address3')?.value,
          address4: this.form.get('address.address4')?.value,
          county: this.form.get('address.county')?.value,
          postcode: this.form.get('address.postcode')?.value,
          },
};
```

If the property and the **formControl** are the same, then we can shorten the code:

```
this.user = {
        firstName: this.form.value,
        lastName: this.form.value,
        email: this.form.value,
        mobile: this.form.value,
        address: {
          address1: this.form.value,
          address2: this.form.value,
          address3: this.form.value,
          address4: this.form.value,
          county: this.form.value,
          postcode: this.form.value,
          },
  };
```

With our page working, now we can start to add the validation to the controls, and we do this in the TypeScript code.

```
        this.form = this.formBuilder.group({
              firstName: [
                this.user.firstName,
                [Validators.required, Validators.minLength(2)],
              ],
              lastName: [
               this.user.lastName,
               [Validators.required, Validators.minLength(2)],
              ],
              email: [this.user.email, [Validators.required,
                     Validators.pattern()]
```

```
      ],
      mobile: [this.user.mobile, [Validators.required]],
      address: this.formBuilder.group({
        address1: [this.user.address.address1, [Validators.
        required]],
        address2: [this.user.address.address2, [Validators.
        required]],
        address3: [this.user.address.address3],
        address4: [this.user.address.address4],
        county: [this.user.address.county, [Validators.
        required]],
        postcode: [this.user.address.postcode, [Validators.
        required]],
      }),
    });
```

We are using the **FormBuilders** group to create our controls. We add the validation as an array of **Validators** (as we could have more than one), this sets up the validation for each control. If we were not using the **FormBuilder**, then we would add the validators to the form control like so:

```
this.form = new FormGroup({
      firstName: new FormControl(this.user.firstName, [
        Validators.required,
        Validators.minLength(2)])
    });
```

Let's now add HTML to our page to display the error messages.

```
<div>
    <label class="asterisk" for="firstName">First Name</label>
    <input type="text" id="firstName" formControlName="firstName" />
    @if (
      form.get("firstName")?.invalid &&
      (form.get("firstName")?.dirty || form.get("firstName")?.touched)
    ) {
      @if (form.get("firstName")?.hasError("required")) {
        <div class="error">Firstname is a required field.</div>
      }
      @if (form.get("firstName")?.hasError("minlength")) {
        <div class="error">Firstname must be two or more
        characters</div>

      }
    }
  </div>
```

There shouldn't be anything new here as this is the same as the template-driven forms, other than we are getting the control from the **FormGroup**.

Let's finish off by looking at the pattern validator.

```
email: [this.user.email,
        [Validators.required,
          Validators.pattern('^[a-z0-9._%+-]+@[a-z0-9.-]+\\.[a-z]
          {2,4}$'),

         ],
       ],
```

The HTML for the email address.

```
<div>
    <label class="asterisk" for="email">Email</label>
    <input type="text" formControlName="email" id="email" />
    @if (
      form.get("email")?.invalid &&
      (form.get("email")?.dirty || form.get("email")?.touched)
    ) {
      @if (form.get("email")?.hasError("required")) {
        <div class="error">Email is a required field.</div>
      }
      @if (form.get("email")?.hasError("pattern")) {
        <div class="error">
          Email address must be a properly qualified email address.
        </div>
      }
    }
  </div>
```

We provide the regular expression to the pattern validator in the code file and check whether the email control has an error.

Adding and Removing Validators

There are times when given a certain condition in our form that we may want to add or remove a validator at runtime. To achieve this, we can use the **addValidator** method. For this example, we'll make address 3 optional by adding a checkbox to the top of the form.

```
<div>
    <label for="addValidator">Add validator for address 3</label>
    <input type="checkbox"
      formControlName="validate"
      id="addValidator"
      [value]="selected"
      (click)="addValidator()"
```

```
        />
      </div>
```

We'll also update our **userModel** and the reactive form setup:

```
user: UserModel = {
    firstName: '',
    lastName: '',
    email: '',
    mobile: '',
    validate: false, // add this
          address: {
            address1: '',
            address2: '',
            address3: '',
            address4: '',
            county: '',
            postcode: '',
       },
  };


mobile: [...],
validate: [this.selected], // add this to the reactive control setup
address: this.formBuilder.group({...});
```

And finally, add the event handler to turn on/off the validation:

```
addValidator(): void {
    this.selected = !this.selected;
    if (this.selected) {
       this.form.get('address.address3')?
       .addValidators(Validators.required);
           } else {
      this.form.get('address.address3')?.clearValidators();
    }
this.form.get('address.address3')?.updateValueAndValidity();
}
```

This will allow us to add and remove a control validation at runtime, when making a change, by either adding or removing a validator, we need to call **updateValueAndValidity()** method, otherwise, the changes won't be applied.

Creating Custom Validators

There are times when the built-in validators do not meet our validation needs and we need to create a custom validation. For example, we need to ensure a username is unique, or a password and confirm password needs to match before being stored. As an example of how to add a custom validator, we'll add a password and a confirm password field to our form and create a custom validator that checks to see if the password and confirm password match in our **UserModel** interface, by adding the password and **confirmPassword** properties.

```
export interface UserModel {
  firstName: string;
  lastName: string;
  email: string;
  mobile: string;
  validate: boolean;
  password: string;
  confirmPassword: string;
  address: {
    address1: string;
    address2: string;
    address3: string;
    address4: string;
    county: string;
    postcode: string;
  };
}
```

Then update the **UserModel**, initially setting the values to an empty string.

```
user: UserModel = {
    firstName: '',
    lastName: '',
    email: '',
    mobile: '',
    validate: false,
    password: '',
    confirmPassword: '',
    address: {
      address1: '',
      address2: '',
      address3: '',
      address4: '',
      county: '',
      postcode: '',
    },
  };
```

Next, add the password and **confirmPassword** to our **formGroup**:

```
validate: [this.selected],
password: [this.user.password, Validators.required],
confirmPassword: [this.user.confirmPassword, Validators.required],
address: this.formBuilder.group({...})
```

Let's also update the **onSubmit()** event, add these two lines:

```
password: this.form.get('password')?.value,
confirmPassword: this.form.get('confirmPassword')?.value,
```

Next, let's add the HTML to our form:

```
<div>
  <label class="asterisk" for="password">Password</label>
  <input type="text" formControlName="password" id="password" />
  @if (
    form.get("password")?.invalid &&
    (form.get("password")?.dirty || form.get("password")?.touched)
  ) {
    @if (form.get("password")?.hasError("required")) {
      <div class="error">Password is a required field.</div>
    }
  }
</div>
<div>
  <label class="asterisk" for="confirmPassword">Confirm
  Password</label>
  <input type="text" formControlName="confirmPassword"
    id="confirmPassword" />
  @if (
    form.get("confirmPassword")?.invalid &&
    (form.get("confirmPassword")?.dirty ||
      form.get("confirmPassword")?.touched)
  ) {
    @if (form.get("confirmPassword")?.hasError("required")) {
      <div class="error">Confirm Password is a required field.</div>
    }
    @if (form.get("confirmPassword")?.hasError("passwords
    DontMatch")) {
      <div class="error">Passwords do not match</div>
    }
  }
</div>
```

Next, we'll set up the `**passwordMatch**` validator now, and then we'll create the validator itself.

In the providers section in our `**reactive-forms.component.ts**` file, add the providers:

```
@Component({
  selector: 'app-reactive-forms',
  standalone: true,
  imports: [ReactiveFormsModule, JsonPipe],
```

```
  // add this line
  providers: [{ provide: Validators, useValue: passwordMatch
  Validator }],

  templateUrl: './reactive-forms.component.html',
  styleUrl: './reactive-forms.component.scss',
})
```

The most notable difference here is that we have added the **`passwordMatchValidator`** validator to the provider's array. Using the providers section of the decorator is the same as calling a service, instead of **'`providing in root`'** in our service, we can provide the service when this component is created.

We'll build the **`passwordMatchValidator`** *in just a moment.*

To call the validation, we need to add the validator as part of the **`formBuilder`**:

```
this.form = this.formBuilder.group(
{
 firstName: [...],
 lastName: [...],
 email: [...],
 mobile: [...],
 validate: [...],
 password: [...],
 confirmPassword: [...],
 address: this.formBuilder.group({...}),
},
{
 validators: passwordMatchValidator('password', 'confirmPassword'),
}
```

This doesn't affect the validation for individual form controls. As we need to validate two form controls, we need to be able to get access to both, so we use the control group validation.

With the validation setup complete, let's create the **`passwordMatch`** validator.

In our validator's directory, create a new file called **`password-match.validator.ts`**, and add the following code:

```
import { AbstractControl, ValidationErrors, ValidatorFn } from '@angu-
lar/forms';

export function passwordMatchValidator(
  password: string,
  confirmPassword: string,
): ValidatorFn {
  return (abstractControl: AbstractControl): ValidationErrors |
  null => {
```

```
        const passwordControl = abstractControl.get(password);
        const confirmPasswordControl = abstractControl.get(confirm
        Password);
        if (confirmPasswordControl!.errors &&
          !confirmPasswordControl!.errors?.['passwordsDontMatch']
        ) {
          return null;
        }
        if (passwordControl!.value !== confirmPasswordControl!.value) {
          const error = { passwordsDontMatch: true };
          confirmPasswordControl!.setErrors(error);
          return error;
        } else {
          const error = { passwordsDontMatch: false };
          confirmPasswordControl!.setErrors(error);
          return null;
        }
      };
    }
```

In this function, we pass in the names of our two form controls as strings (**password** and **confirmPassword**), using these names we create an abstract control of each, so we can get access to check the error object and the value of the two controls. If the **confirmPasswordControl** has an errors object attached, but not one with the name **passwordsDontMatch,** then we exit the function and return null. Otherwise, we check to see if the value of the **passwordControl** and the **confirmPasswordControl** are not equal. If they are not, then we create an errors objcct with a namc of **passwordsDontMatch** and a value of `true` then pass this error object to the **setErrors** method on the **confirmPasswordControl** and return the error, else we set the error object with the same name of **passwordsDontMatch** but with a value of **false**.

What about custom validators for template-driven forms? Let's add a password validation check to our template-driven form. We'll start with the validator this time.

```
function validatePassword(): ValidatorFn {
  return (control: AbstractControl) => {
    let isValid: boolean = false;
    if (control && control instanceof FormGroup) {
      let group = control as FormGroup;
      if (
        group.controls['user.password'] &&
        group.controls['user.confirmPassword']
      ) {
        isValid =
          group.controls['user.password'].value ===
          group.controls['user.confirmPassword'].value;
```

```
      }
    }
    return isValid ? { passwordCheck: false } :
    { passwordCheck: true };
  };
}
```

We'll use the same **password-match.validator** form we used in the reactive section. Here we are creating a validation function, this is like the validator we created in the reactive section, but here we are checking for an instance of a **formGroup** and getting access to the **password** and **confirmPassword** controls and comparing the values, and returns an object that is either true or false. Underneath this code, let's create a directive:

```
@Directive({
  selector: '[passwordCheckDirective]',
  standalone: true,
  providers: [
    {
      provide: NG_VALIDATORS,
      useExisting: CheckPasswordDirective,
      multi: true,
    },
  ],
})
export class CheckPasswordDirective implements Validator {
  private valFn;
  constructor() {
    this.valFn = validatePassword();
  }
  validate(c: AbstractControl): ValidationErrors | null {
    return this.valFn(c);
  }
}
```

This directive calls the **validatePassword** method, as we are implementing the **Validator** interface, we need to implement the validate method and return our function. The HTML for the password and confirm password fields is very similar to what we've written previously, but with a few changes.

```
<div
    ngModelGroup="passwords"
    #passwords="ngModelGroup"
    passwordCheckDirective
  >
    <div>
      <label class="asterisk" for="password">Password</label>
```

```
    <input type="text"
      [(ngModel)]="user.password"
      name="user.password"
      id="password"
      #password="ngModel"
      required
    />
    @if (password?.invalid && (password?.dirty || password?.
    touched)) {
      @if (password.hasError("required")) {
        <span class="error">Password is a required field.</span>
      }
    }
  </div>
  <div>
    <label class="asterisk" for="confirmPassword">Confirm
     Password</label>
    <input type="text"
      [(ngModel)]="user.confirmPassword"
      name="user.confirmPassword"
      id="confirmPassword"
      #confirmPassword="ngModel"
      required
    />
    @if (confirmPassword.invalid && (password.dirty || password.
    touched))    {
     <div class="error">Please confirm password</div>
    }
    @if (passwords.errors?.["passwordCheck"] &&
      (confirmPassword.dirty || confirmPassword.touched)
    ) {
      <div class="error">Passwords do not match</div>
    }
    @if (confirmPassword?.invalid &&
      (confirmPassword?.dirty || confirmPassword?.touched)
    ) {
      @if (confirmPassword.hasError("required")) {
        <span class="error">Confirm Password is a required
        field.</span>
      }
    }
  </div>
</div>
```

The HTML is like what we coded in the template driven section, but there are a few subtle differences. Firstly, we have wrapped both **password** and **confirmPassword** in a

div, applied the **ngModelGroup** directive, and given it the name of a template variable called **#passwords**. We also apply our directive here for the password validator. We have made both controls required and also added an additional check on the **confirmPassword** control. If the user has entered a password but not confirmed the password, then we display a message. We've also added the password validator; here we are checking the errors object with the name **passwordCheck** (this is what we return from our **validatePassword** function) and if the passwords don't match, then we display the error message.

In a real-world application, there would be other checks, like ensuring the casing of both passwords matched, that there was a minimum/maximum number of required characters or to include specific special characters.

Conclusion

In this chapter, we have introduced you to validation and covered reactive and template-driven forms. We have learned how to apply validation to various scenarios, including applying validators in our HTML, adding validation to our TypeScript code, and using a directive to perform validation.

Coming up in the next chapter, Routing is how we can navigate between pages in our applications, we'll look at creating routes, consuming routes, controlling navigation and lazy loading.

Resources

Here is some resources on regular expressions:

A list of tools and documentation that will help you build and test your regular expressions.

- https://regexr.com/
- https://regex101.com/
- https://developer.mozilla.org/en-US/docs/Web/JavaScript/Guide/Regular_expressions
- https://regex.sketchengine.eu/

Alternatives for template driven forms: As mentioned in this chapter it is possible that the HTML for a page with a lot of controls and validation could become hard to read or maintain.

There is a 3rd party library called VestJS which applies validation to the model rather than the form controls. This set up allows for a more centralised validation process and offers greater flexibility by removing the validation logic from the template. The validation itself is written similar to how unit tests are written. By making this more centralised validation can be shared across components. For more information, check out the product page at https://vestjs.dev/docs/get_started

CHAPTER 9
Routing

Introduction

By now, you are now familiar with component creation, reactive data flow, data and form manipulation, and more from the previous chapters.

As your application grows over time, it will include more features with different scopes and use cases. Web applications often split the features among several different pages, accessible at different URLs, each serving a distinct purpose.

Angular comes with powerful tools and utilities to manage routing such as a router, conditional access, route information, lazy loading, and much more.

In this chapter, we will explore how to leverage these features to create pages, restrictions, and other advanced practices to enhance both the user and the developer experience, both for Angular applications relying on standalone components and modules.

Structure

In this chapter, we will cover the following topics:

- Creating Routes
- Consuming Routes
- Controlling Navigation
- Lazy Loading Fundamentals

Creating Routes

Creating a multi-page application starts by defining the routes it will accept.

If you are not familiar with the concept of route, think of it as the way an application reacts to a specific URL or location change.

For instance, on GitHub, you expect your homepage to be located at `'https://github.com/'`, while `'https://github.com/JohnDoe'` should display John Doe's profile. If **github.com** was our Angular application, then '/' would be the route that displays the homepage, and **'/JohnDoe'** the one displaying the user profile. In other words, a route can be seen at the URL of a specific page within an application.

Before defining the routing itself, we first need to set up this mechanism in our project.

Configuring Routing

Routing is fairly straightforward to configure in any Angular application, be it relying on **NgModules** or **standalone** components.

In both cases, we will first need to define the routes on which our Angular application will perform any action.

Initially, we don't have such routes, so it will simply be an empty array of type **Routes**, a type we will be explore in more detail later:

```
import { Routes } from '@angular/router';

const routes: Routes = [];
```

Once created, we can now instruct Angular that the routing of our application will be based on the routes we defined by telling the router what our routes are.

For standalone applications, this configuration is done from the provider's array during the application's bootstrap process:

```
import { bootstrapApplication } from '@angular/platform-browser';
import { provideRouter } from '@angular/router';

bootstrapApplication(AppComponent, {
  providers: [provideRouter(routes)],
});
```

For module-based applications, this can be done by configuring Angular's **RouterModule**:

```
import { NgModule } from '@angular/core';
import { RouterModule } from '@angular/router';

@NgModule({
  declarations: [AppComponent],
  imports: [RouterModule.forRoot(routes)],
  bootstrap: [AppComponent],
})
class AppModule {}
```

With these two steps, Angular is now aware that it should use routing and knows what our routes are – even if none are defined yet.

While the underlying mechanism is configured and the framework knows which elements it should show, we also need to tell it *where* it should display them.

We might want the whole page to change based on the routes, but most of the time, there are some common elements, such as a navbar, footer, or sidebar, that you don't want to disappear when the location changes. In our case, we will display a title at the top of the page.

To define where Angular should change components, we need to provide an anchor for the router, indicating where it can show elements. To do so, we can use the `router-outlet` selector, which acts as a placeholder that the Angular Router will dynamically replace by the appropriate components based on the current route. In standalone components, we must also import the **`RouterOutlet`** we will be using, while in module-based applications, it is already provided through the import of the **`RouterModule`**.

```
import { Component } from '@angular/core';
import { RouterOutlet } from '@angular/router';

@Component({
  selector: 'app-component',
  standalone: true,
  imports: [RouterOutlet],
  template: `
    <h1>Angular Routing</h1>
    <router-outlet />
  `,
})
class AppComponent {}
```

Using **`NgModules`**, the code is merely the same but without the imports:

```
import { Component} from '@angular/core';

@Component({
  selector: 'app-component',
  template: `
    <h1>Angular Routing</h1>
    <router-outlet></router-outlet>
  `,
})
class AppComponent {}
```

Note: *Since the header is defined outside of the routing mechanism, it will be displayed regardless of the route.*

Now that the foundations are properly set, we can define the actual routes for our application to display.

Defining Routes

For now, our routes are only an empty array of **Routes**. In Angular, routing is done based on an array of Route, which Routes is an alias for:

```
export declare type Routes = Route[];
```

With everything set up, let's have a closer look at what a Route actually is and how to define one.

Creating a Homepage

In essence, a route is an object that defines which component the router should display and on which route.

To route a new page, two properties must be specified:

- The **path**, which is the location on which the router will activate the route.
- The **component** that should be displayed where the router outlet is defined.

For example, if we would like to display a home page on '**/home**', the routing configuration would be the following:

```
const routes: Routes = [
  {
    path: 'home',
    component: HomeComponent,
  },
];
```

Note: *Notice that our route does not start with a forward slash. If you add one, Angular will throw a runtime error.*

Additionally, the `Route` object accepts a lot of other properties for advanced routing configuration, some of which we will see in this chapter.

Activation Order and Fallback

Even if our route is defined, we won't see the **HomeComponent** being displayed when accessing our application until we go to **/home**.

To understand why, let's break down what is happening step by step:

1. The user goes to '/'
2. The router detects that this application uses routing and a new navigation has ended on '/'

3. The router goes through each routes defined, and checks if any path matches the current location
4. No route matches the current location, so the router doesn't perform any action

Step 3 is particularly important to note: the router goes through the list of routes that have been provided and activates the first one that matches. For each route, if a route does not match, the router will look at the following one, continuing until one eventually matches or it reaches the end of the route.

In some scenarios, we don't have a specific route on which we would like to display something: if a user navigates to an unknown page, we might want to show a "**`404 Not found`**" page. In that case, it's impossible to predict what location he attempted to reach and we could not define every route for a 404 page.

Hopefully, Angular exposes a special path that can match any route, also known as wildcard routes. A wildcard route is defined as two asterisks:

```
const routes: Routes = [
  {
    path: 'home',
    component: HomeComponent,
  },
  {
    path: '**',
    component: NotFoundComponent,
  },
];
```

Note: *Since the wildcard will match any route, and the router displays the first route that matches the location, be sure to define it as the* ***last*** *route in your configuration. Otherwise, the router will always resolve the* **`NotFoundComponent`** *and display it regardless of the current route.*

Route Matching

Angular routes iteratively evaluate each defined route path against the current URL to determine the matching route. A matcher is used to compare the current path with the route path and can work in two ways.

The first one, which is also the default, is the **exact matching**. It means that a route is activated only if the URL and the path are an exact match. This behavior can also be explicitly used if you specify **`pathMatch: 'full'`** on your route. For example, in this mode, **`/home`** would match **`/home`** but not / or **`/home/about`**.

The second one is the **prefix matching**. This type of matching causes a route to activate if the URL starts with the given path. For instance, **`/product`** would match **`/product`**, **`/`**

product/3, and **/product/order**. You can use this behavior by specifying **pathMatch: 'prefix'** on the route level.

Let's have a look at an example of these modes in action:

```
const routes: Routes = [
  { path: 'home', component: HomeComponent },
  { path: 'about', component: AboutComponent, pathMatch: 'full' },
  { path: 'products', component: ProductsComponent, pathMatch:
  'prefix' },
];
```

In this example:

- The first route (**/home**) requires the URL to be exactly **/home** since it is using the default exact match.
- The second route (**/about**) also requires an exact match since it explicitly uses **pathMatch: 'full'**.
- The third route (**/products**) will match any URL that starts with **/products** because it uses a prefix match.

Redirection and Aliases

Instead of activating a specific component, a route can define where it should point to, acting as an alias for another one.

In our example, instead of showing an error page when a user goes to **/**, it might be better for his navigation experience to redirect him to the homepage.

To do so, we can add a new route specifying what path is targeted, and the location to redirect to:

```
const routes: Routes = [
  {
    path: 'home',
    component: HomeComponent,
  },
  {
    path: '',
    pathMatch: 'full',
    redirectTo: '/home',
  },
  {
    path: '**',
    component: NotFoundComponent,
  },
];
```

Note: *Since this is a redirection, it is defined at the end of the routes but* **before** *the wildcard route.*

By default, the router checks if the beginning of the route matches any route defined. In the case of an empty string, this would result in all routes matching the redirection. We can instruct the router to check for the whole URL by specifying the **`pathMatch: 'full'`** strategy, so this redirection only happens if the location is empty, and only in that case.

Note: *Watch out for your redirection, you might cause an unexpected infinite redirect loop. For example, if* **`'/home'`** *redirects to* **`'/'`**, *and* **`'/'`** *redirects to* **`'/home'`**. *Hopefully, Angular will help you by throwing the following runtime error if that happens:*

```
Error: NG04016: Detected possible infinite redirect when redirect-
ing from '/home' to '/'.
```

With this route configuration, we now have a working Angular application with routing:

- When first landing on `'/'`, the user will be redirected to **`'/home'`**
- **`'/home'`** will show the **`HomeComponent`**
- Any other route will show the **`404 Not Found`** page

With the bases set up, let's push the routing a bit further.

Changing the Title

One of the useful additional properties a route can have is **`title`**, which allows us to dynamically change the tab title of the browser:

```
const routes: Routes = [
  {
    path: 'home',
    component: HomeComponent,
    title: 'Homepage',
  },
];
```

The title can be either a string or a function, allowing us to dynamically compute the title when the page is resolved:

```
const routes: Routes = [
  {
    path: 'home',
    component: HomeComponent,
    title: () => `Homepage at ${new Date().toISOString()}`,
  },
];
```

Whenever the route is activated, the title will be recomputed to display the current date. This feature doesn't require much code but is often a nice thing to add to an application, offering users a comprehensive overview of the current page as well as a clear indication of their location within the application.

Configuring Parameters

On its own, a route is often used to display a slice of the application based on its name. However, this name can also carry important information for our page to show.

For instance, when navigating to **'/contact/john-doe'**, we expect the application to display the information related to the user named John Doe.

We could create a new route for this user:

```
{
   path: 'contact/john-doe',
   component: JohnDoeContactDetailsComponent,
}
```

However, this will only be applicable to that specific user, and if more users are registered, it will quickly get out of hand with one component and one route per user.

Fortunately, the Angular router has our back, and it is possible to specify that part of a route is unknown and will contain a parameter when accessed - in our example, the username.

To create a new parameterized route, all we need to do is to prepend the segment that will contain the parameter with a colon, followed by the name of the parameter:

```
{
   path: 'contact/:username',
   component: UserContactDetailsComponent,
}
```

With our updated path, this route will now display the **UserContactDetailsComponent** on any route that matches **'/contact/...'** and assign the value of the segment to a route parameter named **username**. We will see how to retrieve this parameter in the next section, "*Consuming Routes*".

Creating Children Routes

We are now able to display a contact based on its name, but it would be great to be able to edit it as well.

As we just did, we can recreate a parametrized route for editing a contact:

```
{
   path: 'contact/:username/edit',
   component: EditUserContactDetailsComponent,
},
{
   path: 'contact/:username',
   component: UserContactDetailsComponent,
}
```

This would indeed work but might make it hard to see that the display and editing of a contact are related pages.

Angular offers a way to regroup related routes by nesting them under an existing one. Nested routes are just like any other routes, but defined in the `children` array of the parent route.

Using this, we can now rework our routes:

```
{
  path: 'contact/:username',
  children: [
    { path: 'edit', component: EditContactDetailsComponent },
    { path: '', component: ContactDetailsComponent },
  ],
},
```

This configuration is equivalent, but now both these routes are regrouped under the same prefix. Apart from that, the two components don't share any other elements.

If we would like to display something in common for these two components, we can also specify the parent component and define where the children should be displayed by adding the router outlet the same way we did for the **`AppComponent`**:

```
@Component({
  selector: 'app-contact-page',
  standalone: true,
  imports: [RouterOutlet],
  template: `
    <h2>Contact Page</h2>
    <router-outlet />
  `,
})
class ContactPageComponent {}
```

Note: *If you are using* **`NgModules`**, *don't specify the* `standalone` *and* `imports` *properties.*

Once done, we can use it as our parent component for the two child routes:

```
{
  path: 'contact/:username',
  component: ContactPageComponent,
  children: [
    { path: 'edit', component: EditContactDetailsComponent },
    { path: '', component: ContactDetailsComponent },
  ],
},
```

With this modification, the child routes will now be displayed under the title "**`Contact Page`**" of the **`ContactPageComponent`**.

Consuming Routes

We are now able to create complex routes with various behaviors, but your user mostly won't navigate using the address bar to enter a specific URL each time, and navigation will need to happen on our end, directly from the application.

From our components, there are two ways to use routing: either from the template or from the component's logic.

Template Navigation

Let's start with the navigation from the template, the visual part of the component.

Nowadays, in any web application, it's likely that you will have links to other pages within the application. Our application is no different from others, so let's add some navigation:

```
@Component({
  selector: 'app-component',
  standalone: true,
  imports: [RouterOutlet],
  template: `
    <h1>Angular Routing</h1>

    <nav>
      <ul>
        <li>
          <a href="http://localhost:4200">Home</a>
        </li>
        <li>
          <a href="http://localhost:4200/contact/JohnDoe">John
          Doe</a>
        </li>
      </ul>
    </nav>

    <router-outlet />
  `,
})
class AppComponent {}
```

While this will indeed link to our application at the desired route, this approach won't work once deployed on another URL, or even if we change the port.

For internal routing, Angular also provides us with a built-in mechanism to indicate to the router that the current link leads to another page of our application, using the **RouterLink** directive.

Using the **RouterLink** Directive

The **RouterLink** directive replaces the **href** tag on a link and only needs to know the path of the targeted route. With this directive, our example now works using Angular's router instead of plain HTTP hyperlinks:

```
@Component({
  selector: 'app-component',
  standalone: true,
  imports: [RouterOutlet, RouterLink],
  template: `
    <h1>Angular Routing</h1>

    <nav>
      <ul>
        <li>
          <a routerLink="/">Home</a>
        </li>
        <li>
          <a routerLink="/contact/JohnDoe">John Doe</a>
        </li>
      </ul>
    </nav>

    <router-outlet />
  `,
})
class AppComponent {}
```

Note: *Using the* **RouterLink** *directive requires importing it when using standalone components.*

Here **'JohnDoe'** is written as a raw value, but when navigating, we might have some dynamic data that we would like to pass along.

To build routes based on a path that contains both the route segments and dynamic data, **routerLink** also accepts an array of strings and parameters from which the router will reconstruct the route.

For instance, if the name of the contact is an attribute of our component, here is how we could parametrize the route:

```
@Component({
  selector: 'app-component',
  standalone: true,
  imports: [RouterOutlet, RouterLink, RouterLinkActive],
  template: `
    <h1>Angular Routing</h1>
```

```
    <nav>
      <ul>
        <li>
          <a
            routerLink="/"
            routerLinkActive="active"
            [routerLinkActiveOptions]="{ exact: true }"
          >
            Home
          </a>
        </li>
        <li>
          <a [routerLink]="['/contact', contactName]">
            {{ contactName }}
          </a>
        </li>
      </ul>
    </nav>

    <router-outlet />
  `,
  styles: ['.active { color: red }'],
})
class AppComponent {
  readonly contactName = 'JohnDoe';
}
```

Notice that in both cases we used `'/'` as our route to the homepage. The **RouterLink** accepts both absolute and relative paths. When specifying the route using a forward slash, it indicates that this path is relative to the root path.

As an example of how to provide a relative path to the **RouterLink**, let's add a link from the details of a contact to its edit page:

```
@Component({
  selector: 'app-contact-details',
  standalone: true,
  imports: [RouterLink],
  template: `
    <h2>Contact Details</h2>
    <a routerLink="edit">Edit</a>
  `,
})
class ContactDetailsComponent {}
```

Unlike the previous ones, the value provided to **RouterLink** does *not* start with a forward slash, indicating it is a relative link. Since this component is displayed when the route matches **'contact/:username'**, appending **'edit'** will indicate to the router that the targeted URL is **'contact/:username/edit'**.

Note: *Since the route is relative, we could also have written* **'./edit'** *to tell the router we are starting this route from the current one. This means that to specify the location of a route, either* '/', './', *and* '../' *are valid prefixes, indicating that the route starts from the root, the current route, or the parent route, respectively.*

Using the RouterLinkActive Directive

While the routing is handled by the **RouterLink** directive we just discussed, sometimes we might also want to track which route is active from our template to differentiate it.

We could use JavaScript code to detect the activated route based on the current location and add custom classes, but Angular exports a **RouterLinkActive** directive that will apply the given class to the element whenever the route of the **RouterLink** of the same element is active.

Let's take advantage of it to change the color of the link to red if it points to the current page:

```
@Component({
  selector: 'app-component',
  standalone: true,
  imports: [RouterOutlet, RouterLink, RouterLinkActive],
  template: `
    <h1>Angular Routing</h1>

    <nav>
      <ul>
        <li>
          <a routerLink="/home" routerLinkActive="active">Home</a>
        </li>
        <li>
          <a routerLink="/contact/JohnDoe" routerLinkActive="active">
            John Doe
          </a>
        </li>
      </ul>
    </nav>

    <router-outlet />
  `,
  styles: ['.active { color: red }'],
})
class AppComponent {}
```

When we navigate to **'http://localhost:4200'**, we can now observe the **Home** link turns red.

However, when we browse John Doe's profile, both the links are active. This might not be the desired behavior but Angular is right: `'/'` is indeed part of **'/contact/JohnDoe'**.

To tell the **RouterLinkActive** directive that we only want this link to have the `active` class when the location is `'/'`, we can add some options to specify that the route should exactly match the one of the **RouterLink** by configuring the **RouterLinkActiveOptions**:

```
@Component({
  selector: 'app-component',
  standalone: true,
  imports: [RouterOutlet, RouterLink, RouterLinkActive],
  template: `
    <h1>Angular Routing</h1>

    <nav>
      <ul>
        <li>
          <a
            routerLink="/"
            routerLinkActive="active"
            [routerLinkActiveOptions]="{ exact: true }"
          >
            Home
          </a>
        </li>
        <li>
          <a routerLink="/contact/JohnDoe" routerLinkActive="active">
            John Doe
          </a>
        </li>
      </ul>
    </nav>

    <router-outlet />
  `,
  styles: ['.active { color: red }'],
})
class AppComponent {}
```

With that change, if we navigate once again to John Doe's profile, the Home link no longer appears as active.

TypeScript Navigation

Navigating from the template is only one part of the router's routing capabilities. Another one is to trigger navigation from our component's logic.

We mentioned the **Router** frequently in the previous sections, and indeed, we have been configuring and calling through the directives. However, we can also directly inject it to work with it.

The Angular **Router** can be injected like any other service through dependency injection:

```
// Using inject
private readonly router = inject(Router);

// Using constructor-based injection
constructor(private router: Router) {}
```

Using this instance, we can create a method navigating imperatively to the contact by calling **navigateByUrl**. As the name implies, this method takes an absolute path in the form of a URL and navigates to it:

```
goToContact(): void {
  this.router.navigateByUrl('/contact/JohnDoe');
}
```

Invoking this method will result in the user being redirected to the provided location, in this case, **'/contact/JohnDoe'**.

In the previous section, we saw that the **RouterLink** directive could accept both plain paths and parameterized ones. Since it uses the `Router` under the hood, it is no surprise that it can as well.

To navigate to a different location based on dynamic parameters, the `Router` exposes the `navigate` method. It performs the same function as **navigateByUrl** but accepts an array of path segments instead of a string.

For instance, here is how we can navigate a contact whose name is wrapped by the **contactName** property:

```
readonly contactName = 'JohnDoe';

goToContact(): void {
  this.router.navigate(['/contact', this.contactName]);
}
```

We can now call **goTocontact** and the user will automatically be redirected to '/ **contact/JohnDoe**'.

Retrieving Route Data

For now, we have successfully configured routes and defined navigation both from the template and the component's logic and even passed dynamic data in the routes.

However, we never actually consumed the data of the route itself. As an example, when navigating to the contact page of a user at '**contact/:username**', the user's name is known as the `username` route parameter.

Based on that name, we might want to execute some logic in the **ContactPageComponent**, such as retrieving information from the backend from this ID or simply displaying it.

With the ActivatedRoute

In Angular, the route that is currently activated has such importance that an entire service exists for interacting with it: **ActivatedRoute**.

A lot of information can be accessed through that service, most as **Observables**, such as the current URL, the parameters, the query parameters, and much more.

In our case, to retrieve the `username` of the user, we can take advantage of the **paramMap Observable**, which exposes a map of all the required and optional parameters of a route as a map, in order to display the contact name in the template:

```
@Component({
  selector: 'app-contact-page',
  standalone: true,
  imports: [RouterOutlet, AsyncPipe],
  template: `
    <h2>{{ username$ | async }}'s Contact Page</h2>
    <router-outlet />
  `,
})
class ContactPageComponent {
  username$ = inject(ActivatedRoute).paramMap.pipe(
    map((params) => params.get('username'))
  );
}
```

Note: *If you are using standalone components like in this example, remember to also import the* **AsyncPipe** *to display the* **Observable's** *value.*

If we navigate to a contact's details page, we can now see its name being displayed!

With Router Features

With the introduction of standalone components, the Angular team has worked on making great improvements to the framework's API, including the router one.

They noticed that retrieving data from the activated route was a fairly common task that systematically required RxJS boilerplate.

As an alternative, they offered a new `Router` feature to be configured in the **`provideRouter`** that automatically binds information from the **`Router`** into a component's `Input` based on its name.

To enable it, all we need to do is, in a standalone application, activate the **`withComponentInputBinding`** feature:

```
import { bootstrapApplication } from '@angular/platform-browser';
import {
  provideRouter,
  withComponentInputBinding,
} from '@angular/router';

bootstrapApplication(AppComponent, {
  providers: [provideRouter(routes, withComponentInputBinding())],
});
```

Once configured, we can now remove the observable logic from our component and replace it with a simple input with the same name:

```
@Component({
  selector: 'app-contact-page',
  standalone: true,
  imports: [RouterOutlet],
  template: `
    <h2>{{ username }}'s Contact Page</h2>
    <router-outlet />
  `,
})
```

```
class ContactPageComponent {
  @Input() username: string = '';
}
```

Note: *Not only is our component smaller, but it also enables us to remove the reference to the* **AsyncPipe**, *RxJS methods, and the* **ActivatedRoute** *service!*

With this feature activated, the route parameter will be bound to our **ContactPageComponent's** input, reducing the overall boilerplate without changing its behavior.

Lazy Loading Fundamentals

The routing is now fully functional, but examining the compilation result, we can notice that a single JavaScript file is generated by Angular, containing our whole application.

While this might be suitable in some cases, we might also want to ship some pages as separate bundles.

Introduction to Lazy Loading

When a feature is not used frequently by some users, it doesn't make much sense to make them download the associated code when they open our application.

For such scenarios, lazy loading is often considered as an alternative.

Lazy-loading is a technique that consists of loading certain elements or data only when they are actually needed or queried.

In the context of web applications, it means postponing the downloading of some JavaScript to lighten the weight of the initial one needed to render the page. In general, this helps make the application faster as only the required code is downloaded by the browser.

Note: *Lazy loading is not a silver bullet, it does have an overhead and should not be systematically used. The good question to ask yourself before making a decision is "Will my users use this a lot? If this feature is loaded, does it mean that another feature has a huge chance of being used as well?" Understanding what features relate to one another will help you adequately split your pages.*

Creating a Lazy-Loaded Route

With Angular, lazy loading does not require a lot of code or overhead on our side.

For this part, we will assume that users won't always query the contact pages and that it makes sense to lazy load them.

In Standalone-based Applications

Since the route and the components it activates will be lazy-loaded, the first step is to move them out of the main file, which means creating a new file only for the routes of our contacts feature:

```
export const contactRoutes: Routes = [
  {
    path: '',
    component: ContactPageComponent,
    children: [
      { path: 'edit', component: EditContactDetailsComponent },
      { path: '', component: ContactDetailsComponent },
    ],
  },
];
```

Note: *Don't forget to export the routes as we will need to indicate to the router what route it should look for.*

It is really important for the code you want to lazy-load not to be called in any other part that is not. If a reference exists between them, Angular will include it in the main bundle.

Since the route is now defined in a separate file that will be bundled in a separate JavaScript file, we need to indicate the router where to look for it without directly referencing it, or we will lose the advantage of lazy loading:

```
const routes: Routes = [
  {
    path: 'home',
    component: HomeComponent,
  },
  {
    path: 'contact/:username',
    loadChildren: async () =>
      (await import('./lazy-loaded')).contactRoutes,
  },
  {
    path: '',
    pathMatch: 'full',
    redirectTo: '/home',
  },
  {
    path: '**',
    component: NotFoundComponent,
  },
];
```

By using **`loadChildren`** in our route configuration, the router won't evaluate the route until it is actually activated. If that's the case, Angular will then execute the asynchronous code to load the file at the given path and retrieve the missing route's information.

We can easily verify that this is working by looking at the network tab of our application. When started, navigate to the root page. No change should be visible for now:

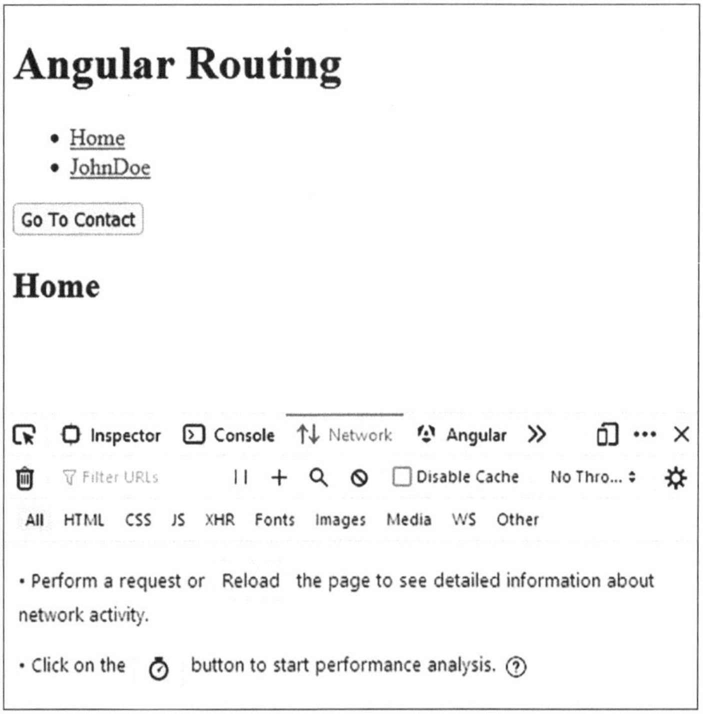

***Figure 9.1**: Angular routing*

However, if we click the "**`Go to Contact`**" button, we can notice that an extra piece of JavaScript is loaded before the page is displayed:

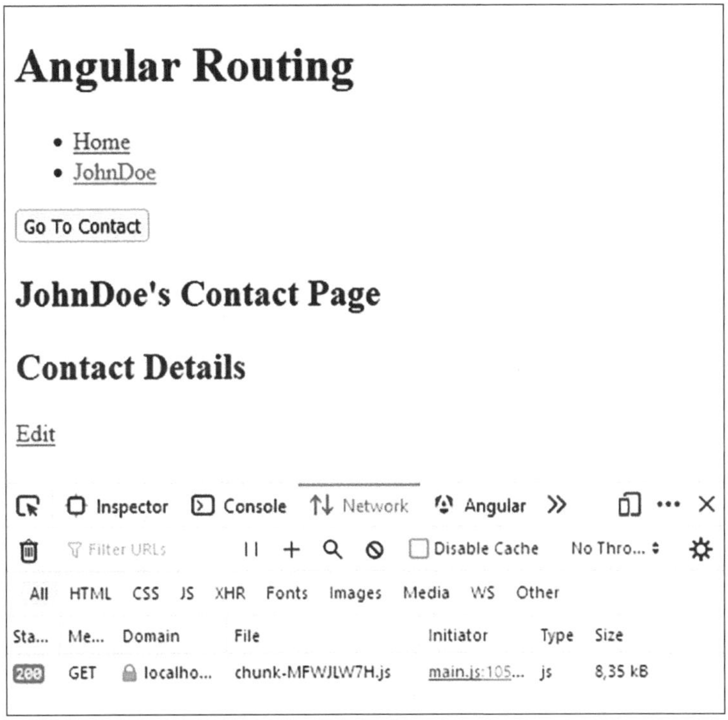

Figure 9.2: *Lazy loading*

The extra chunk of JavaScript is in fact the part that we extracted in a separate part of our Angular application.

In fact, during the compilation process, we can notice that Angular has prepared the JavaScript chunks our application is made of:

```
> ng serve


Initial Chunk Files | Names         | Raw Size
polyfills.js        | polyfills     | 82.71 kB |
main.js             | main          |  5.77 kB |
chunk-X42SQIIA.js   | -             |  1.65 kB |
styles.css          | styles        | 95 bytes |

                    | Initial Total | 90.23 kB

Lazy Chunk Files    | Names         | Raw Size
chunk-MFWJLW7H.js   | lazy-loaded   |  4.19 kB |
```

Figure 9.3: *Showing lazy loaded files*

And that's all, we successfully extracted the code of a feature into its dedicated lazily-loaded chunk of data in our standalone-based Angular application!

If you would like to lazy-load a specific standalone component instead of a subsection of routes, you can use the **loadComponent** method instead of **loadChildren**. The syntax is exactly the same but the dynamic import should resolve a component instead of routes. For instance, if we were to lazy-load a standalone **AboutComponent**, here is how we would do it:

```
const routes: Routes = [
  {
    path: 'about',
    loadComponent: async () =>
      (await import('./about/about.component')).AboutComponent,
  },
  ...
];
```

In Module-based Applications

For Module-based applications, things are slightly different but stay the same in essence.

Instead of just extracting the route and the components into a dedicated file, this time we will also wrap both of them in a dedicated feature module. In our example, since we are working with the contact pages, we will create a new **ContactPage** module:

```
@NgModule({
  declarations: [
    ContactPageComponent,
    EditContactDetailsComponent,
    ContactDetailsComponent,
  ],
  imports: [
    CommonModule,
  ],
})
export class ContactModule {}
```

However, to reference our routes, we cannot use **RouterModule.forRoot** like we previously did, since this configuration is only to be used to configure the initial setup of the router. Instead, the **RouterModule** exposes a second static method named **forChild**, which allows you to specify additional routes without recreating the Router service itself.

The usage, however, is quite similar, and we can provide it with the whole routes we extracted from the initial routes configuration:

```
@NgModule({
  declarations: [
    ContactPageComponent,
```

```
    EditContactDetailsComponent,
    ContactDetailsComponent,
  ],
  imports: [
    CommonModule,
    RouterModule.forChild([
      {
        path: '',
        component: ContactPageComponent,
        children: [
          { path: 'edit', component: EditContactDetailsComponent },
          { path: '', component: ContactDetailsComponent },
        ],
      },
    ]),
  ],
})
export class ContactModule {}
```

To lazily register this module, we will then call **loadChildren** as we did for the standalone-based applications, but this time we will target the newly created module instead of the routes:

```
const routes: Routes = [
  {
    path: 'home',
    component: HomeComponent,
  },
  {
    path: 'contact/:username',
    loadChildren: async () =>
      (await import('./lazy-loaded.module')).ContactModule,
  },
  {
    path: '',
    pathMatch: 'full',
    redirectTo: '/home',
  },
  {
    path: '**',
    component: NotFoundComponent,
  },
];
```

With that last change, we have now successfully implemented the lazy-loading of the contact feature as we did for the standalone-based application.

If you now open your network tab in the browser window, you should see an additional chunk of JavaScript being downloaded when navigating to the contact details page.

Controlling Navigation

Navigating also comes with its deal of issues: what if a user navigates to a route he is not supposed to see, like an admin panel? What if a user attempts to perform an invalid action, such as navigating to an edited page without having the right to? Or even, how to prevent a user from leaving a page if he is currently in the middle of a process?

For all those questions and other use cases, the Angular Router comes with a built-in client-side navigation security mechanism, named `Guards`.

Note: *Client-side is to be stressed here. The guards and their logic are only executed by Angular within the client application, and an extra layer of security will still be needed on your back end to prevent unauthorized usage of your application.*

Introduction to Route Guards

Route guards are a set of classes and/or functions that control and manage routing and navigation within your Angular application. They provide a way to protect routes, enforce certain constraints such as authentication, or perform other checks on specific routes.

In module-based applications, guards are defined as interfaces to be implemented by a service, but in standalone-based applications, guards are defined as functions, taking advantage of the **`inject`** function and offering a way to write shorter and much more concise guarding logic.

Guard's logic is defined as a function that takes the current route and the current router state as parameters. For its return value, a guard returns either a **`boolean`** or a route to redirect the user to, in the form of an **`UrlTree`**.

Like many other Angular APIs, `Observables` and asynchronous calls are first-class citizens, so the data returned from the guard can also be wrapped in an `Observable` or a `Promise`.

Note: *Formerly, guards were written by Angular services implementing the appropriate interface. However, since version 15, this way of writing guards has been deprecated in favor of functional guards. This is the syntax we will see in this chapter.*

There are several guard types, each serving a different purpose. Let's review each of them by intent.

Preventing Access to a Route

The first kind of guard we can expect is one that prevents access to a route.

Consider the following route configuration:

```
[
  {
    path: 'login',
    component: LoginComponent
  },
  {
    path: 'home',
    component: HomeComponent
  }
]
```

The **HomeComponent** might display information based on the current user, but if the user is not currently logged in, it does not make much sense for them to access this page.

For this purpose, the **CanActivate** guard can be used. This guard is one of the most common ones since it checks whether certain conditions are met before allowing the user to process, such as if the current user is logged in, has sufficient rights to access a page, and more.

To create a new **CanActivate** guard, we need to create a new variable of type **CanActivateFn** that returns either a **boolean** or an **UrlTree** as a synchronous or asynchronous value.

In our case, here is what the guard can look like if we want to grant access if the current user is logged in but redirect him to the login page if he is not:

```
const loggedInGuard: CanActivateFn = (
  route: ActivatedRouteSnapshot,
  state: RouterStateSnapshot
) => {
  const currentUser = inject(CurrentUserService).currentUser;

  const isUserLoggedIn = currentUser !== null;
  if (isUserLoggedIn) return true;

  const router = inject(Router);
  return router.createUrlTree(["/login"]);
};
```

As we did here, guards can take advantage of Angular's dependency injection mechanism to retrieve other services and use them.

To actually use the **loggedInGuard**, we need to pass it in the array of the guards of this type on the route we actually want to act on:

```
[
  {
    path: 'login',
    component: LoginComponent
  },
  {
    path: 'home',
    canActivate: [loggedInGuard],
    component: HomeComponent
  }
]
```

Guards that are applied on a route are specified in an array, allowing to combine multiple of them. Only if *all* the guards return true, will the **Router** proceed on activating the route.

With our guard guarding the **'home'** route, an anonymous user will now be automatically redirected to the login page when attempting to navigate to it.

Note: *Once again, keep in mind that this security only prevents a user from displaying a page, not from making* HTTP *calls. You also need to have back-end validation if some operations are sensitive or restricted.*

Preventing Leaving a Route

Our user is now successfully on the **'/cart/checkout'** route, which displays a summary of the items in their basket along with the delivery details. While in the middle of the checkout process, they inadvertently click the "**back**" button of their browser.

Fortunately, there is an Angular guard that prevents navigating out of a route: the **CanDeactivate** guard.

The code is very similar to the **CanActivate** guard, except that this one is evaluated when leaving the route instead of when activating it.

This guard is very useful when you want to add a "*safety mechanism*" that will help the user not to lose progress unintentionally. However, it is important to note that it does not completely block navigation. For example, the user could simply change the URL in the address bar to navigate somewhere else.

This guard has the particularity of taking the component's instance as a parameter, allowing it to check its state and methods since it is of type **CanDeactivateFn<TComponent>**.

In a simpler example, we can update the **EditContactDetailsComponent** component we wrote in the previous chapter to mimic an editing state:

```
@Component({
  selector: 'app-edit-contact-details',
  standalone: true,
  template: `
    <h2>Edit Contact Details</h2>
    <button (click)="isEditing = !isEditing">
      isEditing: {{ isEditing }}
    </button>
  `,
})
class EditContactDetailsComponent {
  isEditing = false;
}
```

We can then write a guard taking advantage of the editing property to ask for confirmation before leaving the page:

```
const ongoingEditionGuard: CanDeactivateFn<EditContactDetails-
Component> = (
  component: EditContactDetailsComponent,
  currentRoute: ActivatedRouteSnapshot,
  currentState: RouterStateSnapshot,
  nextState: RouterStateSnapshot
) => {
  const isEditing = component.isEditing;
  if (!isEditing) return true;

  return window.confirm(
    'You have unsaved changes. Do you really want to leave?'
  );
};
```

As we did for the **`CanActivate`** guard, we can now add this guard to the **`canDeactivate`** guards array of the associated route:

```
{
  path: 'edit',
  component: EditContactDetailsComponent,
  canDeactivate: [ongoingEditionGuard],
}
```

When **`EditContactDetailsComponent#isEditing`** is true and if we click another link or on the back button of our browser, a confirmation window will appear asking if we really want to leave, successfully preventing unwanted navigation.

Note: *This guard is heavily coupled with the* **`EditContactDetailsComponent`** *component. If the deactivation logic is shared among several components, a good alternative would be to type this guard using a common interface instead of a single component.*

Keep in mind that this guard should not be used too often. From a user experience perspective, being prevented by the application itself to freely navigate within a website can be a frustrating experience.

Preventing Loading Other Routes

The **CanActivate** and **CanDeactivate** guards already cover most of the use cases you might face when wanting to control user navigation. However, for now, we are still facing an issue.

Consider the following route configuration:

```
{
  path: "admin",
  canActivate: [adminGuard],
  loadChildren: await () =>
    (async import('./admin-feature/route')).then(m => m.adminRoutes)
}
```

In this route, the admin feature is lazy-loaded; however, the **CanActivate** guard has a snapshot of the route itself as a parameter, which means that it needs to know what the route is. For a lazy-loaded route, this means fetching the feature routes *before* evaluating the guard.

In the previous example, if the user is not an administrator, he will still download the feature before being rejected by the router.

In some scenarios, you might not need to download the route at all to evaluate whether the user can access it or not. In our case, if the current user is not an administrator, we can directly reject the routing.

For such cases, Angular routes have a third kind of guard: the **canMatch** guard.

This guard is of type **CanMatchFn** and takes as parameters a snapshot of the current route and the router. It returns true if the user is allowed to download the lazy-loaded route:

```
const adminGuard: CanMatchFn = (route: Route, segments: Url
Segment[]) => {
  const currentUser = inject(CurrentUserService).currentUser;
  return currentUser?.isAdmin === true;
};
```

We then need to use it in the **canMatch** array instead of the **canActivate** one:

```
{
  path: "admin",
```

```
    canMatch: [adminGuard],
    loadChildren: await () =>
      (async import('./admin-feature/route')).then(m => m.adminRoutes)
  }
```

With this change, the lazy-loaded feature won't be loaded when this guard rejects navigation.

Note: *In older Angular versions,* **`canLoad`** *and* **`canLoadFn`** *were in charge of controlling if a route could be activated and loaded. They are now deprecated and you should prefer* **`canMatch`** *and* **`canMatchFn`** *instead.*

This kind of guard is particularly helpful to keep the advantage of lazy-loading while still controlling the user navigation.

Prefetching Data Using Resolvers

In Angular, Resolvers are a special kind of guard that can fetch data before the actual rendering of the component. Until that data is fetched, the router won't proceed with the navigation.

This has the downside of blocking navigation for a short period of time, but the advantage of being able to display the necessary information without the need for some kind of loader or placeholders.

In our contact application, for example, when navigating to a specific page, we could pre-fetch its details before showing its contact page.

A **`Resolver`** is of type **`ResolveFn<TResolved>`**, where **`TResolved`** is the type of data that is retrieved. As parameters, the resolver takes a snapshot of the current route and of the router state. The expected return type is **`TResolved`** as a synchronous or asynchronous value.

In our case, here is what the resolver for the contact looks like:

```
const contactResolver: ResolveFn<Contact> = (
  route: ActivatedRouteSnapshot,
  state: RouterStateSnapshot
): Contact => {
  const contactName = route.paramMap.get('username')!;

  const contactService = inject(ContactService);
  return contactService.getContactByName(contactName);
};
```

Using them, however, slightly differs from the other route guards since Resolvers are not used in an array but in a map:

```
{
  path: '',
  component: ContactPageComponent,
  resolve: {
    contact: contactResolver,
  },
  children: [
    ...
  ],
},
```

When a resolver executes, the resulting data is placed in the route's **data** property. By assigning a name for the resolver's usage in our route, we can then consume its result from the **ActivatedRoute** from our component:

```
@Component({
  // ...
  template: `
    <h2>{{ username }}'s Contact Page</h2>

    @if (contact$ | async; as contact) {
      <p>Name: {{ contact.name }}</p>
      <p>Address: {{ contact.email }}</p>
    }

    <router-outlet />
  `,
})
class ContactPageComponent {
  @Input() username: string = '';

  contact$: Observable<Contact> = inject(ActivatedRoute).data.pipe(
    map((data) => data['contact'])
  );
}
```

In the same way, a route parameter can be retrieved by using an input of the same name, the resolver's information can also be retrieved in the same way if you used **withComponentInputBinding** in your router configuration.

If that's the case, the previous code can be replaced by a much more concise version:

```
@Component({
  // ...
  template: `
    <h2>{{ username }}'s Contact Page</h2>
```

```
    <p>Name: {{ contact.name }}</p>
    <p>Address: {{ contact.email }}</p>

    <router-outlet />
  `,
})
class ContactPageComponent {
  @Input() username: string = '';
  @Input() contact!: Contact;
}
```

With this configuration, the **ContactPageComponent** component will now immediately display the contact's information when shown, at the cost of the navigation being stopped while Angular asynchronously fetches the data.

As for other guards, be careful not to overuse them as they can introduce a feeling of latency in your application as well as make unnecessary loadings if the component comes to evolve but its route does not.

Conclusion

In this chapter, we went through most of Angular's `Router` capabilities.

We explored how to configure routing both for standalone and module-based applications. We then went through the details of a `Route` to see how they were built and how to pass them parameters.

We reviewed how to navigate from the template or the component's logic, and how to consume the route parameters.

We saw how to optimize our application's bundle size by lazily loading parts of our routes and when it is relevant to do so.

Finally, we saw how to control and secure client-side navigation with route guards along with their main drawbacks. We also saw how to pre-fetch data for the components that benefit from it.

In the next chapter, we will discover the fundamental testing concepts of Angular. By leveraging these, we will ensure that our code not only works but does so reliably.

Exercise

Since you are now familiar with routing, let's go back to the TODO application we developed in *Chapter 6, Component Communication and Data Flow*.

Update the application so it will serve multiple pages:

- `/` should display all TODO items.
- `/?status=pending` should display all TODO items that are not completed.
- `/:id` should display the TODO item with the same ID. Additionally, the data of the associated TODO item should have been pre-fetched before the page is actually displayed.
- `/new` should display a form to create a new TODO item. If the user attempts to leave the page while the form has been partially filled, a pop-up or an alert should be displayed to warn them that they will lose his progress.

CHAPTER 10
Unit Testing

Introduction

When developing software applications, we must ensure that our applications will work as we expect when we deploy them to production and that we can say, with some certainty, that our application will function as it was intended to. It also creates a baseline when maintenance and new features are developed that may modify existing parts of the code. If unit tests start failing, we know we have broken something and either need to fix our code or update the unit test to accommodate the new changes.

The main types of testing in software development are:

- Unit testing
- Component testing
- End-to-End testing

There are many other types, including integration, user acceptance, and regression tcsting.

Usually, the developer writing the code also writes the unit tests. If you are lucky enough to have a dedicated QA team, then they usually write the end-to-end tests, along with others, such as regression, integration, compatibility, smoke tests, and automation tests. In this chapter, we'll cover how to write unit tests and how to configure Angular to use Karma, Jest, and whatever the future has in store for Angular testing.

Note: *Karma has been Angular's flagship unit testing library since AngularJS (formerly Angular 1.x), but it has now been deprecated from Angular version 16. There are a lot of new libraries on the market that use a more modern approach to testing.*

This was also the same for Protractor, the end-to-end testing suite that was deprecated and finally removed in August 2023, various end-to-end testing framework alternatives are Cypress or more recently Playwright.

Karma uses Jasmine as the underlying framework for writing unit tests and runs in the browser or Node and has the look and feel of JavaScript. Jasmine is also the underlying framework for many other testing frameworks and is also well-known as a behavior-driven development tool (BDD) and used in programming languages, such as Ruby and Python.

Structure

The topics we'll cover in this chapter are as follows:

- Setting up Karma: Get up and running with the default unit testing framework
- Setting up Jest: Get up and running with Jest is a popular alternative
- The Future of Angular Testing: Web Test Runner, Vitest, Playwrite

Setting up Karma

As Karma is the default unit testing suite for Angular (for the moment, at least), it will come as no surprise that there isn't anything to set up, it just works out of the box. Versions of Angular prior to version 15 supplied a karma.config.js file this has been removed, but can be added back if we need to make configuration changes, to add this back to your project run:

```
ng generate config karma
```

This will add the following config to the project's root.

```
module.exports = function (config) {
  config.set({
    basePath: '',
    frameworks: ['jasmine', '@angular-devkit/build-angular'],
    plugins: [
      require('karma-jasmine'),
      require('karma-chrome-launcher'),
      require('karma-jasmine-html-reporter'),
      require('karma-coverage'),
      require('@angular-devkit/build-angular/plugins/karma')
    ],
    client: {
      jasmine: {},
      clearContext: false
    },
    jasmineHtmlReporter: {
      suppressAll: true
    },
    coverageReporter: {},
    reporters: ['progress', 'kjhtml'],
    browsers: ['Chrome'],
    restartOnFileChange: true
  });
};
```

When we run our unit tests (which we will do later in this chapter), Karma runs our tests in a Browser, (which is what it was designed to do) but using Karma this way can become a little frustrating when running and debugging unit tests.

It can be a bit slow to run unit tests, it also opens a new browser when trying to close it (in fact, it does these three times before eventually giving up), which is most frustrating. Also, when we run our tests in our CI/CD environment, we don't need to open a browser.

To get around this, let's install the karma-spec-reporter as a dev dependency to the project, this displays all our unit results in the terminal, not in the browser. This is easier to read, it's a lot faster and ready for our CI/CD environment, but if you prefer to see the unit results in the browser you can skip this part.

If your application was built with a version of Angular before version 15, your karma.config.js file will already be in the application root, hence you can skip the next part.

Tip: If you have multiple projects in your application workspace, (that is, you are using a mono-repo), then you will need to specify which project you want to add the Karma config file, to do that specify the project name:

```
ng generate config karma --project <name-of-project>
```

Next, let's install the karma-spec-reporter.

```
// install karma spec reporter as dev dependency

npm install -D karma-spec-reporter
```

Next, change the **`karma-config.js`** file to include the **`karma-spec-reporter`** as a plugin, update the reporter's section, and change the browsers to be **`ChromeHeadless`**.

```
module.exports = function (config) {
  config.set({
    basePath: "",
    frameworks: ["jasmine", "@angular-devkit/build-angular"],
    plugins: [
      require("karma-jasmine"),
      require("karma-chrome-launcher"),
      require("karma-jasmine-html-reporter"),
      require("karma-coverage"),
      require("karma-spec-reporter"), // add spec reporter here
      require("@angular-devkit/build-angular/plugins/karma"),
    ],
    client: {
      jasmine: {},
      clearContext: false,
    },
    jasmineHtmlReporter: {
      suppressAll: true,
    },
```

```
    coverageReporter: {},
    reporters: ["spec"], //<-- add "spec" remove -->"progress", "kjhtml"],
    browsers: ["Chrome", "ChromeHeadless"], // add ChromeHeadless
    restartOnFileChange: true,
  });
};
```

When we run our tests, the results will be shown in the terminal instead of opening a browser. The command to run our tests from the project command line is:

```
npm run test
```

Tip: *It's also possible to set up the script section in our* **`package.json`** *file to set whether we run with or without the browser open, for example*:

```
// scripts section in package.json file
"test:headless": "ng test --browsers=ChromeHeadless"
```

There are many other configurations and plugins we can add to control how Karma works. Though a lot of these are out of scope for this chapter, before we move on to the Jest setup, we will discuss code coverage. As our application develops and we add more features and unit tests, it becomes harder to track what is covered by unit tests and what isn't, Karma has us covered. Part of the default configuration is the **`coverageReporters`** (not shown in the preceding examples), when we run the code coverage Karma outputs the following to the terminal (the results will be different as the projects grow):

- Statements: 100% (3/3)
- Branches: 100% (0/0)
- Functions: 100% (1/1)
- Lines: 100% (2/2)

The preceding output is a breakdown of our application and shows how many functions we have and how many are covered by unit tests, for example. This isn't particularly easy to read, especially on larger projects, so at the same time the code coverage creates a new directory in the root of the project and generates a static HTML page (there are also some styling and JavaScript files as well), the index.html file provides a Graphical User Interface (GUI) version. Opening the index.html file will open the page in a browser and show the same output as the terminal but in a nicer format with the ability to drill into each file to see exactly what code is covered by a test. To run and generate the code coverage from the project terminal type:

```
npm run test --code-coverage
```

We have explored how to set up Karma and make changes to the configuration. Let's now look at writing some unit tests. When creating a new project or adding a new component, service, directive, or pipe, we will get a spec file with the same name as our component (service, directive, and pipe), unless we pass the skip tests flag when creating them.

When writing unit tests, we contain them in blocks. These blocks are called describe blocks and describe the tests contained, let's see an example:

```
describe('unit tests for the app component page', () => {


}
```

Tip: *You can think of a* ***describe*** *as the container to suite of tests. The* ***it*** *block is the test itself and* ***expect*** *is the results. A* ***describe*** *can be nested with* ***it*** *blocks at each level.*

It's possible to nest **describe** blocks but don't create empty **describe** or **it** blocks as it will throw a warning.

Within the **describe** block, let's add an **it** block; this is where we write the test. When writing unit tests, we should try and follow the three A's, these are:

- **Arrange**: The Arranging stage is where we set things up, create any variables, objects and mocks.
- **Act**: This is where we would invoke what is being tested.
- **Assert**: This is where we would check the results from the method, and match what we expected back.

```
describe('unit tests for the app component page', () => {
  it('should create the app', () => {
    // Arrange
    const fixture = TestBed.createComponent(AppComponent);
    // Act
    const app = fixture.componentInstance;
    // Assert
    expect(app).toBeTruthy();
  });
}
```

In the preceding example, we are setting up the environment to the **AppComponent**. Next, we create an instance of the **AppComponent**, and if this is successful, then we would expect to have an instance of the **AppComponent** created in the app variable and we check to see if that is true.

Setting up everything in our tests each time will become repetitive very quickly. We need a place where we can set up (and tear down afterward) so that each test is run in a known state and not influenced by previous tests. Karma has a **beforeEach** and **afterEach** method as the names imply these get called before and after each test has run, allowing us to set common variables, methods, and so on and to destroy them afterward.

```
let component: ReactiveDrivenComponent;
let fixture: ComponentFixture<ReactiveDrivenComponent>;

beforeEach(async () => {
    await TestBed.configureTestingModule({
      imports: [
        RouterTestingModule
      ],
      declarations: [
        ReactiveDrivenComponent
      ],
    }).compileComponents();
    fixture = TestBed.createComponent(ReactiveDrivenComponent);
    comp = fixture.componentInstance;
}

afterEach(() => {
  fixture = null;
  component = null;
}
```

Within the **beforeEach** we set up our **TestBed**, which is the main API for writing unit tests for components and libraries. Next, we import any modules. Even with standalone components, the Karma testing suite still uses some modules. In the preceding example, we're including the **RouterTestingModule** and importing the **ReactiveDrivenComponent**.

Using the application, we've been using throughout this book, let's add a new test for our reactive forms page and our data service, in your IDE of choice, right-click the reactive-driven directory and select the new file.

Note: *The CLI is not able to create spec files on their own, there are third party libraries that will do this for you, so we will need to create these manually.*

Give the file a name **reactive-driven.component.spec.ts** and within this file, let's add a describe block, a **beforeEach**, **aftereach** block, and an it block.

```
let component: ReactiveDrivenComponent;
let fixture: ComponentFixture<ReactiveDrivenComponent>;

describe('reactive-driven-component', () => {
  beforeEach(async () => {
    await TestBed.configureTestingModule({
      imports: [
        RouterTestingModule
      ],
      declarations: [
        ReactiveDrivenComponent
```

```
      ],
    }).compileComponents();
    // if we need to create a new instance for multiple tests
    // we would add it here in the beforeEach.
    // fixture = TestBed.createComponent(ReactiveDrivenComponent);
    // component = fixture.componentInstance;
  });

  afterEach(() => {
    fixture = null;
    component = null;
  }

  it ('should create the app', () => {
    // Arrange
    const fixture = TestBed.createComponent(ReactiveDrivenComponent);
    // Act
    const component = fixture.componentInstance;
    Assert
    expect(component).toBeTruthy();
  });
  Add additional blocks here, can be described and it.
});
```

In this test, we create the environment for testing an instance of the **ReactiveDrivenComponent** (the **Arrange**), then we get an instance of the **ReactiveDrivenComponent** (the **Act**), and finally, we check to see if the variable component exists (the **Assert**).

Karma provides several different options we can choose from to test our expectations, almost all these start with **tobe...** for example: **tobetrue**, **tobefalse**, **tobegreaterthan**, **tobelessthan**. While we are testing this form let's add an h1 element to the top of the HTML page and then write a test to check that an h1 element is there and the text content reads **'Reactive driven forms'**.

Underneath the previous it block, add the following unit test.

```
it('should have an h1 element', () => {
    // only add if the fixture and component are not in the beforeEach
    // const fixture = TestBed.createComponent(ReactiveDrivenComponent);
    // const component = fixture.nativeElement as HTMLElement;
    expect(component.querySelector('h1')?.textContent).toContain(
      'Reactive driven forms'
    );
  });
```

In this test, we create the environment for testing an instance of the component, and then we get the native element from the root of the component. In the expect, we are using a **querySelector** to search for the h1 element and if it finds one, we get the text content and check to see if it contains the specified text.

Note: *The* **querySelector** *will only return the first matching element it discovers, if you have multiple elements with the same selector, then you will need to select on something else like a class or a specific id.*

Let's finish this section by testing our data service, in a real-world application when testing APIs; we should try and avoid calling the actual API endpoint, as this may require some form of authentication to gain access, which we might not be able to provide in a unit test.

Note: *Keep in mind that we are not testing the API or the call to the server, these should be covered by the API unit tests. All that we are interested in testing is that our code called the correct method in our service and that we got a response with some data.*

There are a few ways in which we can do this, for example, we could use our environment files.

```
imports: [...],
providers:[{provide: DataService,
  useClass: environment.prod ? DataService: MockApiService
}],
```

Here we would create a **MockApiService** and if the application is in development mode and we run our unit tests, then our **MockApiService** is called instead. When we deploy our application to QA/UAT testing, having the environment files configured for each environment will make the process much easier to manage.

In our example though, we are using the Json-Server, which will call the API endpoint. Let's first create some mock data in our spec file for this service, this will mimic the data in the **db.json** file and give us something to compare with. In our **data.service.spec.ts** file, create a **mockdata** object and add some fake data, (for a passing test the data needs to match what you have in your **db.json** file).

```
// populate the fields with data, for a passing test the field needs to
// match the field in the db.json file, to make a failing test change the
// mockdata to be something different.
const mockdata: UserModel = {
    firstName: '', // add data to the fields to match db.json
    lastName: '',
    email: '',
    telephone: [
      {phoneNumber: '',},
      {phoneNumber: '',},
      {phoneNumber: '',},
      {phoneNumber: '',},
    ],
```

```
    address: {
      address1: '',
      address2: '',
      address3: '',
      address4: '',
      county: '',
      postcode: '',
    },
  };
```

Now let's create **describe**, **beforeEach**, and **it** blocks .

```
describe('DataService', () => {
  let service: DataService;

  beforeEach(async () => {
    await TestBed.configureTestingModule({
      imports: [HttpClientModule],
      providers: [],
      declarations: [],
    }).compileComponents();
    service = TestBed.inject(DataService);
  });

  it('should call the GET method and return data', () => {
    service.getUser().subscribe((data) => {
      expect(data.firstName).toEqual('Duncan');
      expect(data).toEqual(mockdata);
    });
  });
});
```

Here we are injecting the **DataService** and assigning it to the variable service. In our test, we are calling the service and subscribing to that service, and we are running a couple of expects. We expect the **firstName** to equal "**Duncan**" and that our data (from **db.json**) is equal to our **mockdata**. One of the items we should test for is whether our API has been called; to test this we need to add the following to our **data.service.spec.ts** file:

```
import { HttpTestingController } from '@angular/common/http/testing';
describe('DataService', () => {
  let httpController: HttpTestingController;
  let url: string = 'http://localhost:3000/';

  beforeEach(async () => {
    ...
    // add
    httpController = TestBed.inject(HttpTestingController);
```

```
  }

  it('should call the GET method and return data', () => {
    ...
    /// add
      const req = httpController.expectOne('/userModel');

      expect(req.request.method).toEqual('GET');

      req.flush(service);

      // this could move to the afterEach function
      httpController.verify();
  }
}
```

In the preceding example, we have added the **httpTestingController**, allowing us to mock a request (and subsequently flush the request). The **httpController.expectOne**, expects that one request has been made that matches the method and url options and returns a mock. This confirms that our endpoint has been called, at least once. Let's now set up a failing test:

```
it('should throw a 404 error', () => {
    const message: string = 'force a 404 not found';

    service.getUser().subscribe({
      next: () => fail('this should fail with a 404 not found error'),
      error: (error: HttpErrorResponse) => {
        expect(error.status).withContext('status').toEqual(404);
        expect(error.error).withContext('message').toEqual(message);
      },
    });

    const req = httpController.expectOne(`${url}/userModel`);
    req.flush(message, { status: 404, statusText: 'Not Found' });
  });
```

Even though we are setting this up to be a failing test, it still passes, why? We subscribe to the service (**DataService**) as before, but this time we explicitly set it to fail, then in the error, we check that the status code returned is equal to **404** and the **statusText** is equal to '**Not Found**', which it should do and so the test passes.

Setting up Jest

In this section, we're going to look at replacing Karma for Jest in versions prior to Angular 17 as this is changing (albeit still very experimental at the time of writing), and then, we'll discuss what the plan is post-version 17.

Karma has been marked as deprecated since early 2023, with it likely to be removed in a later version.

Why replace Karma with Jest?

Karma has been around for several years (it was originally part of the Angular 1 release, in 2010) and over the years the web has changed considerably. Since then, Karma, like Angular has evolved over the years, but other testing frameworks have been able to take advantage of these changes making them a more viable alternative. Karma is effectively an http server that runs our tests in a browser and as mentioned earlier in this chapter, this can become problematic, not just when debugging but also when you have lots of tests to run.

This is where Jest shines because it doesn't need to run tests in the browser, Jest uses Node and JSDom. The JSDOM is a JavaScript interpretation of a browser; this has its advantages in that. It doesn't need to spin up an actual browser, just a virtual one. By using a virtual browser, the performance can be significantly improved. The downside to this is that some things can't be tested as they require an actual browser, but these are edge cases and specific to browsers.

We'll set up our example Angular application to use Jest and remove Karma completely from our standalone project. If we want to migrate a real-world application that has lots of existing unit tests written using Karma, this may appear at first to be a daunting task, but the good news is that Jest is also built on top of Jasmine, and therefore, has a very similar syntax to Karma and would only require some minor changes to certain parts of the syntax.

In the standalone application, let's start by uninstalling Karma and Jasmine. In a terminal window for the project at the root where the **`package.json`** file is located, enter:

```
npm uninstall -D @types/jasmine jasmine-core karma karma-chrome-launcher
karma-coverage karma-jasmine karma-jasmine-html-reporter karma-spec-re-
porter
```

Next, we can delete the **`karm.conf.js`** file, then the test object from **`angular.json`** file, and finally the **`test.ts`** file.

Ncxt, install

```
// the -D saves the packages to the dev-dependencies section
npm install -D jest, @types/jest and jest-preset-angular
```

Create **`jest.setup.ts`** file and add the following to the file:

```
import 'jest-preset-angular/setup-jest';
```

In the **`tsconfig.spec.json`** file, change the types array from:

```
{
```

```
  "extends": "../../tsconfig.json",
  "compilerOptions": {
    "outDir": "../../out-tsc/spec",
    "types": ["jasmine"]
  },
rc/j
  "include": ["src/**/*.spec.ts", "src/**/*.d.ts"]
}
To
{
  "extends": "../../tsconfig.json",
  "compilerOptions": {
    "outDir": "../../out-tsc/spec",
    "types": ["jest", "node"]
  },
  "files": ["src/setup.jest.ts"],
  "include": ["src/**/*.spec.ts", "src/**/*.d.ts"]
}
```

Then, add the configuration to a new file called **jest.config.ts** in the root directory.

```
export default {
  displayName: 'standalone-app',
  preset: 'jest-preset-angular',
  setupFilesAfterEnv: ['<rootDir>/projects/standalone-app/src/jest.set-
up.ts'],
  coverageDirectory: '../../coverage/apps/',
  transform: {
    '^.+\\.(ts|mjs|js|html)$': [
      'jest-preset-angular',
      {
        tsconfig: '<rootDir>/projects/standalone-app/tsconfig.spec.json',
        stringifyContentPathRegex: '\\.(html|svg)$',
      },
    ],
  },
  transformIgnorePatterns: ['node_modules/(?!.*\\.mjs$)'],
  snapshotSerializers: [
    'jest-preset-angular/build/serializers/no-ng-attributes',
    'jest-preset-angular/build/serializers/ng-snapshot',
    'jest-preset-angular/build/serializers/html-comment',
  ],
};
Lastly, in the scripts section of the package.json file, add:
"test": "jest",
"test:watch": "jest --watch",
"test:coverage": "jest --coverage"
```

This is all the configuration required to get Jest running in an Angular application prior to Angular 17, the only change we need to make to our tests is in the **`data.service.spec.ts`** where we need to replace the two expects, with the following:

```
it('should throw a 404 error', () => {
    const message: string = 'force a 404 not found';
    service.getUser().subscribe({
      next: () => fail('this should fail with a 404 not found error'),
      error: (error: HttpErrorResponse) => {
 // remove the .withContext('') from the next two lines
        expect(error.status).toEqual(404);
        expect(error.error).toEqual(message);
      },
    });

    const req = httpController.expectOne(`${url}/userModel`);
    req.flush(message, { status: 404, statusText: 'Not Found' });
  });
```

There are a few subtle differences between Karma and Jest, for example: **`toBeTrue()`** is **`toBe(true)`** in Jest, or instead of **`spyOn()`** it's **`jest.spyOn()`**.

Most of this has been covered, we just need to create a **`jest.config.ts`** file. This can be created and modified by using the following command:

```
npm init jest@latest
```

The install will ask us a number of questions and create a config file based on those answers. For example, Jest uses this file to know where to place the code coverage files.

The Future of Angular Testing

The Angular team has always provided developers with the tools for creating unit tests, but over time, Karma has fallen behind to more modern testing frameworks, such as Jest, Cypress, and more recently Vitest and Playwright. All these frameworks have all made big strides ahead of Karma and it's fair to say it's probably had its day and time to pass on the baton.

With that in mind, it was announced in Angular 16 that Karma will be deprecated and removed in a future version. Angular team has been working on adding Jest with plans to add Web Test Runner later (this will probably become the default) and are currently at the experimental stage. This is subject to change, but the idea is to add unit testing to your projects in the same way we currently add CSS to a project, for example, by selecting an option during the application generation. Though that is a little way off at the time of writing, we hope to get more details on this feature, but it may be some time before we see a developer preview.

In the meantime, we can try out the experimental version of Jest (this is subject to change), remove the following packages:

```
npm remove karma karma-chrome-launcher karma-jasmine karma-jasmine-ht-
ml-reporter karma-coverage jasmine-core @types/jasmine
```

Note: *The experimental part of this is how it's enabled in the Angular framework and not Jest. If you had removed Karma and installed Jest prior, then uninstall Jest and delete any files we created.*

Next, we need to install the Jest:

```
npm install -D jest @types/jest @angular-builders/jest
```

Then we need to replace the test section in the angular.json file (for each project):

```
"test": {
          "builder": "@angular-devkit/build-angular:jest",
          "options": {
            "tsConfig": "projects/standalone-app/tsconfig.spec.json",
            "polyfills": ["zone.js", "zone.js/testing"]
          }
        }
```

Note: *Setting this up on our example project doesn't work. Initially, it was considered an issue with the project. When testing a new single project application and the steps above to remove Karma and install Jest all work fine, create a new multiple project application, and this again failed.*

After some research into this, I found this bug report in the Angular CLI GitHub repository Experimental Jest not working in multiple projects, so it looks like there is an issue with multiple project applications using the experimental version of Jest, which will be surely fixed in the future.

Conclusion

In this chapter, we talked about setting up Karma in our Angular projects, we walked through several examples of writing unit tests for components, services, directives, and pipes using our example application. We also discussed ways to improve Karma's output instead of using the browser. Closely followed by looking at removing Karma and setting up Jest, we talked about what the future has in store for unit testing in Angular and looked at using the experimental version that comes with Angular 17.

References

Experimental version of Jest not working in multiple project applications. https://github.com/angular/angular-cli/issues/25308

Index

L

N

O

P

R

U

V